AAT

TECHNICIAN

NVQ AND DIPLOMA PATHWAY
(ADVANCED CERTIFICATE)

COMBINED **COMPANION**   Unit 15

Cash Management
and Credit Control

LEARNING MEDIA

Third edition April 2007
First edition 2004

ISBN 9780 7517 2898 9 (previous edition 0 7517 2617 7)

British Library Cataloguing-in-Publication Data
A catalogue record for this book is available from the British Library

Published by

BPP Learning Media Ltd
BPP House,
Aldine Place,
London, W12 8AA

Printed in Great Britain by Martins the Printers, Berwick-upon-Tweed

Your learning materials, published by BPP Learning Media Ltd, are printed on paper sourced from sustainable, managed forests.

CONTENTS

Course Companion

Revision Companion

INTRODUCTION

This is BPP Learning Media's Combined Companion for AAT Unit 15: Operating a Cash Management and Credit Control System. It has been carefully designed to enable students to practise all aspects of the requirements of the Standards of Competence and performance criteria, and ultimately be successful in their assessments.

The book first contains a Course Companion section containing these key features:

- clear, step by step explanation of the topic

- logical progression and linking from one chapter to the next

- numerous illustrations and practical examples

- interactive activities within the text itself, with answers supplied

- a bank of questions of varying complexity again with answers supplied.

The Revision Companion section contains:

- graded activities corresponding to each chapter of the Course Companion, with answers

- a practice simulation with answers

- the AAT's Sample Simulation for Unit 15

Tutors adopting our Companions (minimum of ten Course Companions and ten Revision Companions per Unit, or ten Combined Companions as appropriate) are entitled to free access to the Lecturers' Area resources, including the Tutor Companion. To obtain your log-in, e-mail lecturersvc@bpp.com.

Home Study students are also entitled to access to additional resources. You will have received your log-in details on registration.

If you have any comments about this book, please e-mail pippariley@bpp.com or write to Pippa Riley, Publishing Projects Director, BPP Learning Media Ltd, BPP House, Aldine Place, London W12 8AA.

Diploma Pathway

This book is ideal for all students studying for Unit 15, whether via the NVQ route or the Diploma Pathway.

UNIT 15 STANDARDS OF COMPETENCE

The structure of the standards for unit 15

Each Unit commences with a statement of the **knowledge and understanding** which underpin competence in the Unit's elements.

The Unit of Competence is then divided into **elements of competence** describing activities which the individual should be able to perform.

Each element includes:

a)   A set of **performance criteria**. This defines what constitutes competent performance.

b)   A **range statement**. This defines the situations, contexts, methods etc in which competence should be displayed.

c)   **Evidence requirements**. These state that competence must be demonstrated consistently, over an appropriate time scale with evidence of performance being provided from the appropriate sources.

d)   **Sources of evidence**. These are suggestions of ways in which you can find evidence to demonstrate that competence. These fall under the headings: 'observed performance; work produced by the candidate; authenticated testimonies from relevant witnesses; personal account of competence; other sources of evidence.'

The elements of competence for Unit 15 are set out below. Knowledge and understanding required for the unit as a whole are listed first, followed by the performance criteria and range statements for each element. Performance criteria are cross-referenced below to chapters in this Companion.

Unit 15: Operating a Cash Management and Credit Control System

What is the unit about?

This Unit consists of four elements. Element 15.1 is concerned with the monitoring and forecasting of cash receipts and payments, the consultation with appropriate staff and the appropriate corrective action in accordance with organisational policy. The second element, Element 15.2, focuses on the management of cash balances. Element 15.3 considers the granting of credit, using valid internal and external sources of information. The final element, Element 15.4, addresses the management and control of the debt-collection process.

Although they are presented as four separate elements, there are significant interrelationships between the four. In particular, Elements 15.1 and 15.2 consider cash management and 15.3 and 15.4 address the credit control function. Significantly, Unit 15 requires students to have an understanding of legal, organisational and banking issues as well as the ability to apply accounting techniques to cash management and credit control activities for a wide range of organisations.

Guidance by element

Element 15.1 Monitor and control cash receipts and payments

Guidance

The first criterion is concerned with the basic business of regularly monitoring (daily, weekly, monthly) cash receipts and payments against a cash budget. The fifth criterion requires students to identify cash shortfalls or surpluses and to identify the most appropriate means to manage the situation. Therefore, students require a clear knowledge of the main types of cash receipts and payments.

- regular receipts and payments, such as cash and credit sales
- payroll and operating costs
- capital costs, such as the purchase of new equipment or premises
- drawings
- dividends
- financial payments
- instances of exceptional receipts and payments

Students also need to be able to distinguish between cash and non-cash elements (such as depreciation and provisions).

The second and third criteria require students to appreciate how cash forecasts are put together using a synthesis of information from accounting, sales and technical staff. The fourth criterion requires students to be aware of the two different forms of cash budgets – ie modifying profit and loss account and balance sheet data to calculate cash flow, and also using a simple cashier's forecast of receipts and payments.

Alongside developing a cash forecast, students need to be able to apply basic statistical techniques for estimating future trends, including moving averages and the ability to apply different inflation factors to a forecast. Students should also be able to understand the appropriateness of computer models, such as spreadsheets, to assess the sensitivity of the forecast to changes in individual elements.

Element 15.2 Manage cash balances

Guidance

The first, second, fourth and fifth criteria are concerned with relating the cash forecast to the action required to manage the cash deficit or surplus predicted. In the case of a cash deficit, students are required to be aware of the different ways of funding such a deficit, including bank overdrafts, medium and long-term loans, and leasing or asset-based financing. This will also require an understanding of the structure of the UK banking system and the relationships between different types of financial institutions.

Students also need to be aware of different alternatives for investing surplus cash. These might include bank deposits and investment in marketable securities such as bills of exchange, certificates of deposit, government securities and local authority short loans. Although management of a portfolio of securities is beyond the scope of the Standards of Competence required at this level, students should have an understanding of the terms and conditions attached to each of these investments and their specific risks.

All of this is set in the context of an organisation's structure, systems and procedures and the nature of its business transactions.

Element 15.3 Grant credit

Guidance

The first three criteria are concerned with establishing a customer's credit status and the credit-granting decision. In making this decision, students are expected to be able to make use of both internal and external sources of information. These might include analysing accounting information, or informal information from sales staff or trade contacts. External information would include information from credit reference agencies, banks and official publications. In making the credit-granting decision, students are expected to be able to manage the paradox of conflicting information and make a suitable credit decision. The fourth criterion concerns how the credit-granting decision is communicated to the customer – in all instances in a courteous and tactful manner.

The element has a significant legal element and students are expected to be aware of the terms and conditions relating to the granting of credit and the effect of the Data Protection Act 1998 on credit control information. Students are also required to be able to calculate the cost of discounts for prompt payment and understand why such discounts are offered to credit customers.

Element 15.4 Monitor and control the collection of debts

Guidance

Criteria A-C are concerned with the monitoring and communication to other individuals of the status of debtors' accounts. Such an analysis might make use of an age analysis of debtors, the calculation of average periods of credit given and received and of the incidence of bad and doubtful debts.

Criterion D focuses on communication with debtors, emphasising the need for courtesy but also with due regard for the need to recover amounts due. As with Element 15.3, there is an important legal component to Element 15.4. In this respect, students are required to understand the legal remedies for breach of contract and the legal and administrative procedures for the collection of debts. In addition, an elementary understanding of the effect of bankruptcy and insolvency is required.

The fifth criterion addresses the need to identify the most appropriate debt-recovery method. In this regard, students are expected to have an understanding of the costs and benefits of other (external) means of debt collection, including factoring arrangements and debt insurance.

Knowledge and understanding

The Business Environment	Chapter
1 The main types of cash receipts and payments: regular revenue receipts and payments; capital receipts and payments; drawings/dividends and disbursements; exceptional receipts and payments (Element 15.1)	1,2
2 The basic structure of the banking system and the money market in the UK and the relationships between financial institutions (Element 15.2)	4
3 Bank overdrafts and loans; terms and conditions; legal relationship between bank and customer (Element 15.2)	4

Accounting principles and theory | Chapter

24 Cash flow accounting and its relationship to accounting for income and expenditure (Element 15.1) — 2

25 Liquidity management (Elements 15.2, 15.3 & 15.4) — 4

The organisation

26 Understanding that the accounting systems of an organisation are affected by its organisational structure, its administrative systems and procedures and the nature of its business transactions (Elements 15.1, 15.2, 15.3 & 15.4) — 1, 2

27 Understanding that recording and accounting practices may vary in different parts of the organisation (Elements 15.1 & 15.4) — 2

28 An understanding that practice in this area will be determined by an organisation's specific financial regulations, guidelines and security procedures (Element 15.2) — 4

29 An understanding that in public sector organisations there are statutory and other regulations relating to the management of cash balances (Element 15.2) — 4

30 Understanding that practice in this area will be determined by an organisation's credit control policies and procedures (Element 15.3) — 5, 6

31 An understanding of the organisation's relevant policies and procedures (Elements 15.1, 15.3 & 15.4) — 2, 6, 8

Element 15.1 Monitor and control cash receipts and payments

Performance criteria | Chapter

A Monitor and control cash receipts and payments against budgeted cash flow — 1

B Consult appropriate staff to determine the likely pattern of cash flows over the accounting period and to anticipate any exceptional receipts or payments — 2, 3

C Ensure forecasts of future cash payments and receipts are in accord with known income and expenditure trends — 3

D Prepare cash budgets in the approved format and clearly indicate net cash requirements — 2

E Identify significant deviations from the cash budget and take corrective action within defined organisational policies — 1

Range statement

Cash flows to be monitored: regular revenue receipts and payments; capital receipts and payments; drawings or dividends and disbursements; exceptional receipts and payments

Element 15.2 Manage cash balances

Performance criteria	Chapter
A Arrange overdraft and loan facilities in anticipation of requirements and on the most favourable terms available	4
B Invest surplus funds in marketable securities within defined financial authorisation limits	4
C Ensure the organisation's financial regulations and security procedures are observed	4
D Ensure account is taken of trends in the economic and financial environment in managing cash balances	4
E Maintain an adequate level of liquidity in line with cash forecasts	4

Range statement

Maintain liquidity through the management of: cash, overdrafts and loans

Element 15.3 Grant credit

Performance criteria	Chapter
A Agree credit terms with customers in accordance with the organisation's policies	6
B Identify and use internal and external sources of information to evaluate the current credit status of customers and potential customers	6
C Open new accounts for those customers with an established credit status	6
D Ensure the reasons for refusing credit are discussed with customers in a tactful manner	6

Range statements

1 Internal information derived from: analysis of the accounts; colleagues in regular contact with current or potential customers or clients

2 External information derived from: credit rating agencies; supplier references; bank references

Element 15.4 Monitor and control the collection of debts

Performance criteria	Chapter
A Monitor information relating to the current state of debtors' accounts regularly and take appropriate action	7
B Send information regarding significant outstanding accounts and potential bad debts promptly to relevant individuals within the organisation	7
C Ensure discussions and negotiations with debtors are conducted courteously and achieve the desired outcome	7
D Use debt recovery methods appropriate to the circumstances of individual cases and in accordance with the organisation's procedures	8
E Base recommendations to write off bad and doubtful debts on a realistic analysis of all known factors	8

Range statements

1   Information on debtors: age analysis of debtors; average periods of credit given and received; incidence of bad and doubtful debts

2   Appropriate action: information and recommendations for action passed to appropriate individual within own organisation; debtor contacted and arrangements made for the recovery of the debt

ASSESSMENT STRATEGY

Unit 15 is assessed by a **skills test**, in the form of a simulation usually.

A skills test is a means of collecting evidence of your ability to carry out practical activities and to **operate effectively in the conditions of the workplace** to the standards required. Evidence may be collected at your place of work or at an Approved Assessment Centre by means of simulations of workplace activity, or by a combination of these methods.

If the Approved Assessment Centre is a **workplace** you may be observed carrying out accounting activities as part of your normal work routine. You should collect documentary evidence of the work you have done, or contributed, in an **accounting portfolio**. Evidence collected in a portfolio can be assessed in addition to observed performance or where it is not possible to assess by observation.

Where the Approved Assessment Centre is a **college or training organisation**, skills based assessment will be by means of a combination of the following.

a)   Documentary evidence of activities carried out at the workplace, collected by you in an **accounting portfolio**

b)   Realistic **simulations** of workplace activities; these simulations may take the form of case studies and in-tray exercises and involve the use of primary documents and reference sources

c)   **Projects and assignments** designed to assess the Standards of Competence

If you are unable to provide workplace evidence, you will be able to complete the assessment requirements by the alternative methods listed above. Note that the Diploma Pathway route to the AAT qualification does not require the presentation of any workplace evidence.

COURSE COMPANION UNIT 15

chapter 1:
MONITORING CASH RECEIPTS AND PAYMENTS

chapter coverage

In this opening chapter of the Course Companion for Unit 15 we will consider the importance of cash to a business and the important control element of the monitoring of cash receipts and payments. The topics that are to be covered are:

✍ the importance of cash to a business

✍ differences between cash and profit

✍ cash and credit transactions

✍ types of cash flows

✍ the purpose and format of cash flow forecasts

✍ monitoring cash flows

✍ using cash flow forecasts

KNOWLEDGE AND UNDERSTANDING AND PERFORMANCE CRITERIA COVERAGE

Performance criteria – element 15.1

■ monitor and control cash receipts and payments against budgeted cash flow
■ identify significant deviations from the cash budget and take corrective action within defined organisational policies

knowledge and understanding – accounting principles and theory

■ the main types of cash receipts and payments: regular revenue receipts and payments; capital receipts and payments; drawings/dividends and disbursements; exceptional receipts and payments
■ form and structure of cash budgets
■ understanding that the accounting systems of an organisation are affected by its organisational structure, its administrative systems and procedures and the nature of its business transactions

INTRODUCTION

Unit 15, Operating a cash management and credit control system, consists of four separate elements but there are significant interrelationships between them. The first two elements concern cash management and this will be considered in the first four chapters of this Course Companion. Elements 15.3 and 15.4 relate to the credit control function and the management of debtors which will be considered in Chapters 5 to 8 of this Course Companion.

Cash management

In this first chapter we will introduce you to the concept of cash management and indeed the importance of cash to a business. This will be followed by more detailed consideration of how and why businesses manage their cash balances and the tools and instruments that are available in order for them to do this successfully.

CASH AND THE BUSINESS

When you think about a business the first question that you might reasonably ask about that business is 'Is it profitable?'. The aim of most businesses is of course to make a profit for its owners whether the business is that of a sole trader, a partnership or a company making profits for its shareholders.

If a business is profitable this means that it is making more by selling its goods or services than it is expending on the purchase of goods and the payment of expenses. However profit is not always enough! In order for a business to succeed it must have cash in its bank account (or an agreed overdraft with its bank) in order to pay all of its costs and expenses as they fall due. If not the business could be in trouble and might eventually flounder.

HOW IT WORKS

Jo Kennedy has just set up a jewellery, gifts and cards business. She buys in materials, makes the jewellery, gifts and cards and then sells them to a few private customers but largely to a small number of retail outlets. She started the business on 1 March with £1,000 in her business bank account and during that month wrote cheques for materials for £800.

Jo felt that she had a good month in March as she made sales to private customers totalling £300 and further sales of £900 to various retail outlets. The private customers paid either by cash or cheque and Jo paid these into the business bank account immediately. However the retail customers were not prepared to pay the amount they owed until May.

In April Jo needs to replenish her stock of materials at a cost of a further £800 and to pay two months rent on her studio totalling £350. How will she be able to do this?

Jo Kennedy - Cash summary

	March £	April £	May £
Opening balance	1,000	500	
Payments	(800)	(1,150)	
Receipts from private trade	300		
Receipts from retailers			900
Closing balance	500	(650)	

By the end of March Jo still has £500 in the business bank account but her payments due in April are £1,150. Although there is £900 receivable in May from her March retail sales, without substantial cash receipts from private sales in April Jo will either not have enough money to continue in business or must approach her bank for a substantial overdraft.

This illustrates that in order to carry on in business it is important not only to be profitable but also to have the cash available to meet the business payments when they fall due.

Cash and profit

The previous simple example showed that there is a distinct difference between making a profit and having available cash. So now we will remind you of the reasons for the difference between profit and cash.

The accruals concept

The profit for a period is calculated using the accruals concept. Under the ACCRUALS CONCEPT revenue from sales and the cost of goods and expenses are accounted for in the period in which they are earned or incurred rather than in the period in which the cash is received or paid. Therefore even though a business may appear to have made a profit in a period it may not yet have the cash to show for it.

Non-cash expenses

Generally expenses of a business will reduce the amount of cash that the business has as these expenses will have to be paid for. However there are some expenses which have no effect on cash at all, NON-CASH EXPENSES. The most obvious of these is the annual depreciation charge on fixed assets. Although this is an expense of the business it is not an amount of cash leaving the business.

Another example of a non-cash expense is that of a provision. Provisions are set up under accounting rules for expenses payable in the future which are probable but as yet either the amount or the timing of these expenses are uncertain. Therefore although they are an expense of the business they do not represent cash going out of the business just yet.

Receipts/payments not affecting profit

Many businesses will find that on occasions they have receipts of cash into the business which do not affect profit. For example if a sole trader pays more capital into his business or a company issues additional shares for cash there are receipts of cash into the business but the profit of the business is not affected.

Conversely if a sole trader takes drawings out of his business or a company pays its shareholders a cash dividend then these are reductions in the cash balance of the business but not in the profit level of the business.

Purchase of fixed assets

When fixed assets are purchased by a business this will often mean a large payment of cash in order to acquire the asset. However as you will have seen in your earlier accounting studies this does not affect the profit and loss account. Only the annual depreciation charge on the new asset is an expense rather than the full cash cost.

Sale of fixed assets

When a fixed asset is sold then this will mean cash coming into the business, being the selling price of the asset. However the profit of the business is only increased or decreased by any amount of profit or loss on the sale of this asset rather than the cash received.

Activity 1

Think of two other types of transaction or event which affects profit in a different way to the effect it has on the amount of cash in the business.

Cash and credit transactions

When we have talked about cash so far in this chapter we have generally meant the amount of money that the business has in its bank account. However we must be quite clear about the distinction between transactions which are for cash and those which are on credit.

A CASH TRANSACTION is one that takes place either with coins and notes, a cheque, a credit card or a debit card. Cash transactions are basically those for which money will be available in the business bank account almost immediately once the amounts have been paid into the bank.

A CREDIT TRANSACTION is one where the receipt or the payment is delayed for a period of time which is agreed between the two parties to the transaction. Many business sales and purchases are made on credit whereby the goods are delivered or received now but payment is agreed to be received or made in say 30 or 60 days time.

Activity 2

In each of the following cases decide whether the transaction is a cash or credit transaction:

i)   cheque made out for £100 for the payment of rent

ii) credit card sales of £800

iii) goods purchased for £250 with payment to be made on receipt of the invoice

iv) goods and an invoice delivered to a customer today for payment in 30 days

---

TYPES OF CASH FLOWS

Now that we have considered the importance of cash and the differences between cash and profit we must consider the different types of cash transactions or cash flows that a business will have.

Regular cash flows

The vast majority of the cash flows of a business will be REGULAR CASH FLOWS. This means that they will generally take place every week, every month, every quarter or annually.

For example if a business has weekly paid employees then they will be paid on Friday of every week. If a business has an agreement with its credit customers that goods are paid for at the end of the month after they are delivered then it will have receipts from customers at the end of each month. A business pays rent every quarter in advance so every three months there is a rental cash flow. Most companies pay their Corporation Tax liability for the year nine months after the year end so each year this payment will have to be made.

Irregular cash flows

Some cash flows of a business however are likely to be IRREGULAR CASH FLOWS. For example the purchase of new fixed assets is not necessarily something that is done every six months but as and when required.

Exceptional cash flows

Some of the cash flows of a business could also be regarded as EXCEPTIONAL CASH FLOWS or unpredictable cash flows. For example if a machine breaks down the costs of mending or replacing it could not have been predicted.

Variable and fixed cash flows

Some cash flows will be variable in amount although regular in time scale. For example the amount of cash sales or receipts from debtors is likely to vary each period. However other cash flows are likely to be fixed in amount as well as regular. For example the quarterly rent that a business pays for its building will be the same each quarter until there is a rent review and any amounts paid under a hire purchase agreement will be the same amount each period.

Types of cash receipt

Most cash receipts will be receipts from:

- cash sales
- credit sales
- interest on money on deposit

All of these are fairly regular (though the amount in each time period may vary considerably). However other cash receipts might be irregular such as:

- receipts of dividends from investments
- additional capital raised
- loan finance taken out
- receipts from sale of fixed assets

It is also possible that there may be exceptional receipts such as:

- insurance monies received after theft of a company asset
- receipt of a government grant newly introduced

Types of cash payment

Again as with cash receipts most cash payments are likely to be regular but there will tend to be a wider variety of payments than there generally are of receipts. Regular cash payments (of varying amounts) might include:

- cash payments for purchases
- . payments for purchases made on credit
- payments of wages and salaries
- payments for expenses
- payments for VAT, PAYE and NIC
- payments for corporation tax
- interest payments on loans

Irregular payments might include:

- drawings by a sole trader or partners in a partnership
- dividends to shareholders in a company
- payments to acquire new fixed assets

Exceptional payments might include:

- emergency expenses such as repair costs
- bank charges on early withdrawal of funds

Different types of business

It must be appreciated that different types of business will incur different types of cash flows.

The structure of the business will initially affect the type of cash flows. For example a company may make regular annual dividend payments to its shareholders whereas the amount and frequency of drawings that a sole trader takes out of the business will be his decision. A company will have to pay corporation tax on an annual basis whereas a sole trader pays his income taxes out of his personal income rather than out of the business.

The trade of the business will also affect the type of cash flows that the business has. For example a supermarket will have a large amount of cash sales and purchases on credit but little or no sales on credit. In contrast a manufacturing business may make all of its sales on credit with no immediate receipts of cash for goods sold.

Service industries will tend to have large, monthly expenses for wages and salaries but only a few payments for purchases either on credit or for cash.

Activity 3

Give an example of an exceptional receipt and an exceptional payment that a business might have.

CASH FLOW FORECASTS

It is generally argued that the management of a business have three main roles:

- planning
- decision making
- control

PLANNING is the formation of a strategy for the long term future and then detailed financial and non-financial plans of how the business is to operate over the short and medium term future.

DECISION MAKING can range from day to day operating decisions to long term strategic decisions.

CONTROL is about comparing the actual performance of the business to the planned performance and taking actions to correct any deviations from the plan.

The production of cash flow forecasts is a useful management tool particularly for planning and control purposes.

What is a cash flow forecast?

A CASH FLOW FORECAST is a method of determining the expected net cash flow for a future period and the expected cash or overdraft balance at the end of that future period. Cash flow forecasts can be prepared daily, weekly, monthly, quarterly or even annually depending upon the amount of detail required by management and the amounts of cash involved. Cash flow forecasts are often also referred to as CASH BUDGETS.

There are two main types of cash flow forecast:

- a RECEIPTS AND PAYMENTS CASH BUDGET

- a PROFIT AND LOSS ACCOUNT AND BALANCE SHEET CASH FLOW FORECAST

Receipts and payments cash budget

In this type of cash flow forecast the expected receipts for a period are listed and totalled as are the expected payments in the period. The NET CASH FLOW is determined by deducting the payments from the receipts and this net movement is applied to the opening cash balance in order to find the anticipated closing cash balance.

A typical cash budget of this type is shown below:

	March £	April £	May £
Receipts			
Cash sales	X	X	X
Receipts from credit customers	X	X	X
Proceeds from sale of fixed assets		X	
Total receipts (a)	X	X	X
Payments			
Cash purchases	X	X	X
Payments to credit suppliers	X	X	X
Wages	X	X	X
Operating expenses	X	X	X
Purchase of fixed assets	X		
Dividend			X
Total payments (b)	X	X	X
Net cash flow (a - b)	X	X	X
Opening cash balance	X	X	X
Closing cash balance	X	X	X

Note how the closing cash balance each month becomes the opening cash balance at the start of the following month.

The detailed lines making up the receipts and payments may differ from business to business depending upon the nature of their business and transactions.

Profit and loss account and balance sheet cash flow forecast

This type of cash flow forecast requires a forecast profit and loss account for the period and forecast balance sheet information at the start and end of the period.

Under this method of determining net cash flow for a future period and the cash balance at the end of the period the starting point is the anticipated operating profit for the period. This is then adjusted for non-cash expenses such as depreciation and also for changes in working capital (debtors, creditors and stocks). The resulting total is the net cash flow from operating activities. This can then be adjusted for other anticipated non-operating cash flows such as the purchase of fixed assets or the issue of shares.

A typical example of such a cash flow forecast would be like this:

	March £
Net operating profit	X
Adjustments for:	
Depreciation	X
Profit on sale of fixed assets	(X)
Working capital adjustments:	
Increase in stocks	(X)
Decrease in debtors	X
Increase in creditors	X
Net cash flow from operations	X
Non-operating cash flows	
Interest payments	(X)
Purchase of fixed assets	(X)
Proceeds from sale of fixed assets	X
Issue of shares	X
Payment of dividend	(X)
Net cash flow	X
Opening cash balance	X
Closing cash balance	X

In the next chapter we will consider how to prepare these two types of cash flow forecast in detail.

Note that the first method, the cash receipts and payments method, of preparing a cash forecast or budget is more common than the second method.

Activity 4

Briefly explain the difference between a receipts and payments cash budget and a cash flow forecast based upon a forecast profit and loss account and balance sheets.

MONITORING CASH FLOWS

We have already seen that one of the important roles of management is that of control of operations and transactions. One way of controlling the operations of the business is to compare the actual effects of the operations to those that were anticipated in the plans for the business.

It has already been noted that cash is a vital element of any business and therefore it is an important management role to compare the actual cash flows for a period to the expected cash flows as shown in the cash flow forecast. If there are significant differences between the actual and expected cash flows then management can investigate the reasons for these differences and consider any action that is necessary in order to ensure that cash flows and cash balances revert to plan.

There are two main methods of comparing the actual cash flows and position to the budgeted cash flows and budgeted balance:

- comparison of each individual cash flow
- reconciliation of the actual cash balance to the budgeted cash balance

Comparison of individual cash flows

Under this method of monitoring the actual cash flows of a business, for each individual line of the cash forecast the actual cash flow for the period is compared to the budgeted cash flow and the difference is recorded. This difference is often known as the VARIANCE.

HOW IT WORKS

SC Fuel and Glass is a company based in the south of England which sells and distributes oil and petrol and also has a glass making division. SC prepares monthly cash flow forecasts and monitors the actual cash flows compared to the budgeted cash flows shortly after the end of each month.

Given below is the cash budget for the fuel division of SC for the month of June together with the actual cash flows for the month.

Cash budget: June

	Budgeted cash flows £	Actual cash flows £
Receipts:		
Cash sales	110,000	106,500
Receipts from credit customers	655,000	633,000
Proceeds from sale of fixed assets	–	15,000
Total receipts	765,000	754,500
Payments:		
Payments to credit suppliers	550,000	589,000
Wages	108,000	108,000
Rent	10,000	10,500
Advertising	12,000	9,000
Purchase of fixed assets	–	27,000
Dividend payment	20,000	20,000
Total payments	700,000	763,500
Net cash flow	65,000	(9,000)
Opening cash balance	10,000	10,000
Closing cash balance	75,000	1,000

Note how the actual net cash flow is a cash outflow, shown in brackets, as the total payments in the month were greater than the total receipts.

We can now compare the actual and budgeted figures for each line of the cash flow statement to discover the differences or variances.

	Budgeted cash flows £	Actual cash flows £	Variance £
Receipts:			
Cash sales	110,000	106,500	(3,500)
Receipts from credit customers	655,000	633,000	(22,000)
Proceeds from sale of fixed assets	–	15,000	15,000
Total receipts	765,000	754,500	
Payments:			
Payments to credit suppliers	550,000	589,000	(39,000)
Wages	108,000	108,000	–
Rent	10,000	10,500	(500)
Advertising	12,000	9,000	3,000
Purchase of fixed assets	–	27,000	(27,000)
Dividend payment	20,000	20,000	
Total payments	700,000	763,500	
Net cash flow	65,000	(9,000)	(74,000)
Opening cash balance	10,000	10,000	–
Closing cash balance	75,000	1,000	(74,000)

Any difference which is good news, such as receipts being higher than budgeted or payments being lower, are known as FAVOURABLE VARIANCES.

Any differences which are bad news where receipts are less than budgeted or payments are greater than budgeted are known as ADVERSE VARIANCES. The adverse variances are shown in brackets.

Further investigation

At this stage it is likely that some or all of these variances would be investigated.

Receipts
Cash sales   – why are these less than budgeted?

Receipts from customers – why are these less than budgeted?

Sale of fixed asset   – this is an unexpected receipt but why has the sale taken place if it was not planned for?

Payments
Payments to creditors – why are these greater than budgeted?

| Rent | – this is probably a rent increase that was not included in the forecast |

Advertising — why are these costs lower than budgeted?

Purchase of fixed assets — why has this taken place when it was not budgeted for? was the purchase to replace the fixed asset that was sold?

The overall effect of all of these variances from the cash forecast figures is that the net cash flow for the period is £74,000 and the forecast cash balance is therefore £74,000 lower than anticipated.

Management action to be taken

Having discovered the variances between the actual cash flows and the budgeted cash flows management may wish to take actions to try to bring the cash position back in line with the budgeted position. What possible actions might they take with the fuel division of SC?

Receipts from credit customers — credit control might be improved to encourage earlier payments from debtors

Payments to credit suppliers — these may be delayed longer

Purchase of fixed assets — these should be considered to determine if they are necessary and if there is another form of financing that does not require so much cash to be spent immediately

Activity 5

Receipts from credit customers for a period were £186,000 compared to the budgeted figure of £168,000. Is this a favourable or an adverse variance?

Reconciliation of actual cash balance to budgeted cash balance

This method of comparing actual to budgeted cash flows uses many of the same calculations as in the method above but presents the final information in a slightly different manner. Again each line in the cash flow forecast is compared to the actual figure and the variance is calculated. However these variances are then used to reconcile the final actual cash balance to the final budgeted cash balance.

HOW IT WORKS

Again we will use the cash flow forecast and actual figures for June for the fuel division of SC.

	June Budgeted cash flows £	Actual cash flows £
Receipts:		
Cash sales	110,000	106,500
Receipts from credit customers	655,000	633,000
Proceeds from sale of fixed assets	–	15,000
Total receipts	765,000	754,500
Payments:		
Payments to credit suppliers	550,000	589,000
Wages	108,000	108,000
Rent	10,000	10,500
Advertising	12,000	9,000
Purchase of fixed assets	–	27,000
Dividend payment	20,000	20,000
Total payments	700,000	763,500
Net cash flow	65,000	(9,000)
Opening cash balance	10,000	10,000
Closing cash balance	75,000	1,000

Again the variance for each line of the cash flow forecast is calculated:

	June		
	Budgeted cash flows	Actual cash flows	Variance
	£	£	£
Receipts:			
Cash sales	110,000	106,500	(3,500)
Receipts from credit customers	655,000	633,000	(22,000)
Proceeds from sale of fixed assets	–	15,000	15,000
Total receipts	765,000	754,500	
Payments:			
Payments to credit suppliers	550,000	589,000	(39,000)
Wages	108,000	108,000	–
Rent	10,000	10,500	(500)
Advertising	12,000	9,000	3,000
Purchase of fixed assets	–	27,000	(27,000)
Dividend payment	20,000	20,000	–
Total payments	700,000	763,500	
Net cash flow	65,000	(9,000)	(74,000)
Opening cash balance	10,000	10,000	–
Closing cash balance	75,000	1,000	(74,000)

These figures are then used to explain why the actual cash balance at the end of June was £1,000 when it had been budgeted to be £75,000.

This is normally done by starting with the budgeted cash balance and adding any favourable variances and deducting any adverse variances.

June Reconciliation of actual cash balance to budgeted cash balance

	£
Budgeted cash balance	75,000
Shortfall in cash sales	(3,500)
Shortfall in receipts from customers	(22,000)
Additional receipt from sale of fixed asset	15,000
Additional payments to credit suppliers	(39,000)
Additional rent	(500)
Lower advertising cost	3,000
Additional fixed asset purchase	(27,000)
Actual cash balance	1,000

Activity 6

If the budgeted cash balance is to be reconciled to the actual cash balance is an adverse variance added to or subtracted from the budgeted cash balance?

USING CASH FLOW FORECASTS

As well as using a cash flow forecast or cash budget to monitor any differences between actual cash flows and what had been anticipated, the cash flow forecast can also be used for other purposes.

Identifying cash surpluses or deficits

If a cash flow forecast is prepared for a number of periods in advance then the anticipated cash balance at the end of each of those periods can be forecast. The management of the business can then plan ahead as to how to invest any anticipated cash surplus and how to fund any anticipated cash deficit. These areas will be considered in more detail in Chapter 4 of this Course Companion.

Taking action to improve the budgeted position

A cash flow forecast shows what the cash position is expected to be given the current and planned circumstances and operations of the business. However if the cash flow forecast indicates an excessive surplus or, perhaps more importantly, an overdraft which exceeds the agreed overdraft limit, then the advance warning gives management the opportunity to change policies or operating practices in order to improve the position that is indicated in the cash flow forecast.

Suppose that an excessive overdraft was predicted by the cash flow forecast. The types of actions that could be taken include:

- improving credit control procedures to ensure money is received from credit customers sooner

- increasing the proportion of cash sales in comparison to credit sales

- selling surplus fixed assets

- increasing the period of credit taken from suppliers therefore paying suppliers later

- negotiating credit terms for expenses that are currently paid in cash

student notes✍

- ■ delaying payments for fixed assets

- ■ changing the method of financing the purchase of fixed assets

- ■ waiving or delaying dividend payments

Discretionary and non-discretionary payments

Some care has to be taken when making suggestions as to how to improve a forecast cash flow position as there are some payments that must be made on time, NON-DISCRETIONARY PAYMENTS, whereas there are others, DISCRETIONARY PAYMENTS, which could validly be delayed.

HOW IT WORKS

SC Fuel and Glass have now prepared their cash flow forecasts for the fuel division for the quarter ending 30 September on the basis that the opening cash balance is the actual closing balance of £1,000 at the end of June. The company has an agreed overdraft limit of £50,000.

The cash budget for the three months to 30 September appears as follows:

	July £	August £	Sept £
Receipts:			
Cash sales	80,000	94,000	98,000
Receipts from credit customers	612,000	588,000	561,000
Proceeds from sale of fixed assets	–	–	22,000
Total receipts	692,000	682,000	681,000
Payments:			
Payments to credit suppliers	520,000	500,000	520,000
Wages	108,000	108,000	108,000
Rent	10,500	10,500	10,500
Advertising	12,000	2,000	2,000
Purchase of fixed assets	25,000	37,000	–
VAT	22,000		
Corporation tax	–	90,000	
Total payments	697,500	747,500	640,500
Net cash flow	(5,500)	(65,500)	40,500
Opening cash balance	1,000	(4,500)	(70,000)
Closing cash balance	(4,500)	(70,000)	(29,500)

There is an anticipated overdraft at the end of each of the three months but the main problem is that in August the agreed overdraft limit is exceeded by £20,000. Is there anything that can be done to improve this position and try to keep the division within its agreed overdraft limit?

Receipts

Cash sales receipts	– there is probably little that can be done over such a short space of time to improve the cash sales position
Receipts from debtors	– it might be possible to tighten credit control procedures and collect money earlier from debtors
Sale of fixed assets	– if this asset is surplus to requirements it may be possible to sell it in July or August or if it is being sold on credit to collect the money sooner

Payments

Payments to credit suppliers	– it may be possible to extend the period of credit to suppliers and pay them later thereby improving the cash position
Wages	– wages are non-discretionary and must be paid in full and on time
Rent	– it is unlikely that there could be any renegotiation of the payment terms for the rent
Advertising	– there is a large cost in July. Could this be postponed or alternatively paid for over a number of months rather than in one go?
Purchase of fixed assets	– large amounts of purchases in July and August. It may be possible to delay these purchases, negotiate credit terms for the payment or change the purchase method to hire purchase or leasing.
VAT	– this is a non-discretionary payment and must be paid when due otherwise financial penalties will be incurred
Corporation tax	– this is a non-discretionary payment and must be paid when due otherwise financial penalties will be incurred

Activity 7

Give an example of a discretionary payment and a non-discretionary payment.

CHAPTER OVERVIEW

- as a starting point for this Unit it is important to realise how vital cash is to a business even if the business is profitable as it must be able to meet its payments as and when they fall due

- there are a number of differences between profit and cash due to the accruals concept, non-cash expenses, receipts or payments which do not affect profit, purchases and sales of fixed assets

- cash transactions are where a form of money is received immediately whereas in a credit transaction goods are received or sent immediately but payment is delayed by agreement between the buyer and the seller

- cash flows may be regular, irregular, exceptional, variable or fixed

- a cash flow forecast predicts the net cash flows for a future period and the expected cash balance at the end of the period and is useful to management for planning and control purposes

- a receipts and payments cash flow forecast is one where the cash receipts and cash payments are listed and totalled and the net cash flow for the period is applied to the opening cash balance in order to find the closing cash balance

- a profit and loss account and balance sheet cash flow forecast is one where net operating profit is used initially and adjusted for non-cash figures and working capital movements to arrive at net cash flow from operating activities

- as part of the management role of control it is important to compare the actual cash flows for a period to the budgeted or forecast cash flows – this can be done by calculating variances on a line by line basis or by reconciling the actual cash balance to the budgeted cash balance

KEY WORDS

Accruals concept revenue and expenses are accounted for in the period in which they are incurred rather than the period in which the cash is received or paid

Non-cash expenses expenses of the business which are charged to profit but do not affect the amount of cash in the business

Cash transaction a transaction by cash, cheque, credit card or debit card

Credit transaction a transaction where receipt or payment of cash is delayed for a period of time

Regular cash flows cash flows that take place on a regular basis be it daily, weekly, monthly, quarterly or annually

Irregular cash flows cash flows which occur fairly infrequently and with no set pattern

Exceptional cash flows unusual or unpredictable cash flows

Planning the management task of setting long, medium and short term plans for the business

Decision making the management task of making long and short term decisions regarding the business

Control the management task of controlling the operations and performance of the business

Cash flow forecast or **cash budget** a method of determining the expected net cash flow for a future period and the cash balance at the end of that period

CHAPTER OVERVIEW cont.

- once the variances between actual and budgeted cash flows have been determined they may be investigated and appropriate actions taken

- a cash flow forecast, once prepared, can indicate to management future cash surpluses or deficits and can also indicate areas where procedures and policies can be altered or improved in order to improve the cash position

KEY WORDS

Receipts and payments a list of all cash receipts and payments for the cash flow forecast period netted off to find the net cash flow for the period

Profit and loss account and balance sheet cash flow forecast a method of determining net cash flow from operations by adjusting net operating profit

Net cash flow determined by deducting the payments from the receipts, then applying this net movement to the opening cash balance in order to find the anticipated closing cash balance

Variance the difference between actual results and budgeted results

Favourable variances variances which represent greater income or less expense than budgeted

Adverse variances variances which represent less income or greater expenses than budgeted

Discretionary payments payments which can validly be cancelled or delayed

Non-discretionary payments payments which must be made for the business to continue

HOW MUCH HAVE YOU LEARNED?

1   Explain why it could be argued that a healthy cash balance is as important to a business as making profits.

2   What are the factors that account for the difference between the amount of profit a business makes and its cash balance?

3   i)   Give five examples of regular cash flow payments for a business
    ii)   Give an example of an exceptional receipt and an exceptional payment

4   Complete the following proforma cash flow forecast with examples of the adjustments required.

	£
Net operating profit	X
Adjustments for:	
i)	
ii)	
iii)	
iv)	
v)	
Net cash flow from operating activities	X

5   Given below is the budgeted cash flow statement for Glenn Security Systems for the month of May together with the actual cash flows for the month.

    i)   Identify three significant differences between the actual cash flow for the month and the budgeted cash flow

    ii)   Suggest three actions that the company could have taken to avoid using its overdraft facility

Cash flow forecast May

	Budget £	Actual £
Cash sales receipts	43,000	45,000
Credit sales receipts	256,000	231,000
Credit suppliers	(176,000)	(189,000)
Wages	(88,000)	(88,000)
Overheads	(43,200)	(44,500)
Capital expenditure	–	(40,000)
Movement for the month	(8,200)	(85,500)
Bank b/f	53,400	52,100
Bank c/f	45,200	(33,400)

6 Given below is the budgeted cash flow statement for Glenn Security Systems for the month of May together with the actual cash flows for the month.

	Budget £	Actual £
Cash sales receipts	43,000	45,000
Credit sales receipts	256,000	231,000
Credit suppliers	(176,000)	(189,000)
Wages	(88,000)	(88,000)
Overheads	(43,200)	(44,500)
Capital expenditure	–	(40,000)
Movement for the month	(8,200)	(85,500)
Bank b/f	53,400	52,100
Bank c/f	45,200	(33,400)

Reconcile the actual cash balance at 31 May to the budgeted cash balance at that date.

7 Given below are the cash flow forecasts for the quarter ending 30 June for Davies Engineering. The company has an agreed overdraft facility of £20,000.

Cash flow forecast

	April £	May £	June £
Receipts:			
Cash sales	64,000	75,000	78,000
Receipts from credit customers	489,000	470,000	449,000
Proceeds from sale of fixed assets	–	10,000	–
Total receipts	553,000	555,000	527,000
Payments:			
Payments to credit suppliers	426,000	437,000	425,000
Wages	84,000	84,000	84,000
Rent	8,000	8,000	8,000
Capital expenditure	26,000	28,000	–
VAT	–	12,200	
Training costs	20,000		
Repairs and maintenance	10,400		
Total payments	574,400	569,200	517,000
Net cash flow	(21,400)	(14,200)	10,000
Opening cash balance	2,600	(18,800)	(33,000)
Closing cash balance	(18,800)	(33,000)	(23,000)

What could be done to improve the cash forecast position and keep the company within its agreed overdraft limit?

chapter 2:
PREPARING CASH BUDGETS

chapter coverage 📖

In this chapter we will be considering the preparation of cash flow budgets (the term can be used interchangeably with cash flow forecast). This is a topic that will almost definitely appear in every assessment as it is the core topic of the first part of the syllabus for Unit 15. The preparation of cash budgets can seem daunting at first as you will be provided with a lot of information. However in this chapter we will deal with each area of the preparation of the budget separately and you will see that with a logical approach this will quickly build into the ability to prepare a complete cash budget.

The topics that are to be covered are:

✎ information required to prepare a cash budget

✎ sales receipts

✎ payments for purchases

✎ other cash payments and receipts

✎ overdraft interest

✎ preparing a cash budget in a manufacturing organisation

✎ preparing a cash flow forecast from a budgeted profit and loss account and balance sheets

Note that we use the term 'cash budget' for a statement produced from details of sales and production etc, and 'cash flow forecast' for a statement based on forecast profit and loss account and balance sheets. Note carefully the wording that is used in every simulation.

Performance criteria – element 15.1

- consult appropriate staff to determine the likely pattern of cash flows over the accounting period and to anticipate any exceptional receipts or payments
- prepare cash budgets in the approved format and clearly indicate net cash requirements

knowledge and understanding

- the main types of cash receipts and payments: regular revenue receipts and payments; capital receipts and payments; drawings/dividends and disbursements; exceptional receipts and payments
- form and structure of cash budgets
- lagged receipts and payments
- cash flow accounting and its relationship to accounting for income and expenditure
- understanding that the accounting systems of an organisation are affected by its organisational structure, its administrative systems and procedures and the nature of its business transactions
- understanding that recording and accounting practices may vary in different parts of the organisation
- an understanding of the organisation's relevant policies and procedures

INTRODUCTION

In the previous chapter we saw the format that cash budgets can take. The most common is that of a receipts and payments type cash flow forecast and we will be concentrating on this for most of the chapter. However we will also consider how to determine net cash flow and cash position using a forecast profit and loss account and forecast balance sheets.

Information for a cash budget

When we considered the types of cash flows that a typical business might have in the previous chapter we saw that these are many and varied. They include sales cash flows, purchases cash flows, overheads or expenses cash flows, capital expenditure and receipts, and other payments and receipts such as additional capital and dividends or drawings.

As an accounting technician you will not necessarily have a detailed knowledge of all of these areas therefore you will require expert and detailed information from other personnel within the business in order to be able to prepare a cash budget. In particular you will typically need input from the following functions within the business:

- sales staff regarding the anticipated future levels of sales

- production staff regarding the expected levels of production and associated purchasing and other costs

- accounting personnel regarding prices, costs, wages, overheads etc

- senior personnel regarding capital expenditure and sales, and plans for items such as the raising of additional capital or the payment of a dividend.

Different types of business

The format of a cash budget will depend upon the particular types of cash flow of that business.

Equally the preparation of a cash budget will depend upon the type of business. For a retail business the cash flows will involve the purchase of goods which are then resold either for cash or on credit. However in a manufacturing business the materials required for production will have to be purchased and processed and then the finished goods will be sold. These different types of business will require different techniques in order to prepare the cash budget. In this chapter we will consider the budgeting techniques to prepare a cash budget for both a retail-type organisation and a manufacturing organisation.

Preparation of a cash budget

The preparation of a cash budget, both in practice and in assessments, will require information from a variety of sources and this information must be brought together in order to determine the figures for each line of the cash budget.

We will start with one of the more complicated areas, which is determining the cash to be received from sales in each future period.

SALES RECEIPTS

Cash sales

Most businesses will have a mixture of cash sales and sales on credit. When preparing the cash budget the starting point will be the total expected sales for the period which will probably be provided by the sales department. Of these total sales a certain amount, either reported as an absolute amount or as a percentage of total sales, will be cash sales which means that the cash inflow will take place at the same time as the sale.

Credit sales

When a business makes sales on credit this means that the cash for the sale will be received at some point in time after the sale. The detailed terms of sales on credit will be considered in Chapter 6 of this Course Companion, but typical examples would be 30 days after the invoice date or 60 days after the invoice date. The receipt of money some time after the invoice date is known as a LAGGED RECEIPT.

Whatever credit terms are set for credit customers there will be some customers who do not adhere to them and will pay later than they are meant to. This problem will be dealt with later in the Course Companion in Chapter 7.

However at this stage it is important to realise that some cash from credit sales will be received according to the stated credit terms but some will be received later. This means that of the credit sales in one particular month certain proportions of the cash will often be received in a number of different months after the sale.

HOW IT WORKS

The fuel division of SC Fuel and Glass is preparing its quarterly cash flow forecast for each of the three months of October, November and December.

The sales of the fuel division for these three months are expected to be as follows:

October	£680,000
November	£700,000
December	£750,000

Of these sales, 20% are cash sales and the remainder are sales on credit. Experience has shown that on average the debtors for credit sales pay the money due with the following pattern:

The month after sale	20%
Two months after sale	50%
Three months after sale	30%

Therefore the cash for the October credit sales will be received in November, December and January. If we are preparing the cash flow forecast for the period from October to December then some of the cash inflows will be from credit sales in earlier months therefore you will also require information about the credit sales for these earlier months.

The total sales in July to September for the fuel division (again 20% of these were cash sales) are:

July	£600,000
August	£560,000
September	£620,000

We can now start to piece together the information required to prepare the cash from sales for October to December:

Cash budget – October to December

	October £	November £	December £
Cash receipts:			
Cash sales			
(20% of month sales)	136,000	140,000	150,000

Now we need to deal with sales on credit which are more complicated and will require a working:

WORKING – Cash from credit sales

	October £	November £	December £
July sales			
(80% x 600,000 x 30%)	144,000		
August sales			
(80% x 560,000 x 50%)	224,000		
(80% x 560,000 x 30%)		134,400	
September sales			
(80% x 620,000 x 20%)	99,200		
(80% x 620,000 x 50%)		248,000	
(80% x 620,000 x 30%)			148,800
October sales			
(80% x 680,000 x 20%)		108,800	
(80% x 680,000 x 50%)			272,000
November sales			
(80% x 700,000 x 20%)			112,000
Cash from credit sales	467,200	491,200	532,800

Cash budget – October to December

	October £	November £	December £
Cash receipts:			
Cash sales	136,000	140,000	150,000
Cash from credit sales	467,200	491,200	532,800

Activity 1

A company makes credit sales with a typical payment pattern of 40% of the cash being received in the month after sale, 35% two months after the sale and 25% three months after the sale. Credit sales in August, September and October were £320,000, £360,000 and £400,000 respectively.

What are the cash receipts from credit sales received in November?

PAYMENTS FOR PURCHASES

In a similar way to sales, purchases of the goods that a business buys can be made for cash or on credit. If the purchases are for cash then the cash outflow is at the same time as the purchase. However if the purchase is made on credit then there will be a LAGGED PAYMENT where the cash is paid some time after the purchase is made. As with sales the business will have a typical payment pattern for its credit suppliers which can be used to find the cash outflow for each period.

Settlement discounts

When transactions are made on credit it is common practice for the seller to offer the buyer a SETTLEMENT DISCOUNT (or cash discount or prompt payment discount). This means that if the buyer takes advantage of the discount and pays within a certain time period then a certain percentage is deducted from the amount which is owed.

For cash budget purposes if a settlement discount is taken on purchases then this means that the cash payment will be earlier than normal but will be for the invoice amount less the settlement discount.

HOW IT WORKS

The purchasing manager for SC Fuel and Glass has provided you with the following information about the anticipated purchases of fuel for the fuel division for the period October to December.

October	£408,000
November	£420,000
December	£450,000

The accounts department provides you with the following information about the payment pattern for these purchases which are all made on credit terms.

- 25% of purchases are offered a 2% discount for payment in the month of the purchase and SC Fuels takes advantage of all such settlement discounts offered.

- 60% of purchases are paid in the month following the purchase

- 15% are paid two months after the date of purchase.

This means that 25% of purchases are paid in the month of purchase with 2% deducted. The remaining 75% of purchases are paid for in the following two months therefore we need information about the purchases in August and September in order to complete the cash flow forecast.

August purchases	£340,000
September purchases	£360,000

Again we will need a working in order to determine the payments to suppliers in each of the three months.

WORKING Payments to credit suppliers

	October £	November £	December £
August purchases			
(340,000 x 15%)	51,000		
September purchases			
(360,000 x 60%)	216,000		
(360,000 x 15%)		54,000	
October purchases			
(408,000 x 25% x 98%)	99,960		
(408,000 x 60%)		244,800	
(408,000 x 15%)			61,200
November purchases			
(420,000 x 25% x 98%)		102,900	
(420,000 x 60%)			252,000
December purchases			
(450,000 x 25% x 98%)			110,250
Payments to credit suppliers	366,960	401,700	423,450

We can now start to add figures to the cash payments section of the cash budget.

Cash flow forecast – October to December

	October £	November £	December £
Cash receipts:			
Cash sales	136,000	140,000	150,000
Cash from credit sales	467,200	491,200	532,800
Cash payments:			
Payments for credit purchases	366,960	401,700	423,450

Gross profit margins

In the example above the amount of purchases each month in total was given to you by the purchasing director. It is however possible that you may be given the sales for a month and the gross profit percentage and be expected to work out the relevant figure for purchases. Note that gross profit margin may also be called 'gross profit percentage' and 'gross profit on sales'.

HOW IT WORKS

The fuel division of SC Fuel and Glass operates with a gross profit margin of 40%. This means that the purchases figure (providing that stocks remain constant) is 60% of the sales for the month. Therefore you might have simply been given the sales for October to December and be expected to work out the purchases for each month.

	Sales	Purchases
October	£680,000 x 60%	£408,000
November	£700,000 x 60%	£420,000
December	£750,000 x 60%	£450,000

Activity 2

A business makes all of its purchases on credit and it makes a consistent gross profit on sales of 25%. 60% of the purchases are paid for in the month after purchase and the remainder two months after the purchase.

The business has the following anticipated sales:

July	£200,000
August	£240,000
September	£260,000

What is the cash payment to suppliers in October?

Settlement discounts offered on sales

In just the same way that settlement discounts can be taken on purchases a business may offer a settlement discount on its sales. This will affect the amount of cash inflow from sales on credit as those discounts which are taken up will pay earlier but will pay the invoice amount less the settlement discount.

If a settlement discount of 3% is offered on credit sales which are paid for in the month of sale then for those customers who take up the settlement discount the amount received will be just 97% of the invoiced amount.

Activity 3

A business makes the following sales on credit:

August	£120,000
September	£100,000
October	£150,000

A settlement discount of 2.5% is offered for payment in the month of sale and this is taken up by 10% of customers. A further 50% of total customers pay one month after the sale and the remaining 40% of customers pay two months after the month of sale.

What is the cash inflow from credit customers for the month of October?

OTHER CASH PAYMENTS AND RECEIPTS

In most cash budget calculations the determination of the amount of cash receipts from sales and cash payments for purchases are the hardest elements to deal with. However there will be a number of other types of cash payments and cash receipts that will need to be considered and included in the cash budget.

Wages and salaries

In almost all cases net wages and salaries tend to be paid in the month in which they are incurred and therefore there is no difficulty with either calculation or timing of the cash flows. Amounts due to HM Revenue & Customs in respect of PAYE and NIC, and pension deductions, normally represent the difference between gross and net wages and salaries, and are normally paid in the following month.

Overheads

Expenses or overheads will normally be paid in the month in which they are incurred however care should be taken in an assessment to read the information given as some may be lagged payments.

Care should also be taken with depreciation which is not a cash cost. Often the figure for overheads will include an amount which represents depreciation for the period and this must be excluded in order to find the cash payment.

Irregular or exceptional payments

Other types of payments that are not incurred on a regular basis may be included in the information regarding cash payments. These may include:

- VAT payments (usually quarterly)
- payment details for the acquisition of fixed assets
- dividend payments
- loan repayments

In an assessment details of the precise timing of these payments will be given to you.

Irregular or exceptional receipts

Again detailed information about such receipts will be given in an assessment. The most common type of irregular receipts are cash received from the sale of fixed assets. These are sometimes lagged receipts if the sale is made on credit and the cash is therefore received some time after the sale.

Another possible type of irregular receipt might be the receipt of additional capital. For a sole trader or a partnership this will be additional money paid into the business by the owner or partners. For a company this will be the proceeds from an issue of additional share capital. For a sole trader, partnership or company there might also be a cash receipt from further loan capital being taken out.

HOW IT WORKS

Having dealt with the cash receipts from sales and the cash payments for purchases for the fuel division of SC Fuel and Glass we will now complete the cash budget using the following additional information:

- gross wages and salaries are £113,000 each month, payable at the end of the month in which they are incurred

- 75% of general overheads are paid in the month in which they are incurred with the remainder being paid in the following month. General overheads were £80,000 in each of September and October rising to £87,000 in each of November and December

- included in the general overheads figures is a monthly amount of £12,000 for depreciation of fixed assets

- in January the fuel division is having a new property constructed and in December a down-payment of £120,000 is required to be paid to the building company

- in October the quarterly VAT payment of £45,000 is to be paid

- in October a fixed asset was sold for £18,000 but it was agreed that the asset would be paid for in two equal instalments in November and December

- the cash balance at the end of September was an overdraft balance of £29,500.

You are now to complete the cash budget for the fuel division for the three months ended 31 December.

- Wages and salaries are a straightforward cash payment in the month incurred. As they are gross, we do not need to worry about separating out deductions payable to HMRC and the pension fund

- For the general overheads firstly the depreciation charge must be removed as this is a non-cash expense and then a working will be required to ensure that the correct amount of cash payment is

student notes ✎

shown in each month as 25% of the overheads are paid in the month after they are incurred

WORKING – General overheads

	October £	November £	December £
September overheads			
(25% x (80,000 - 12,000))	17,000		
October overheads			
(75% x (80,000 - 12,000))	51,000		
(25% x (80,000 - 12,000))		17,000	
November overheads			
(75% x (87,000 - 12,000))		56,250	
(25% x (87,000 - 12,000))			18,750
December overheads			
(75% x (87,000 - 12,000))			56,250
Total overhead payment	68,000	73,250	75,000

- The construction down-payment is a straightforward December cash flow

- The VAT is a cash payment in October

- The fixed asset sale cash receipt will be £9,000 in the months of November and December

- Using the opening cash balance at 1 October, the opening and closing balances each month can be calculated

Cash budget October to December

	October £	November £	December £
Cash receipts:			
Cash sales	136,000	140,000	150,000
Cash from credit sales	467,200	491,200	532,800
Sale of fixed assets		9,000	9,000
Total cash receipts	603,200	640,200	691,800
Cash payments:			
Payments for credit purchases	366,960	401,700	423,450
Wages and salaries	113,000	113,000	113,000
General overheads	68,000	73,250	75,000
Capital expenditure			120,000
VAT	45,000		
Total cash payments	592,960	587,950	731,450
Net cash flow for the month	10,240	52,250	(39,650)
Opening cash balance	(29,500)	(19,260)	32,990
Closing cash balance	(19,260)	32,990	(6,660)

Activity 4

A company is preparing its cash flow forecast for the month of November. The estimated cash sales in November are £64,000 and sales on credit in October and November are estimated to be £216,000 and £238,000. It is estimated that 40% of credit customers pay in the month of sale after deducting a 2% discount and the remainder pay one month after the date of sale.

Purchases are all on credit payable in the month following the purchase. Purchases were £144,000 in October and £165,000 in November.

Wages and salaries of £80,000 a month are payable in the month in which they are incurred as are general overheads of £65,000. The general overheads figure includes a depreciation charge of £15,000 each month. A dividend of £20,000 is to be paid to the shareholders in November.

The balance on the cash account at the beginning of November is anticipated to be an overdraft balance of £10,200.

Prepare the cash budget for the month of November.

OVERDRAFT INTEREST

One final adjustment might be required to a cash budget if it is anticipated that the cash balance during the period will be an overdraft balance. If there is an overdraft balance then the bank will charge interest on the amount of the overdraft. This interest will be a cash outflow based upon the overdraft amount, which will normally be paid in the following month.

HOW IT WORKS

We will return to the cash budget for the fuel division of SC Fuel and Glass. The cash budget to date appears as follows:

Cash budget October to December

	October £	November £	December £
Cash receipts:			
Cash sales	136,000	140,000	150,000
Cash from credit sales	467,200	491,200	532,800
Sale of fixed assets		9,000	9,000
Total cash receipts	603,200	640,200	691,800
Cash payments:			
Payments for credit purchases	366,960	401,700	423,450
Wages and salaries	113,000	113,000	113,000
General overheads	68,000	73,250	75,000
Capital expenditure			120,000
VAT	45,000		
Total cash payments	592,960	587,950	731,450
Net cash flow for the month	10,240	52,250	(39,650)
Opening cash balance	(29,500)	(19,260)	32,990
Closing cash balance	(19,260)	32,990	(6,660)

At the end of September there is an overdraft balance of £29,500 and at the end of October an overdraft balance of £19,260. Say that interest is charged at 1% per month on these balances in the following month. Therefore a further cash outflow line must be included for overdraft interest based upon the balance at the end of the previous month. This in turn will have an effect on the net cash flow for the month and the overdraft balance at the end of October.

The overdraft interest cash payment in October will be based upon the overdraft balance at 1 October:

1% x £29,500 = £295

This is entered as a cash outflow which in turn means that the overdraft balance at the end of October will increase to £19,555. Therefore the overdraft interest in November will be:

1% x £19,555 = £196

Cash budget – October to December

	October £	November £	December £
Cash receipts:			
Cash sales	136,000	140,000	150,000
Cash from credit sales	467,200	491,200	532,800
Sale of fixed assets		9,000	9,000
Total cash receipts	603,200	640,200	691,800
Cash payments:			
Payments for credit purchases	366,960	401,700	423,450
Wages and salaries	113,000	113,000	113,000
General overheads	68,000	73,250	75,000
Capital expenditure			120,000
VAT	45,000		
Overdraft interest	295	196	
Total cash payments	593,255	588,146	731,450
Net cash flow for the month	9,945	52,054	(39,650)
Opening cash balance	(29,500)	(19,555)	32,499
Closing cash balance	(19,555)	32,499	(7,151)

Note that the introduction of the overdraft interest has affected each of the month end balances.

MANUFACTURING ORGANISATIONS

The cash budgets that have been prepared so far in this chapter have been based upon a retail-type organisation whereby goods are purchased for cash or on credit and then sold to customers either for cash or on credit. However we also need to consider how to prepare a cash budget for a manufacturing organisation.

Cash payments

In a manufacturing organisation the major difference is in the calculations that are required in order to determine the cash payments for each period, in particular for purchases and for wages.

Purchases

The amount of purchases in each month will depend upon the amount of production in the factory each month. This is turn will be dependent upon the anticipated sales for the month and any changes in stocks. The starting point therefore for this type of cash flow forecast will be a PRODUCTION BUDGET.

Production budget

A production budget is prepared in terms of units of production and shows the amount that is due to be produced in the factory in each period. This will be based upon the quantity that it is anticipated will be sold in the period but with adjustments for any changes in opening and closing stocks of finished goods. The production budget will appear as follows:

	Units
Sales	X
Less: opening stock of finished goods	(X)
Add: closing stock of finished goods	X
Production quantity	X

Purchases budget – units of materials

Once the production quantity for the period has been determined then the PURCHASES BUDGET can be calculated, again in units of materials. The number of units to be purchased will be based upon the production quantity for the period and any changes in opening and closing stocks of raw materials.

	Units
Production quantity	X
Less: opening stocks of raw materials	(X)
Add: closing stocks of raw materials	X
Purchases quantity	X

Purchases budget – £s

Once the quantity of purchases for the period has been determined then the amount in monetary terms can be found by multiplying the quantity by the unit price.

Finally the payment pattern for these purchases can be determined and the cash flows for payments for materials entered into the cash budget.

HOW IT WORKS

We will now consider the glass division of SC Fuel and Glass. The cash flow forecast for this division is to be prepared for the three months of October, November and December. We will start with the most complicated calculations which are for the purchases of materials.

The glass division makes sealed double-glazed units in its factory and the material required is two glazed sheets per unit each costing £16.

Sales quantities of double-glazed units are anticipated to be:

	Units
October	13,200
November	14,100
December	14,800

The number of completed double-glazed units in stock at 1 October are anticipated to be 1,000 units. The closing stocks of completed double-glazed units for each of the three months are planned to be as follows:

	Units
October	1,000
November	1,200
December	900

We are now in a position to prepare the production budget for the three months:

Production budget – units

	October Units	November Units	December Units
Sales	13,200	14,100	14,800
Less: opening stock of completed units	(1,000)	(1,000)	(1,200)
Add: closing stock of completed units	1,000	1,200	900
Production quantity	13,200	14,300	14,500

Note that the closing stock of completed units in one month is of course the opening stock of completed units in the following month. You will also note the following about the production quantities:

■ where there is no change in closing stock levels the production quantity is the same as the sales level

■ where closing stock levels are increasing, the production quantity must be higher than the sales level to provide the additional stocks

■ where closing stock levels are decreasing the production, quantity is lower than the sales quantity as stocks of completed goods are being used up.

Now that we have the production quantity for each month we can move on to calculate the amount of raw materials, sheets of glass in this case, that must be purchased each month in order to meet the production budget. There are two sheets of glass required for each glazed unit but we must also take into account any changes in the stock levels of the raw materials, sheets of glass.

At 1 October there will be 600 sheets of glass in stock. The sheets of glass expected to be in stock at the end of each of the three months are as follows:

	Sheets
October	600
November	400
December	1,000

The purchases budget in units, sheets of glass, is based upon the production quantity and the changes in stock levels.

Purchases budget – quantity

	October Units	November Units	December Units
Required for production quantity			
(13,200 x 2)	26,400		
(14,300 x 2)		28,600	
(14,500 x 2)			29,000
Less: opening stock of raw materials	(600)	(600)	(400)
Add: closing stock of raw materials	600	400	1,000
Purchases in units	26,400	28,400	29,600

As with the production budget, closing stocks at the end of one month are the opening stocks at the start of the next month.

Now that the purchase quantities are known the monetary amount of the purchases can then be calculated as we know that each sheet of glass costs £16.

Purchases budget – £s

	October Units	November Units	December Units
Purchases in units	26,400	28,400	29,600
	£	£	£
Purchases in £s (x £16)	422,400	454,400	473,600

The final stage in the calculation of the cash flow for purchases of materials is to determine the purchasing and payment pattern for these purchases.

SC Fuel and Glass have a policy of purchasing the materials required for production in the month before that production takes place. They pay 40% of their suppliers in the month after the purchase and the remainder two months after the purchase.

We can now think this through:

October's purchases – made in September
Paid for: 40% in October
                         60% in November

This has thrown up an additional problem in that part of the October cash payment for materials will be for 60% of September's purchases. Therefore we will need to produce a production budget and purchases budget for September as well. Suppose we are given the information below for September.

September sales	12,000 units
Opening stock of finished units	700 units
Opening stock of glass sheets	800

Production budget

	September Units
Sales	12,000
Less: opening stock of finished units	(700)
Add: closing stock of finished units	1,000
Production quantity	12,300

Purchases budget – quantity

	September Units
Production (2 x 12,300)	24,600
Less: opening stock of sheets	(800)
Add: closing stock of sheets	600
Purchase quantity	24,400

Purchases budget – £s

	September £
Purchases (24,400 x £16)	390,400

Finally a working is needed to determine the payments to be made for purchases on credit in each of the three months:

WORKING – Payments to credit suppliers

	October £	November £	December £
September production			
(390,400 x 60%)	234,240		
October production			
(422,400 x 40%)	168,960		
(422,400 x 60%)		253,440	
November production			
(454,400 x 40%)		181,760	
(454,400 x 60%)			272,640
December production			
(473,600 x 40%)			189,440
Payments to suppliers	403,200	435,200	462,080

At last we can complete the first line of cash payments in the cash budget for the glass division:

Cash budget – October to December

	October £	November £	December £
Cash payments:			
Payments to suppliers	403,200	435,200	462,080

Wages

In a manufacturing organisation the wages paid to the production workers will often be dependent upon the hours that they work. This in turn is dependent upon the production quantity in each period which will have been calculated in the production budget.

HOW IT WORKS

Returning to SC Fuel and Glass and the glass division cash budget the production director tells you that each glazed unit requires 1.5 labour hours and the payroll department informs you that the workforce are paid at a rate of £8 per hour. Gross wages are paid in the same month as they are incurred.

Using the production budget the wages cash payment each month can be calculated.

Production budget – units

	October Units	November Units	December Units
Sales	13,200	14,100	14,800
Less: opening stock of completed units	(1,000)	(1,000)	(1,200)
Add: closing stock of completed units	1,000	1,200	900
Production quantity	13,200	14,300	14,500

Gross wages payments

	October £	November £	December £
October (13,200 x 1.5 x £8)	158,400		
November (14,300 x 1.5 x £8)		171,600	
December (14,500 x 1.5 x £8)			174,000

These figures can then also be entered onto the cash budget.

Cash budget – October to December

	October £	November £	December £
Cash payments:			
Payments to suppliers	403,200	435,200	462,080
Wages	158,400	171,600	174,000

Cash receipts

Now we have dealt with the complicated bit of a manufacturing organisation's cash flow forecast we can return to the areas which are no different from a retailer such as cash receipts from sales. However we will introduce here the concept of BAD DEBTS.

Bad debts

When sales are made on credit there is always a possibility that some of the credit customers will never pay the amounts due from them. This problem will be considered in more detail in a later chapter of this Course Companion but in this chapter we will consider the effect this has on producing the cash flow forecast.

If it is considered that some invoices will never be actually paid by credit customers then these should be excluded from the cash receipts in the cash flow forecast. From their experience most businesses will have an idea of the percentage of debts which tend to turn bad and as these are likely never to be received then they are not included as cash receipts.

HOW IT WORKS

The glass division of SC Fuel and Glass sells each sealed double-glazed unit for £80. All sales are on credit and the payment pattern from debtors is estimated as follows:

- 30% pay in the month following the invoice

- the remainder pay two months after the invoice date but bad debts are generally about 5% of sales.

As bad debts will never turn into a cash inflow, the amount of cash received two months after the invoice date is 65% of the month's invoices rather than 70%.

Estimated sales for the glass division are:

	Units
August	10,200
September	12,000
October	13,200
November	14,100
December	14,800

Cash receipts from debtors can then be calculated using a working.

WORKING – receipts from sales

	October £	November £	December £
August sales			
(10,200 x £80 x 65%)	530,400		
September sales			
(12,000 x £80 x 30%)	288,000		
(12,000 x £80 x 65%)		624,000	
October sales			
(13,200 x £80 x 30%)		316,800	
(13,200 x £80 x 65%)			686,400
November sales			
(14,100 x £80 x 30%)			338,400
Total receipts from sales	818,400	940,800	1,024,800

These figures can now be entered into the cash budget:

Cash budget – October to December

	October £	November £	December £
Cash receipts:			
Cash from credit sales	818,400	940,800	1,024,800
Cash payments:			
Payments to suppliers	403,200	435,200	462,080
Wages	158,400	171,600	174,000

Other receipts and payments

Finally to complete the cash budget the other cash receipts and payments for the period will be included.

HOW IT WORKS

The remaining figures need to be dealt with in the cash budget for the glass division.

- production expenses are estimated as 15% of the materials and wages payments and are paid in the month in which they are incurred. This figure includes £18,000 of depreciation charge each month

- selling costs are estimated as 10% of the sales revenue for the period and 75% are payable in the month in which they are incurred and the remainder in the following month

- additional machinery has been acquired under a lease (see later in this Course Companion) and the lease payments are £15,000 each month

- in October the corporation tax payment of £290,000 must be paid

- the cash balance at 1 October was anticipated to be £45,000 in credit

- in this example we are ignoring the complication of overdraft interest charges

The cash budget can now be completed:

Cash budget – October to December

	October £	November £	December £
Cash receipts:			
Cash from credit sales	818,400	940,800	1,024,800
Cash payments:			
Payments to suppliers	403,200	435,200	462,080
Wages	158,400	171,600	174,000
Production expenses (W1)	66,240	73,020	77,412
Selling costs (W2)	103,200	111,000	117,000
Lease payments	15,000	15,000	15,000
Corporation tax	290,000		
Total payments	1,036,040	805,820	845,492
Net cash flow for the month	(217,640)	134,980	179,308
Opening cash balance	45,000	(172,640)	(37,660)
Closing cash balance	(172,640)	(37,660)	141,648

student notes✍

WORKINGS

Working 1 – Production expenses

	October £	November £	December £
October ((15% x (403,200 + 158,400)) – 18,000)	66,240		
November ((15% x (435,200 + 171,600)) – 18,000)		73,020	
December ((15% x (462,080 + 174,000)) – 18,000)			77,412

Working 2 – Selling costs

	October £	November £	December £
September costs (10% x (12,000 x £80) x 25%)	24,000		
October costs (10% x (13,200 x £80) x 75%)	79,200		
(10% x (13,200 x £80) x 25%)		26,400	
November costs (10% x (14,100 x £80) x 75%)		84,600	
(10% x (14,100 x £80) x 25%)			28,200
December costs (10% x (14,800 x £80) x 75%)			88,800
Total selling costs	103,200	111,000	117,000

Activity 5

A company anticipates sales of 45,000 units of its product in August. Stocks of finished goods at 1 August are expected to be 4,000 units and this is to be increased by 2,000 units by the end of the month.

Each unit of the finished product requires 5kg of materials each of which cost £7.50 per kg. Stocks of raw materials are expected to consist of 40,000 kg at 1 August decreasing by 10,000 kg by the end of the month.

Purchases are made in the month prior to production and paid for in the following month.

What are the payments to be made in August in respect of purchases?

PREPARING A CASH FLOW FORECAST

In Chapter 1 of this Course Companion we saw that there are two types of cash flow forecast - the receipts and payments type (see above as a cash budget) and the type that is based upon a budgeted profit and loss account and opening and closing budgeted balance sheets. This is produced in a similar format to the Cash Flow Statement produced by financial accountants on the basis of historical data.

We will now consider the preparation of the latter type of budget, which we shall call a cash flow forecast.

Pro-forma

In Chapter 1 we saw the pro-forma for a cash flow forecast based upon a budgeted profit and loss account and balance sheets:

	£
Net operating profit	X
Adjustments for:	
Depreciation	X
Profit on sale of fixed assets	(X)
Working capital adjustments:	
Increase in stocks	(X)
Decrease in debtors	X
Increase in creditors	X
Net cash flow from operations	X
Non-operating cash flows	
Interest payments	(X)
Purchase of fixed assets	(X)
Proceeds from sale of fixed assets	X
Issue of shares	X
Payment of dividend	(X)
Net cash flow	X
Opening cash balance	X
Closing cash balance	X

Most of the figures required for this type of cash flow forecast can be taken from the budgeted profit and loss account or by comparison of the opening and closing budgeted balance sheets. We will consider each figure in turn.

Net operating profit	– budgeted P&L
Depreciation	– budgeted P&L
Profit/loss on sale of fixed assets	– budgeted P&L
Increase/decrease in stocks/ debtors/creditors	– comparison of budgeted balance sheets

Interest payments	– budgeted P&L
Purchase of fixed assets	– comparison of budgeted balance sheets
Proceeds from sale of fixed assets	– additional information
Issue of shares	– comparison of budgeted balance sheets
Payment of dividend	– budgeted P&L and budgeted balance sheets

Operating profit to operating cash flow

The first part of this type of cash flow forecast starts with the net operating profit for the period and makes various adjustments in order to finish with the net cash flow from operating activities.

There are two types of adjustment that are made:

- adjustments for NON-CASH FLOWS – items such as depreciation charges or profits/losses on the sale of fixed assets are charged or credited in determining the net profit for the period but as they are not cash flows then the charges must be added back and any credits deducted in order to get to net cash flow.

- WORKING CAPITAL adjustments – increases or decreases in working capital – stocks, debtors and creditors – must also be adjusted for as the cash movements for these items are not reflected in the sales and cost of sales figures in the profit and loss account.

Non-operating cash flows

The latter part of this type of cash flow forecast deals with the type of cash inflows and outflows that are not reported in the operating part of the profit and loss account. These will include interest and dividend payments, payments and receipts for purchases and sales of fixed assets and changes in long term capital such as share issues or repayment of loans.

HOW IT WORKS

SC Fuel and Glass has a small lubricants division known as SCL. A detailed receipts and payments type of cash flow forecast is not prepared for the division but every six months the management accountant produces a budgeted profit and loss account for the next six month period and a budgeted balance sheet for the end of the period. From this a budgeted cash flow forecast is also prepared.

The budgeted profit and loss account for the six months ending 31 December, and the budgeted balance sheets as at 30 June and 31 December are given below for SCL.

Budgeted profit and loss account – six months ending 31 December

	£000
Sales	840
Cost of sales	(572)
Gross profit	268
Operating expenses	(130)
Operating profit	138
Interest paid	(10)
Profit before tax	128
Tax	(32)
Retained profit	96

The figure for operating expenses includes £24,000 of depreciation charges and an estimated profit of £3,000 on the sale of a fixed asset that is expected to realise £20,000 during the period.

The budgeted balance sheets for SCL at 30 June and 31 December are as follows:

Budgeted balance sheets

	31 December £000	31 December £000	30 June £000	30 June £000
Fixed assets		1,188		1,139
Current assets:				
Stock	47		31	
Debtors	58		62	
Cash at bank	–		4	
	105		97	
Creditors: amounts falling due within one year				
Creditors	41		35	
Tax	32		30	
Bank overdraft	3		–	
	76		65	
Net current assets		29		32
		1,217		1,171
Creditors: amounts falling due after more than one year				
Long term loan		(250)		(300)
		967		871
Share capital		500		500
Retained profits		467		371
		967		871

student notes✍

From the budgeted profit and loss account and the budgeted balance sheets we will now prepare the cash flow forecast. We can see from the balance sheets that it is expected that the cash balance of £4,000 at 30 June will have become an overdraft of £3,000 by 31 December. The budgeted cash flow forecast will explain and predict why this is to happen.

The starting point for the budgeted cash flow forecast is the operating profit for the six month period of £138,000. This is then adjusted for any non-cash items being the depreciation charge for the period and the anticipated profit on sale of a fixed asset.

The depreciation charge will be added back to the profit figure as this is not a cash outflow and the budgeted profit on sale of the fixed asset will be deducted from the profit figure as this is not a cash inflow. The cash inflow for the sale of the fixed asset is the cash expected to be received and this will be dealt with later in the cash flow forecast.

Cash flow forecast for six months ended 31 December

	£000
Operating profit	138
Adjustments for:	
Add: depreciation	24
Less: Profit on sale of fixed asset	(3)

The next step is to make adjustments for the changes in working capital – stock, debtors and creditors. The relevant figures come from comparison of the opening and closing budgeted balance sheets.

If stocks and debtors increase this means that there is a deduction as there is less cash inflow than recorded profit. This is most easily understood by considering debtors. If sales are recorded as £100 in the profit and loss account but debtors increase by £5 then there is £5 less received in cash than has been recorded in the profit and loss account.

The converse is true for creditors for which there will be an addition to profit for an increase and a deduction for a decrease.

Once the adjustments for changes in working capital have been made then the figure we are left with is the CASH FLOW FROM OPERATING ACTIVITIES.

Cash flow forecast for six months ended 31 December

	£000
Operating profit	138
Adjustments for:	
Add: depreciation	24
Less: Profit on sale of fixed asset	(3)
Working capital adjustments:	
Increase in stocks (47 – 31)	(16)
Decrease in debtors (58 – 62)	4
Increase in creditors (41 – 35)	6
Cash flow from operating activities	153

We are now concerned with any other budgeted cash inflows or outflows for the period that are not part of the operating activities of the business.

The first of these are any interest payments and the tax payment for the period.

The interest charge in the profit and loss account is £10,000 and there are no creditors for any accrued interest in the balance sheets so this must be the amount that is forecast to be paid for interest during the period.

The creditor for tax in the balance sheet is the same as the tax charge in the profit and loss account therefore it is expected that the creditor at 30 June for tax of £30,000 will be paid during the six month period.

Cash flow forecast for six months ended 31 December

	£000
Operating profit	138
Adjustments for:	
Add: depreciation	24
Less: Profit on sale of fixed asset	(3)
Working capital adjustments:	
Increase in stocks (47 – 31)	(16)
Decrease in debtors (58 – 62)	4
Increase in creditors (41 – 35)	6
Cash flow from operating activities	153
Non-operating cash flows	
Interest paid	(10)
Tax paid	(30)

By comparing the opening and closing budgeted balance sheets we can see that there are two other items that have changed - fixed assets and the long term loan.

There is quite a lot to consider for cash inflows and outflows regarding fixed assets. Firstly, and the easiest figure, is the cash inflow from the anticipated sale of the fixed asset which we are told is £20,000. Then however we move onto the cash outflow for any purchases of fixed assets. The simplest method of finding this figure is to reconstruct the fixed asset ledger account in order to find the additions to fixed assets as the balancing figure.

We have the opening and closing fixed assets at net book value balances from the balance sheets:

Fixed assets at NBV			
	£'000		£'000
Opening balance	1,139		
		Closing balance	1,188

On the credit side of the account we can also slot in the depreciation charge for the year of £24,000 which we are told about.

Fixed assets at NBV

	£'000		£'000
Opening balance	1,139	Depreciation charge	24
		Closing balance	1,188
	‾‾‾‾		‾‾‾‾

Also on the credit side we need the net book value of the asset to be disposed of. The proceeds from disposal are anticipated to be £20,000 with a profit on disposal of £3,000. Therefore the net book value of the asset to be disposed of must be £17,000.

Fixed assets at NBV

	£'000		£'000
Opening balance	1,139	Depreciation charge	24
		Disposal	17
		Closing balance	1,188
	‾‾‾‾		‾‾‾‾

Finally the account can be balanced and the balancing figure on the debit side is the amount of cash to be spent on additions to fixed assets during the period.

Fixed assets at NBV

	£'000		£'000
Opening balance	1,139	Depreciation charge	24
		Disposal	17
Cash additions (bal fig)	90	Closing balance	1,188
	1,229		1,229

The fixed asset cash inflow of £20,000 and cash outflow of £90,000 can now be entered into the cash flow forecast.

Cash flow forecast for six months ended 31 December

	£000
Operating profit	138
Adjustments for:	
Add: depreciation	24
Less: Profit on sale of fixed asset	(3)
Working capital adjustments:	
Increase in stocks (47 - 31)	(16)
Decrease in debtors (58 - 62)	4
Increase in creditors (41 - 35)	6
Cash flow from operating activities	153
Non-operating cash flows	
Interest paid	(10)
Tax paid	(30)
Proceeds from sale of fixed assets	20
Additions to fixed assets	(90)

Finally the other figure that has changed between the two budgeted balance sheets is the long term loan which is budgeted to be reduced from £300,000 to £250,000. Therefore there is a budgeted repayment that can be inserted in the cash flow forecast.

Once this has been done the cash flow forecast can be totalled to find the increase or decrease in cash during the period.

Budgeted cash flow forecast for six months ended 31 December

	£000
Operating profit	138
Adjustments for:	
Add: depreciation	24
Less: Profit on sale of fixed asset	(3)
Working capital adjustments:	
Increase in stocks (47 - 31)	(16)
Decrease in debtors (58 - 62)	4
Increase in creditors (41 - 35)	6
Cash flow from operating activities	153
Non-operating cash flows	
Interest paid	(10)
Tax paid	(30)
Proceeds from sale of fixed assets	20
Additions to fixed assets	(90)
Loan repayment	(50)
Decrease in cash	(7)

By comparing the two balance sheet figures for cash and overdraft it can be seen that at the start of the period there is a cash balance of £4,000 but at the end of the period there is a budgeted overdraft of £3,000. This is a budgeted decrease in cash of £7,000 as shown by the cash flow forecast.

Activity 6

A business has a budgeted operating profit for the next three months of £269,600. In arriving at this figure depreciation of £31,500 has been charged as well as an anticipated loss of £14,200 on the sale of fixed assets.

During the three month period it is anticipated that stocks will increase by £5,400, debtors will increase by £6,700 and that creditors will increase by £4,200.

What is the net cash flow from operating activities for the three month period?

CHAPTER OVERVIEW

- in order to prepare a cash budget information will be required from many different sources within the organisation

- when preparing a cash budget one of the most complicated areas is normally cash receipts from sales

- receipts from cash sales will take place at the same time as the sale but receipts from credit sales may be spread over a number of subsequent months

- payments for purchases on credit will similarly be typically spread over a number of future months

- if a settlement discount is offered on credit sales then the amount of anticipated cash inflow must be reduced and if settlement discounts are taken on purchases then the amount of the cash outflow must be reduced to reflect the smaller payment

- in some instances the amount of purchases for a period will need to be calculated by reference to anticipated sales in the period and the anticipated gross profit margin

- care must be taken with the timing of other cash flows such as overheads which may not necessarily be all paid in the month incurred – any non-cash flows such as depreciation charges must be excluded from the cash flow forecast

KEY WORDS

Lagged receipt receipt of cash which takes place some time after the related transaction

Lagged payment payment of cash which takes place some time after the related transaction

Settlement discount discount offered by the seller to the buyer in return for early payment of the amount due

Production budget a budget which shows the amount of production each period in the factory in units

Purchases budget a budget showing the purchases required in units to meet the production budget and any planned changes to closing stocks of raw materials

Bad debts invoiced amounts that it is considered will never be received in cash

Non-cash flows charges or credits in the profit and loss account which do not represent cash outflows or inflows

Working capital stocks, debtors and creditors

Cash flow from operating activities the net cash flows caused by the operating activities of the business

- if information is given about overdraft interest then this must be calculated each month based upon the overdraft balance and shown as a cash outflow

- in a manufacturing organisation the amount of payments for purchases will be dependent upon the production budget and the purchases pattern and supplier payment pattern

- the production budget will be affected by changes in stocks of finished goods whereas the purchases budget is affected by changes in raw materials stocks

- in a manufacturing organisation the wages payment for the period may also be dependent upon the production quantity each period

- if bad debts are anticipated then these are amounts that will not be received in cash and are therefore excluded from the cash budget

CHAPTER OVERVIEW cont.

- a cash flow forecast can also be prepared from a budgeted profit and loss account and opening and closing budgeted balance sheets. This type of cash flow forecast starts with operating profit which is adjusted for non-cash flows and for working capital changes, giving the figure for net cash flow from operating activities

- any cash flows from non-operating activities are then included to give the final figure for the overall change in cash balance between the two balance sheet dates

HOW MUCH HAVE YOU LEARNED?

1   A business has estimates of the following sales figures:

	£
October	790,000
November	750,000
December	720,000
January	700,000
February	730,000
March	760,000

Of these total sales figures 10% are likely to be cash sales and the remainder are credit sales. The payment pattern from debtors in the past has been such that 40% of the total sales pay in the month after the sale and the remainder two months after the month of sale. However there are also normally 5% bad debts.

What are the forecast cash receipts from sales for each of the months from January to March?

2   A business has estimates of the following sales figures:

	£
October	790,000
November	750,000
December	720,000
January	700,000
February	730,000
March	760,000

The business operates at a standard gross profit margin of 25%. Purchases are all made in the same month as the sale and are all on credit. 20% of purchases are offered a 2% discount for payment in the month after purchase and the business takes all such discounts. A further 65% of the purchases are paid for two months after the month of purchase and the remaining 15% are paid for three months after the date of purchase.

What are the forecast cash payments for purchases for each of the months of January to March?

3   A business is about to prepare a cash flow forecast for the quarter ending 31 December. The recent actual and estimated sales figures are as follows:

	£
July (actual)	340,000
August (actual)	300,000
September (estimate)	360,000
October (estimate)	400,000
November (estimate)	450,000
December (estimate)	460,000

All sales are on credit and the payment pattern is as follows:

20% pay in the month of sale after taking a 5% settlement discount
30% pay in the month following the sale
40% pay two months after the month of sale
8% pay three months after the month of sale

There are expected to be 2% bad debts.

The purchases of the business are all on credit and it is estimated that the following purchases will be made:

	£
August	200,000
September	220,000
October	240,000
November	270,000
December	280,000

30% of purchases are paid for in the month after the purchase has been made and the remainder are paid for two months after the month of purchase.

Gross wages are expected to be £42,000 each month and are paid in the month in which they are incurred. General overheads are anticipated to be £30,000 for each of September and October increasing to £36,000 thereafter. 80% of the general overheads are paid for in the month in which they are incurred and the remainder in the following month. Included in the general overheads figure is a depreciation charge of £5,000 each month.

Selling expenses are anticipated to be 5% of the monthly sales value and are paid for in the month following the sale.

The business has planned to purchase new equipment for £40,000 in November and in the same month to dispose of old equipment with estimated sales proceeds of £4,000.

If the business has an overdraft balance at the start of the month then there is an interest charge that month of 1% of the overdraft balance. At 1 October it is anticipated that the business will have an overdraft of £50,000.

You are required to prepare the cash budget for the three months ending 31 December.

4   A manufacturing business is to prepare its cash budget for the three months commencing 1 October. The business manufactures a product called the gleep which requires 4kg of raw material X per completed gleep and 2 hours of labour per completed gleep. The raw material cost is anticipated to be £6 per kg and the labour force are paid at a rate of £7.50 per hour. Each gleep sells for £60.

The forecast sales in gleeps are as follows:

	August	September	October	November	December
Forecast sales – units of gleeps	7,000	7,200	6,800	7,400	7,500

Sales are on credit with 60% of debtors paying the month after sale and the remainder two months after the sale.

Stocks of completed gleeps are anticipated to be 800 at the start of September and October but these are to be reduced by 100 units per month at the start of each of the next three months.

The raw materials required for production are purchased in the month prior to production and 40% are paid for in the following month and the remainder two months after purchase. The anticipated stocks of raw materials at 1 September and 1 October are 7,000 kgs and the planned stock levels at the end of each month are:

	Kgs
October	7,400
November	8,000
December	7,600

The production staff gross wages are paid in the month in which they are incurred.

Production overheads are anticipated to be 40% of the materials purchases each month and are paid for in the month in which they are incurred. General overheads are anticipated to be £64,000 in each of October and November increasing to £70,000 in December and are paid in the month in which they are incurred. The figure for general overheads includes £12,000 of depreciation each month.

The cash balance at 1 October is expected to be £20,000 in credit.

You are required to prepare the cash flow forecast for the months of October, November and December.

5   Given below is the forecast profit and loss account for a business for the three months ending 31 December together with forecast balance sheets at that date and also at 30 September.

Forecast profit and loss account for three months ending 31 December

	£000
Sales	720
Cost of sales	468
Gross profit	252
Administration costs	22
Overheads	108
Operating profit	122
Interest paid	12
Profit before tax	110
Tax	28
Retained profit	82

Included in the figure for overheads is £64,000 of depreciation charge for the year.

Forecast balance sheets

	31 December		30 September	
	£000	£000	£000	£000
Fixed assets		822		488
Current assets:				
Stock	81		78	
Debtors	75		60	
Cash	–		12	
	156		150	
Creditors: amounts falling due within one year:				
Trade creditors	104		75	
Bank overdraft	13		–	
Tax	28		40	
Proposed dividend	–		22	
	145		137	
Net current assets		11		13
Creditors: amounts falling due after more than one year:				
Long term loan		(100)		
		733		501
Share capital		500		400
Share premium		50		–
Retained profit		183		101
		733		501

From the forecast profit and loss account and forecast balance sheets prepare a cash flow forecast for the three months ending 31 December.

chapter 3:
FURTHER ASPECTS OF CASH BUDGETING

In the previous chapter we looked at the techniques required to prepare a cash flow forecast and cash budget. In this chapter we will consider in more depth how the figures that are included in the cash budget are estimated, for example for production, sales and wages. We will start with the use of time series analysis in the forecasting of future figures and then consider the effect of inflation on our forecasts. Finally we will recognise that the figures that are included in the cash budget are only estimates and consider what effect changes in those estimates might have on the cash position by using the technique of sensitivity analysis.

The topics that are to be covered are:

✍ time series analysis

✍ graphical presentation

✍ calculating a trend using moving averages

✍ calculating seasonal variations

✍ using time series analysis in cash budgeting

✍ dealing with inflation in cash budgeting

✍ using indices

✍ sensitivity analysis

✍ computer spreadsheets and sensitivity analysis

Performance criteria - element 15.1

- consult appropriate staff to determine the likely pattern of cash flows over the accounting period and to anticipate any exceptional receipts or payments
- ensure forecasts of future cash payments and receipts are in accord with known income and expenditure trends

knowledge and understanding

- basic statistical techniques for estimating future trends: moving averages, allowance for inflation
- computer models to assess the sensitivity of elements in the cash budget to change (eg price, wage rate changes)

TIME SERIES ANALYSIS

When preparing a cash budget an enormous number of figures must be estimated. These include:

- sales figures
- purchases figures
- wages costs
- overheads
- exceptional receipts or payments.

One method of estimating sales and costs figures is to look at the past and determine any pattern there might be in these figures over time in order to estimate the likely future figures. One method of analysing past or historic figures is to use the technique of TIME SERIES ANALYSIS.

Time series

A TIME SERIES is simply a record of figures that have occurred over a past period of time. For example each of the following would be an example of a time series:

- daily takings for the last three months
- weekly labour costs for the last six months
- monthly sales for the last three years
- quarterly sales quantities for the last five years
- annual number of employees for the last fifteen years

Using time series

The figures in a time series can be analysed in a variety of ways in order to produce results that can be used within budgeting. One method of presenting the time series information is to produce a graph of the figures with time plotted along the horizontal axis and the figures on the vertical axis. This can give a useful visual presentation of the figures over the time period.

HOW IT WORKS

At the end of December 2006 the management accountant of SC Fuel and Glass decided to carry out a time series analysis on the quarterly sales of the fuel division for the last three years (2004, 2005 and 2006). The sales figures for each of those quarters are given below (with quarter 1 being the three months ending 31 March, quarter 2 the three months ending 30 June etc).

Time period		Sales £000
2004	Quarter 1	2,030
	Quarter 2	1,570
	Quarter 3	1,620
	Quarter 4	2,100
2005	Quarter 1	2,080
	Quarter 2	1,740
	Quarter 3	1,690
	Quarter 4	2,190
2006	Quarter 1	2,150
	Quarter 2	1,830
	Quarter 3	1,780
	Quarter 4	2,200

From these figures we can see that the fuel business is clearly seasonal with generally higher sales in Quarter 1 and Quarter 4 of each year than in the other two quarters. However these highs and lows can be more easily seen when illustrated on a graph.

SC Fuel and Glass – Fuel division – quarterly sales

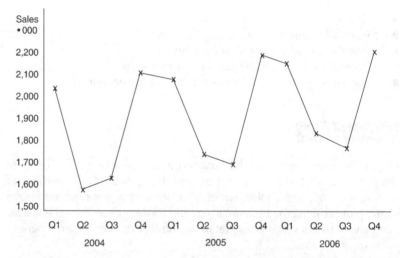

From the graph we can quite easily see that even though the sales do vary each quarter due to the seasonality of the business there is a definite upwards movement of the figures over time or trend.

THE TREND

The TREND of a series of figures in a time series is the way in which the figures are moving in general despite various ups and downs caused by seasonality. One very simple way of determining the trend is to draw a line of best fit on a time series graph which shows in general how the figures are changing.

HOW IT WORKS

Returning to the fuel division sales a TREND LINE could be drawn onto the graph as follows:

SC Fuel and Glass – Fuel division – quarterly sales

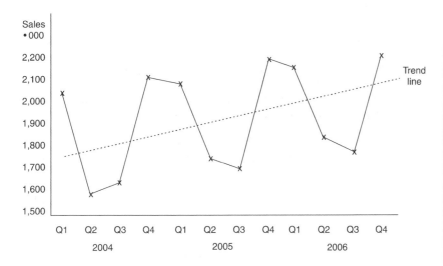

Although this line now gives a graphical presentation of the trend in sales for the fuel division there are more technical methods of determining the trend of a time series and one of these is the technique of using moving averages.

Moving averages

A moving average is the average of each successive group of figures from the time series. A moving average can be taken using either an even or an odd number of figures for each average. Using an odd number is slightly easier so we will start with an illustration of this.

HOW IT WORKS

We return to the sales figures for the fuel division for the last three years.

		Sales £000
Time period		
2004 Quarter 1		2,030
Quarter 2		1,570
Quarter 3		1,620
Quarter 4		2,100
2005 Quarter 1		2,080
Quarter 2		1,740
Quarter 3		1,690
Quarter 4		2,190
2006 Quarter 1		2,150
Quarter 2		1,830
Quarter 3		1,780
Quarter 4		2,200

We have already seen from the graph that there is a general upwards trend in the figures but distinct seasonal variations. In time series analysis we attempt to firstly calculate the trend of the figures using moving averages and then to identify these SEASONAL VARIATIONS.

We will start by calculating a three period moving average for the sales figures. We begin with calculating the average of the first three quarters, Q1 to Q3 2004:

$$\frac{2,030 + 1,570 + 1,620}{3} = 1,740$$

We then move onto the next group of three quarters, Q2 to Q4 2004:

$$\frac{1,570 + 1,620 + 2,100}{3} = 1,763$$

and so on ......

Each of these average figures is shown in the table against the middle quarter for each calculation – therefore the first average of 1,740 is shown against Q2 2004, the next one against Q3 2004 and so on.

Time period		Sales £000	Moving average £000
2004	Quarter 1	2,030	
	Quarter 2	1,570	1,740
	Quarter 3	1,620	1,763
	Quarter 4	2,100	1,933
2005	Quarter 1	2,080	1,973
	Quarter 2	1,740	1,837
	Quarter 3	1,690	1,873
	Quarter 4	2,190	2,010
2006	Quarter 1	2,150	2,057
	Quarter 2	1,830	1,920
	Quarter 3	1,780	1,937
	Quarter 4	2,200	

student notes

The moving average figures show a clear increase and indicate the trend of the figures.

Activity 1

Given below are the monthly costs incurred by a factory:

	£000
January	129
February	138
March	135
April	142
May	150
June	153
July	148
August	151
September	162
October	165
November	172
December	164

Calculate a three month moving average for these cost figures.

Choosing the number of periods in the moving average calculation

In the calculations above we used a three quarter moving average to make the calculations relatively straightforward. However the choice of the best number of periods to include in each moving average will depend upon the circumstances and seasonality of the business. The aim will be to choose the number of periods which cover an entire cycle of seasons.

student notes✍

Therefore if a shop is looking at its daily sales and is open for five days a week with different levels of takings per day a five period moving average would be most appropriate. However if the same shop were open for six days a week then a six period moving average would be better.

HOW IT WORKS

In the case of the fuel division of SC Fuel and Glass there are in fact four quarters in each year with similar movement in results between the quarters in each year.

Therefore a four quarter moving average would be more appropriate and would give us a clearer picture of the trend of the figures as each set of four numbers covers one entire cycle of seasons. The use of an even number for the moving average however adds an additional calculation in order to determine the trend figures.

Centred moving average

When we were using the three quarter moving averages above each average figure related to the middle quarter that had been used. However with an even number of quarters there is of course no middle quarter.

Instead the four quarter moving average is shown in between the two middle quarters and there is another column which in turn averages each pair of moving averages.

HOW IT WORKS

We will now calculate four quarter moving averages for the fuel division sales.

$$\frac{2,030 + 1,570 + 1,620 + 2,100}{4} = 1,830$$

then

$$\frac{1,570 + 1,620 + 2,100 + 2,080}{4} = 1,843$$

etc.

These are shown in the table between the figures for the middle two quarters:

Time period	Sales £000	Moving average £000
2004		
Quarter 1	2,030	
Quarter 2	1,570	
		1,830
Quarter 3	1,620	
		1,843
Quarter 4	2,100	
2005		1,885
Quarter 1	2,080	
		1,903
Quarter 2	1,740	
		1,925
Quarter 3	1,690	
		1,943
Quarter 4	2,190	
2006		1,965
Quarter 1	2,150	
		1,988
Quarter 2	1,830	
		1,990
Quarter 3	1,780	
Quarter 4	2,200	

As each of these moving average figures do not relate to a specific time period a further calculation is required to find the centred moving average. This is done by taking each pair of moving averages in turn and finding their average and plotting them against the time period between them:

$$\frac{1,830 + 1,843}{2} = 1,837$$

$$\frac{1,843 + 1,885}{2} = 1,864$$

etc

student notes✍

Time period	Sales £000	Moving average £000	Centred moving average £000
2004			
Quarter 1	2,030		
Quarter 2	1,570		
		1,830	
Quarter 3	1,620		1,837
		1,843	
Quarter 4	2,100		1,864
2005		1,885	
Quarter 1	2,080		1,894
		1,903	
Quarter 2	1,740		1,914
		1,925	
Quarter 3	1,690		1,934
		1,943	
Quarter 4	2,190		1,954
2006		1,965	
Quarter 1	2,150		1,977
		1,988	
Quarter 2	1,830		1,989
		1,990	
Quarter 3	1,780		
Quarter 4	2,200		

The centred moving average figures are now the trend line for the sales figures which can again be seen to be increasing. We can now remove the other figures and clearly see how the trend line relates to each quarter:

Time period		Sales £000	Trend £000
2004	Quarter 1	2,030	
	Quarter 2	1,570	
	Quarter 3	1,620	1,837
	Quarter 4	2,100	1,864
2005	Quarter 1	2,080	1,894
	Quarter 2	1,740	1,914
	Quarter 3	1,690	1,934
	Quarter 4	2,190	1,954
2006	Quarter 1	2,150	1,977
	Quarter 2	1,830	1,989
	Quarter 3	1,780	
	Quarter 4	2,200	

Note that there are no related trend figures for the first two or last two quarters due to the nature of the calculations we have made.

We can now clearly see that the trend for the sales figures is an increase in each quarter of between £20,000 and £30,000. In fact the average increase in the trend each quarter is about £22,000 ((1,989 – 1,837)/7 changes in trend).

Activity 2

Given below are the quarterly sales for a business:

		£000
2004	Q1	305
	Q2	300
	Q3	352
	Q4	380
2005	Q1	330
	Q2	327
	Q3	369
	Q4	390
2006	Q1	335
	Q2	331
	Q3	377
	Q4	400

Calculate the trend of these figures using a four quarter centred moving average.

SEASONAL VARIATIONS

Each figure in the original time series can be said to be made up of a number of different elements. Technically these are:

- trend
- cyclical variation
- seasonal variation
- random variation

We have already seen that the trend is the general movement of the time series calculated using moving averages. The CYCLICAL VARIATION is the long term variations due to general economic conditions. Such variations typically take place over a period of about seven years and therefore for most practical purposes are ignored when dealing with time series analysis.

The RANDOM VARIATION is variations in the figures due to unexplained or random events. Again by their very nature they tend to be ignored for time series analysis.

Therefore we are left with the trend and the seasonal variation. The trend is the general long term movement of the time series and the seasonal variation is the effect on the actual figure of that particular season. There are two models which are used in time series analysis – the additive model and the multiplicative model.

Additive model

The ADDITIVE MODEL is where each actual figure in the time series is made up as follows:

$$A = T + S$$

where
A = actual figure
T = trend figure
S = seasonal variation

Multiplicative model

The MULTIPLICATIVE MODEL is where each actual figure in the time series is made up as follows:

$$A = T \times S$$

where
A = actual figure
T = trend figure
S = seasonal variation

Whichever model is used the starting point is to calculate the seasonal variation.

Calculating the seasonal variation – additive model

We will start with the additive model:

If $\quad A = T + S$

Then $\quad S = A - T$

So the seasonal variation is found by deducting the trend figure from the actual figure for each quarter.

HOW IT WORKS

We will return to our actual and trend figures for the sales of the fuel division.

		Sales A £000	Trend T £000	Seasonal variation A – T £000
2004	Quarter 1	2,030		
	Quarter 2	1,570		
	Quarter 3	1,620	1,837	– 217
	Quarter 4	2,100	1,864	+ 236
2005	Quarter 1	2,080	1,894	+ 186
	Quarter 2	1,740	1,914	– 174
	Quarter 3	1,690	1,934	– 244
	Quarter 4	2,190	1,954	+ 236
2006	Quarter 1	2,150	1,977	+ 173
	Quarter 2	1,830	1,989	– 159
	Quarter 3	1,780		
	Quarter 4	2,200		

From this we can clearly see that the actual figures for Quarters 1 and 4 are above the trend and the actual figures for Quarters 2 and 3 are below the trend. However at this point we need to average the seasonal variations for each quarter in order to determine one single figure for each season.

	Quarter 1 £000	Quarter 2 £000	Quarter 3 £000	Quarter 4 £000
2004			– 217	+ 236
2005	+ 186	– 174	– 244	+ 236
2006	+ 173	– 159		
	+ 359	– 333	– 461	+ 472
Average – divided by 2	+ 179	– 166	– 230	+ 236

The final stage is to ensure that the four seasonal variations add back to zero. In this case the positive variations total 19 more than the negative variations therefore we will deduct five from three variations and four from the smallest:

	Quarter 1 £000	Quarter 2 £000	Quarter 3 £000	Quarter 4 £000
Adjusted variation	+ 174	– 170	– 235	+ 231

Activity 3

Given below are the quarterly sales for a business used in the previous activity:

		£000
2004	Q1	305
	Q2	300
	Q3	352
	Q4	380
2005	Q1	330
	Q2	327
	Q3	369
	Q4	390
2006	Q1	335
	Q2	331
	Q3	377
	Q4	400

Calculate the seasonal variations given that the trend was based upon a four quarter centred moving average using the additive model.

Calculating the seasonal variation – multiplicative model

Under the multiplicative model:

$A = T \times S$

S is expressed as a proportion or percentage of the trend figure so:

$S = \dfrac{A}{T}$

In order to calculate the seasonal variation using this model the actual figure must be divided by the trend and the result expressed as a percentage.

HOW IT WORKS

We will now calculate the seasonal variations for the fuel division sales using the multiplicative model.

		Sales A £000	Trend T £000	Seasonal variation A/T %
2004	Quarter 1	2,030		
	Quarter 2	1,570		
	Quarter 3	1,620	1,837	88.2%
	Quarter 4	2,100	1,864	112.7%
2005	Quarter 1	2,080	1,894	109.8%
	Quarter 2	1,740	1,914	90.9%
	Quarter 3	1,690	1,934	87.4%
	Quarter 4	2,190	1,954	112.1%
2006	Quarter 1	2,150	1,977	108.8%
	Quarter 2	1,830	1,989	92.0%
	Quarter 3	1,780		
	Quarter 4	2,200		

Again these seasonal variations must be averaged to find a single percentage for each season:

	Quarter 1 %	Quarter 2 %	Quarter 3 %	Quarter 4 %
2004			88.2	112.7
2005	109.8	90.9	87.4	112.1
2006	108.8	92.0		
	218.6	182.9	175.6	224.8
Average – divided by 2	109.3%	91.5%	87.8%	112.4%

At the final stage the four average seasonal variations should add up to 400%.

In this case they add up to 401%, so we will deduct 0.3 from the two highest variations and 0.2 from the two lowest variations. The final result is as follows:

	Quarter 1	Quarter 2	Quarter 3	Quarter 4
Adjusted variation	109.0%	91.3%	87.6%	112.1%

Activity 4

Again you are given the quarterly sales for a business used in the previous two activities:

		£000
2004	Q1	305
	Q2	300
	Q3	352
	Q4	380
2005	Q1	330
	Q2	327
	Q3	369
	Q4	390
2006	Q1	335
	Q2	331
	Q3	377
	Q4	400

This time calculate the seasonal variations using the multiplicative model.

USING TIME SERIES ANALYSIS IN CASH BUDGETING

In the previous sections we have seen how to calculate a trend using moving averages and how to calculate a seasonal variation using either the additive model or the multiplicative model. Now we will consider how this information can be used in the cash budgeting process.

Time series analysis in budgeting is used in order to estimate future figures based upon the past trend and seasonal variations that have been calculated. This process of using the historical information to estimate future figures is known as EXTRAPOLATION.

HOW IT WORKS

The management accountant at SC Fuel and Glass, having carried out the time series analysis on the fuel division sales, decides to use the information to estimate the sales figures for each of the quarters of 2007.

The last trend figure that was calculated was for 2006 Quarter 2 at a figure of £1,989,000. We have already seen that on average the trend is increasing by £22,000 each quarter therefore we can use this information to calculate the trend figure for each quarter of 2007. The figure for Quarter 1 of 2007 is calculated as the last trend figure of £1,989,000 plus 3 additions of £22,000 to cover the last two quarters of 2006 as well as Quarter 1 of 2007 and so on.

	Trend £000
2007 Quarter 1 (1,989 + (3 x 22))	2,055
Quarter 2 (2,055 + 22)	2,077
Quarter 3 (2,077 + 22)	2,099
Quarter 4 (2,099 + 22)	2,121

We now have to take into account the seasonal variations. Under the additive model each seasonal variation is either added to or deducted from the trend to determine the estimated future sales.

Seasonal variation – additive model

	Quarter 1 £000	Quarter 2 £000	Quarter 3 £000	Quarter 4 £000
Adjusted variation	+ 174	– 170	– 235	+ 231

	Trend £000	Seasonal variation £000	Estimated sales £000
2007 Quarter 1 (1,989 + (3 x 22))	2,055	+ 174	2,229
Quarter 2 (2,055 + 22)	2,077	– 170	1,907
Quarter 3 (2,077 + 22)	2,099	– 235	1,864
Quarter 4 (2,099 + 22)	2,121	+ 231	2,352

Under the multiplicative model the trend is multiplied by the seasonal variation percentage in order to estimate the future sales for each quarter.

Seasonal variation – multiplicative model

	Quarter 1	Quarter 2	Quarter 3	Quarter 4
Adjusted variation	109.0%	91.3%	87.6%	112.1%

	Trend £000	Seasonal variation %	Estimated sales £000
2007 Quarter 1 (1,989 + (3 x 22))	2,055	109.0	2,240
Quarter 2 (2,055 + 22)	2,077	91.3	1,896
Quarter 3 (2,077 + 22)	2,099	87.6	1,839
Quarter 4 (2,099 + 22)	2,121	112.1	2,378

Additive model versus multiplicative model

As we have seen, under the additive model the seasonal variation is expressed as an absolute figure whereas under the multiplicative model it is expressed as a percentage. Therefore if the trend of figures is either rising or

student notes ✍

decreasing to any significant degree then the multiplicative model will tend to give rather more accurate estimates of future figures as the seasonal variation is increasing or decreasing in line with the trend rather than by an absolute amount which may quickly become out of date.

Problems with using time series analysis for forecasting

As we have seen in the previous paragraphs time series analysis can be a useful method of attempting to forecast future sales and cost figures. However you should also be aware that the technique does have its limitations:

- the less historic data available the less reliable will be the results

- the further into the future we forecast the less reliable will be the results

- there is an assumption that the trend and seasonal variations from the past will continue into the future

- cyclical and random variations have been ignored.

Activity 5

Continuing with the quarterly sales for a business used in the previous activities and the figures that you have calculated for the trend and seasonal variations you are now to use both the additive model and the multiplicative model to determine the estimated sales figures for the four quarters of 2007.

		£000
2004	Q1	305
	Q2	300
	Q3	352
	Q4	380
2005	Q1	330
	Q2	327
	Q3	369
	Q4	390
2006	Q1	335
	Q2	331
	Q3	377
	Q4	400

INFLATION AND CASH BUDGETS

INFLATION is the increase in prices of goods and services over a period of time. If we are trying to estimate future figures for cash receipts from sales or cash payments for goods or expenses then any increases caused by inflation must be taken into consideration.

Specific increases

In most economies there will be inflation to some degree and this is often dealt with by a one off increase in sales price or for example an annual increase in the hourly rate paid to the work force. Such anticipated increases should be built into the cash budget.

HOW IT WORKS

The glass division of SC Fuel and Glass are preparing their cash budget for the three months ended 31 March 2007. The selling price of the sealed double glazed units has been £80 per unit for more than a year and it has been decided to increase this price by 10% per unit from 1 March 2007.

The work force are currently paid at a rate of £8 per hour and each double glazed unit requires 1.5 hours of labour. From 1 February there is to be a 7.5% increase in the hourly wage rate.

Sales and production for the three months of January to March 2007 are estimated as follows:

	Sales Units	Production Units
January	13,800	13,400
February	13,500	13,600
March	13,900	14,000

The figures that will be used in the cash budget for sales and for wages costs will need to incorporate the planned increases in prices.

Sales

	£
January (13,800 x £80)	1,104,000
February (13,500 x £80)	1,080,000
March (13,900 x (£80 x 1.10))	1,223,200

Wages

	£
January (13,400 x 1.5 x £8)	160,800
February (13,600 x 1.5 x (£8 x 1.075))	175,440
March (14,000 x 1.5 x (£8 x 1.075))	180,600

Activity 6

A business currently sells its single product for a price of £95 per unit. However from 1 November 2006 this price is to be increased by 5%. Sales quantities are anticipated to be 43,000 units in October and 40,000 in November. What is the expected value of the business's sales in October and November?

General price increases

In some cases, particularly when considering expenses, there may not be any known specific increases in prices, however experience may have shown that expenses tend to increase on average at a particular level which may well be in line with the general level of inflation within the economy. Again such general expectations of increased prices should be built into the cash budget.

HOW IT WORKS

The fuel division of SC Fuel and Glass is also preparing its cash budget for the quarter ending 31 March 2007. In December 2006 the overheads were estimated to be £87,000 which included £12,000 of depreciation charges. It is now considered that these overheads, excluding depreciation, will increase by 0.5% each month.

The figures to be included in the cash budget for overheads will therefore be as follows:

	£
January (75,000 x 1.005)	75,375
February (75,375 x 1.005)	75,752
March (75,752 x 1.005)	76,131

Activity 7

A business purchases raw materials at a current cost, September 2006, of £15.80 per kg. It purchases 100,000 kgs each month and it is anticipated that the price will rise by 1.2% each month. What is the expected value of purchases in October and November 2006?

INDICES

One common method of expressing changes in prices is by the use of indices. An INDEX is a measure of the changes over time in the price of an item or a group of items. Index numbers are normally expressed in terms of a BASE YEAR or BASE PERIOD for which the value assigned to the index is 100. Any subsequent increases or decreases in the price of the item are then reflected in the value of the index.

Calculation of an index

The first step in the calculation of an index is to determine the base year and set the price in that year at the value of 100. The price in subsequent years is then expressed as a proportion of 100. If the price is higher than the base year price the index will be greater than 100 but if it is lower than the base year price the index will be less than 100.

HOW IT WORKS

The glass division of SC Fuel and Glass has seen the price of glass sheets vary over the past few years. The average price for glass sheets for the past six years has been as follows:

2001	£14.60
2002	£14.40
2003	£15.20
2004	£15.00
2005	£15.60
2006	£16.00

Using 2001 as the base year an index for these prices can be constructed.

		Index value
2001		100.0
2002	14.40/14.60 x 100	98.6
2003	15.20/14.60 x 100	104.1
2004	15.00/14.60 x 100	102.7
2005	15.60/14.60 x 100	106.8
2006	16.00/14.60 x 100	109.6

Using indices in cash budgeting

In some instances, when preparing a cash budget, you may not know the precise future price of either sales that are to be made or purchases or expenses that are to be paid for. However you may be given a price index for the item and an anticipated value for that index in the future and this can be used to determine the value of the anticipated cash inflow or cash outflow.

Specific and general price indices

A SPECIFIC PRICE INDEX is an index which relates to a specific item such as the goods that a business purchases or the items that it sells. A GENERAL PRICE INDEX is an index which measures the price of a variety of goods and services and is in effect a measure of general inflation.

Retail Price Index

The best known general price index in the UK is the RETAIL PRICE INDEX (RPI) which measures changes in the cost of items of expenditure in the average household and therefore provides a good indication of the general level of inflation in the economy. The RPI is based upon a base month of January 1987 when the index was set at 100. By February 2006 the index was at the level of 194.2.

HOW IT WORKS

Returning to SC Fuel and Glass, the sales for the fuel division were £750,000 in December 2006. This was when the specific price index for fuel stood at 187.4. The quantity of fuel to be sold in January and February is considered to be similar to that in December but the price index is expected to be 190.1 in January and 192.3 in February.

From this information we can forecast the expected sales value of fuel in January and February.

		£
January	£750,000 x 190.1/187.4	760,806
February	£750,000 x 192.3/187.4	769,610

The general overheads of the fuel division (excluding depreciation) in December were £75,000. It is now believed that overheads increase in line with the general inflation rate as indicated by the RPI. In December 2006 the RPI is 196.6. It is anticipated that the RPI will be 197.2 in January and 198.1 in February. Using this information we can determine the estimated overheads figure (excluding depreciation) for each of the two months.

		£
January	£75,000 x 197.2/196.6	75,229
February	£75,000 x 198.1/196.6	75,572

Activity 8

A business believes that its general overheads increase in line with the Retail Price Index. In April 2006 the general overheads were £200,000 and the RPI was 195.3. The RPI is anticipated to be 195.9 in May 2006 and 196.4 in June 2006.

What is the expected general overhead cost in May and June 2006?

SENSITIVITY ANALYSIS

As we have clearly seen in the previous two chapters there are many estimates and assumptions involved in the preparation of cash budgets. What happens to the cash balance if these estimates and assumptions are not accurate?

For example we could ask ourselves many questions:

- what happens if sales only grow by 0.5% per month rather than the 0.8% monthly forecast growth?

- what happens if 80% of debtors take two months to pay rather than 50% of debtors paying one month after the sale as was expected?

- what happens if bad debts increase from 2% to 5%?

- what happens if there is an unexpected increase in raw materials prices?

- what happens if a major supplier offers a settlement discount for payment within one month which is taken up?

- what happens if wage rises are 10% not the forecast 5%?

What is sensitivity analysis?

SENSITIVITY ANALYSIS is a method of changing variables within the cash budget to determine the overall effect that this would have on the final cash balance. For example a cash budget might be produced with the assumption of 1% sales growth each month but then re-produced on the basis of only 0.5% sales growth per month in order to determine how much lower the cash balance would be on this basis.

Settlement discounts

One particular area that can be subject to sensitivity analysis can be the potential introduction of a settlement discount to credit customers. For those customers that take advantage of the settlement discount this means that they will pay earlier but the amount that is received will be the invoice value less the settlement discount. The benefit to the company offering the discount is of course that money is received sooner but a smaller amount in total will be received.

HOW IT WORKS

The glass division of SC Fuel and Glass sells each sealed double-glazed unit for £80. All sales are on credit and the payment pattern from debtors is estimated as follows:

- 30% pay in the month following the invoice

- the remainder pay two months after the invoice date but bad debts are generally about 5% of sales.

Estimated sales for the glass division are:

	£
August	816,000
September	960,000
October	1,056,000
November	1,128,000
December	1,184,000

The cash receipts from debtors have been included in the cash budget as follows:

Cash budget – October to December 2006

	October £	November £	December £
Cash receipts:			
Cash from credit sales	818,400	940,800	1,024,800

The sales director is now considering offering credit customers a settlement discount of 5% for payment made in the month of sale. It is believed that if the discount is offered for sales from October onwards then 50% of customers will pay in the month of sale, 20% in the month following the sale and 25% two months after the month of sale with bad debts remaining at 5%.

The sales director has asked you to prepare calculations to determine the revised receipts from customers for the three months of October, November and December if the settlement discount is offered to customers.

Receipts from sales

	October £	November £	December £
August sales			
(£816,000 x 65%)	530,400		
September sales			
(£960,000 x 30%)	288,000		
(£960,000 x 65%)		624,000	
October sales			
(£1,056,000 x 50% x 95%)	501,600		
(£1,056,000 x 20%)		211,200	
(£1,056,000 x 25%)			264,000
November sales			
(£1,128,000 x 50% x 95%)		535,800	
(£1,128,000 x 20%)			225,600
December sales			
(£1,184,000 x 50% x 95%)			562,400
Total sales	1,320,000	1,371,000	1,052,000

The receipts from sales are substantially greater for these three months than under the original scenario as debtors are paying substantially earlier. However over subsequent months the figures will even out as in fact less money is received from debtors due to the discount despite being received earlier.

COMPUTER MODELS

In a manual system it is usually only possible to change one variable at a time to see the effect on cash flows and even that can mean long-winded calculations. However if computer models and particularly computer spreadsheets are used then it is possible to see the effect of a variety of different changes in estimates at any one time.

HOW IT WORKS

SC Fuel and Glass is considering opening a car distribution division. The company has been in discussions with a particular car manufacturer and has put together detailed forecasts of the income and expenses of such a venture. The management accountant is trying to prepare a cash budget for the first six months of business, 1 January 2007 to 30 June 2007, for the bank, as they will be approached for a loan. The management accountant has decided to carry out the cash flow forecast on a computer spreadsheet.

student notes

The following data has been gathered regarding the expected cash flows of the potential new business:

- the business should start with a balance of £100,000 in the bank

- sales in January 2007 are anticipated to be £300,000 with a growth rate of 5% per month for the first six months. All sales are on credit with no bad debts anticipated and with 60% of customers paying in the month after the sale and 40% two months after the sale

- the average gross profit margin on sales of cars is 10%. Stock is purchased the month before sale and paid for in the month after purchase

- overheads are anticipated to be £15,000 in January rising by 1.5% each month and payable in the month they are incurred

- if the business runs into overdraft then the interest will be 1% per month based upon the overdraft balance at the end of the previous month

- fixed assets costing £60,000 will need to be purchased in January and will be paid for in two equal instalments in January and February.

The spreadsheet rows and columns are like this:

	A	B	C	D	E	F	G
		Jan	Feb	Mar	Apr	May	June
		£000	£000	£000	£000	£000	£000
1	Sales						
2	**Cash receipts**						
3	One month after sale						
4	Two months after sale						
5	Total receipts						
6	**Cash payments**						
7	Purchases						
8	Overhead						
9	Interest						
10	Fixed assets						
11	Tax						
12	Dividends						
13	Total payments						
14	Net cash flow						
15	Opening balance						
16	Closing balance						

This is the basic cash budget but there are also a number of other figures and variables that must be added to the spreadsheet:

- there are a number of constant figures such as the sales, overheads, fixed asset purchases and the opening cash balance in January that can be entered

- the variables such as sales growth rate, overhead growth rate, cost of sales (based upon gross profit margin), overdraft interest rate and debtor payment periods can then also be entered into other cells in the spreadsheet.

	A	B	C	D	E	F	G
		Jan	Feb	Mar	Apr	May	June
		£000	£000	£000	£000	£000	£000
1	Sales	300					
2	**Cash receipts**						
3	One month after sale						
4	Two months after sale						
5	Total receipts						
6	**Cash payments**						
7	Purchases						
8	Overhead	15					
9	Interest						
10	Fixed assets	30	30				
11	Tax						
12	Dividends						
13	Total payments						
14	Net cash flow						
15	Opening balance	100					
16	Closing balance						
17							
18	Sales growth rate	1.05					
19	Overhead growth rate	1.015					
20	Cost of sales	0.9					
21	Debtors within one month	0.6					
22	Debtors within two months	0.4					
23	Overdraft interest	0.01					

At this stage the formulae for the individual figures can be determined based upon the cells in the spreadsheet.

For illustrative purposes we have only inserted the formulae for the first couple of months but the pattern will become clear after this.

February sales	=+B1 * B18
March sales	=+C1 * B18
Receipts within one month:	
February cash receipts	=+B1 * B21
March cash receipts	=+C1 * B21
Receipts within two months:	
March cash receipts	=+B1 * B22
January purchases	=+B1 * B20
February purchases	=+C1 * B20
March purchases	= + D1 * B20
February overheads	=+B8 * B19
March overheads	=+C8 * B19
January total cash receipts	=+B3 + B4
February total cash receipts	=+C3 + C4
January total cash payments	=+B7 + B8 + B9 + B10 + B11 + B12
February total cash payments	=+C7 + C8 + C9 + C10 + C11 + C12
January net monthly cash flow	=+B5 − B13
February net monthly cash flow	=+C5 − C13
January closing cash balance	=+ B14 + B15
February closing cash balance	=+C14 + C15
February opening cash balance	=+B16
March opening cash balance	=+C16

and so on ...

These formulae can now be entered into the spreadsheet so that it starts to take shape like this:

	A	B	C	D	E	F	G
		Jan	Feb	Mar	Apr	May	June
		£000	£000	£000	£000	£000	£000
1	Sales	300	=+B1*B18	=+C1*B18			
2	**Cash receipts**						
3	One month after sale		=+B1*B21	=+C1*B21			
4	Two months after sale			=+B1*B22			
5	Total receipts	=+B3+B4	=+C3+C4	=+D3+D4			
6	**Cash payments**						
7	Purchases	=+B1*B20	=+C1*B20	=+D1*B20			
8	Overhead	15	=+B8*B19	=+C8*B19			
9	Interest						
10	Fixed assets	30	30				
11	Tax						
12	Dividends						
13	Total payments	=+B7+B8 +B9+B10 +B11+B12	=+C7+C8 +C9+C10 +C11+C12				
14	Net cash flow	=+B5–B13	=+C5–C13				
15	Opening balance	100	=+B16	=+C16			
16	Closing balance	=+B14+B15	=+C14+C15				
17							
18	Sales growth rate	1.05					
19	Overhead growth rate	1.015					
20	Cost of sales	0.9					
21	Debtors within one month	0.6					
22	Debtors within two months	0.4					
23	Overdraft interest	0.01					

Spreadsheets and sensitivity analysis

In the example above we have seen how it is relatively easy to set up a computer spreadsheet in order to produce a cash budget. One of the major benefits of using a computer spreadsheet however is not just in the setting up of the budget but in how the spreadsheet package can manipulate the information once the basic budget has been set.

Once the spreadsheet has been set up it is a simple exercise to run a programme to determine the effect on the cash balances if for example the monthly increase in sales is assumed to be only 1% rather than 1.5% and the assumed debtors payment pattern is changed. Indeed any of the variables in the spreadsheet can be changed, and more than one at a time, in order to find a range of possible outcomes depending upon a range of possible economic situations which may prevail.

CHAPTER OVERVIEW

- cash budgets are based upon estimates of future cash inflows and outflows. One method of estimating future figures such as sales or costs is to use time series analysis

- a time series is a series of historical figures over a period of time and the first stage is to determine the trend of these figures using moving averages

- once the trend has been determined the seasonal variations can be calculated either using the additive model or the multiplicative model

- once the trend and any seasonal variations are known then this information can be used to estimate future figures by extrapolating the trend line into the future and applying the appropriate seasonal variation

- in estimating future cash flows account must be taken of any anticipated inflation. This may be in the form of a one-off price increase or a more general period by period increase

- one method of expressing a change in prices is using an index. This could be a specific price index for a particular item of goods or services or a general price index such as the Retail Price Index

- an index, with its associated future estimated value, can be used to convert a current cash flow value to its estimated actual future value

- as cash budgets are prepared using many estimates and variables it is entirely likely that in practice these variables or assumptions may not hold true. Sensitivity analysis is a method of changing variables or assumptions within a budget in order to determine the effect this will have on overall cash flow

- one useful method of both preparing a cash budget and carrying out sensitivity analysis is to use a computer model such as a spreadsheet

KEY WORDS

Time series analysis a method of analysing historic data in order to use the results for future calculations

Time series any record of figures occurring over a past period

Trend the general movement in a time series over time

Trend line a line drawn onto a graph of a time series to indicate the general movements of the figures

Seasonal variations variations of the figures for particular time periods from the trend due to seasonal factors

Cyclical variations long term movements in a time series due to general economic conditions

Random variations variations in time series figures due to random or unexplained events

Additive model a time series model where the actual figure is made up of the trend plus the seasonal variation

Multiplicative model a time series model where the actual figure is made up of the trend multiplied by the seasonal variation

Extrapolation using historic data to make estimates of future figures

Inflation the increase in prices of goods and services over time

Index a measure of changes in price over time

Base year/period the year or period upon which an index is based and to which year the index value of 100 is assigned

Specific price index a price index relating to a specific item of goods or services

CHAPTER OVERVIEW contd.

KEY WORDS cont'd

General price index a price index relating to a variety of goods and services

Retail Price Index a general index which measures changes in the cost of items of expenditure in the average household

Sensitivity analysis a method of changing variables in a budget to determine the overall effect

HOW MUCH HAVE YOU LEARNED?

1   Given below are the daily takings in a restaurant that is open 5 days a week, Tuesday to Saturday.

	Tues £	Wed £	Thurs £	Fri £	Sat £
Week 1	560	600	630	880	930
Week 2	540	590	640	850	940
Week 3	550	560	600	870	970

You are required to calculate a five day moving average for the daily takings.

2   Given below are the quarterly factory costs for a business for the last three years.

		Costs £
2004	Q1	265,400
	Q2	259,800
	Q3	230,400
	Q4	235,600
2005	Q1	258,700
	Q2	254,300
	Q3	228,300
	Q4	230,400
2006	Q1	255,600
	Q2	251,200
	Q3	225,300
	Q4	227,600

i)   Calculate a four quarter centred moving average in order to find the trend in these figures. What can you conclude from your trend calculations?

ii) Determine the seasonal variations for each of the four quarters using the additive model.

iii) Using the trend and seasonal variation information estimate the factory costs for each of the four quarters of 2007.

3   Given below are the units produced in a factory from Monday to Friday for each day for three weeks.

	Mon Units	Tues Units	Wed Units	Thurs Units	Fri Units
Week 1	1,400	1,600	1,800	1,800	1,550
Week 2	1,380	1,620	1,830	1,810	1,500
Week 3	1,450	1,650	1,850	1,840	1,570

i)   Calculate a five day moving average to find the trend of these production figures.
ii) Calculate any seasonal variations (on a daily basis) using the multiplicative model.
iii) Using the trend and seasonal variations estimate the daily production figures for week 4.

4   What are the problems with using time series analysis to estimate future figures for cash budgeting purposes?

5 It is December 2006 and a business is preparing its cash budget for the first quarter of 2007. The following sales and purchases figures have been produced:

	Sales Units	Purchases Units
January	5,000	5,200
February	5,600	5,800
March	5,700	5,500

The current cost of purchases is £20 per unit and these are sold for £35 per unit. The business has been informed by its supplier that purchase prices will be increased from 1 February 2007 by 5% and the business has decided to increase its selling price by 8% from 1 January 2007.

Purchases are all paid for in the month of purchase but the cash receipts from sales all occur in the month following the sale. Sales in December 2006 were 4,800 units.

What are the estimated cash inflows from sales and cash payments for purchases in each of the three months of January, February and March 2007?

6 A business has general overheads of £160,000 in September 2006 but it is anticipated that these will increase by 1.75% per month for the next few months. Overheads are paid the month after they are incurred.

What is the cash outflow for overheads for the month of December 2006?

7 A business makes purchases of a particular raw material which has a cost of £10.80 per kg in September 2006. The actual and estimated specific price index for this material is as follows:

	Price index
September (actual)	148.5
October (estimate)	151.6
November (estimate)	154.2
December (estimate)	158.7

What is the expected price per kg (to the nearest penny) of the raw material in each of the months of October, November and December 2006?

8 A business currently pays its suppliers with the following pattern:

70% one month after the date of purchase
30% two months after the date of purchase

Some suppliers offer a 3% discount for payment during the month of purchase but in the past the business has not taken advantage of this. If it did take advantage then 40% of purchases would be paid for in the month of purchase, 40% in the month following purchase and 20% two months after the date of purchase.

Purchases are estimated to be as follows:

	£
August	330,000
September	380,000
October	400,000
November	440,000
December	390,000

You are required to calculate the payments to suppliers for each of the three months of October, November and December on the following bases:

i)   the current situation continues where no settlement discounts are taken

ii)   the settlement discounts are taken from those suppliers who are paid in the month of purchase (assume that this policy begins in October).

9   The management accountant of a business has decided to produce the cash budget for the quarter ending 31 March 2007 using a computer spreadsheet. The following data is available for this cash budget:

■   the balance on the bank account is anticipated to be £45,000 at 1 January 2007

■   sales in November 2006 were £470,600 and in December 2006 were £480,000. It is anticipated that there will be a growth rate in these sales of 2% per month. 10% of the sales are for cash and of the remainder half will pay in the month after the sale and the other half in the following month

■   purchases are all paid for in cash in the month of their sale and they are generally 70% of the sales value of that month

■   overheads in December 2006 were £80,000 and these have generally increased at a rate of 0.8% per month

■   a dividend payment of £40,000 is due in March 2007

You are required to set up the columns and rows of the spreadsheet and produce formulae for all of the figures that will appear in the spreadsheet. Enter the numbers calculated by the formulae for January into the appropriate cells in the spreadsheet.

chapter 4:
MANAGING CASH BALANCES

chapter coverage 📖

In the first three chapters of this Course Companion we have considered in detail the process of producing cash budgets and cash flow forecasts, and monitoring actual cash flows and balances compared to these. One of the main reasons for the preparation of cash budgets and forecasts is in order to identify whether the business is likely to have a deficit of funds or a surplus of funds.

If the business is likely to have a deficit at some point in the future then it must consider methods of raising additional finance to cover this deficit. If, in contrast, the business is likely to have surplus funds then these should be invested in order to make profits for the business.

In this chapter we will consider the main sources of additional funds for any deficit and the main types of investment for any surplus. However we will start the chapter with a look at the banking system which allows such transactions to take place and the legal relationship between a customer and its bank.

The topics that are to be covered are:

✍ the banking system

✍ the relationship between the bank and the customer

✍ the operations of the money markets

✍ dealing with a cash deficit

✍ raising additional finance

✍ overdraft finance

✍ short and medium term loans

✍ leasing or hire purchase

✍ dealing with a cash surplus

✍ types of investments

✍ government monetary policy

✍ public sector accounting

✍ dealing with cash

Performance criteria - element 15.2

- arrange overdraft and loan facilities in anticipation of requirements and on the most favourable terms available
- invest surplus funds in marketable securities within defined financial authorisation limits
- ensure the organisation's financial regulations and security procedures are observed
- ensure account is taken of trends in the economic and financial environment in managing cash balances
- maintain an adequate level of liquidity in line with cash forecasts

knowledge and understanding

- the basic structure of the banking system and the money market in the UK and the relationships between financial institutions
- bank overdrafts and loans; terms and conditions; legal relationship between bank and customer
- types of marketable security (bills of exchange, certificates of deposit, government securities, local authority short term loans); terms and conditions; risks
- government monetary policies
- managing risk and exposure
- liquidity management
- an understanding that practice in this area will be determined by an organisation's specific financial regulations, guidelines and security procedures
- an understanding that in public sector organisations there are statutory and other regulations relating to the management of cash balances

THE BANKING SYSTEM

If a business is to raise additional funds or invest surplus funds then this will be done either through a bank or within the money markets. Therefore we will begin this chapter with a look at the banking system in the UK and the money markets.

Banks

There are two main types of banks in the UK, primary and secondary banks.

PRIMARY BANKS are those which operate the money transmission service in the economy. This means that they are the banks which operate cheque accounts and deal with cheque clearing. They are sometimes also known as the commercial banks, retail banks or clearing banks.

The SECONDARY BANKS are made up of a wide range of merchant banks, other British banks and foreign banks in the UK. They do not tend to take part in the cheque clearing system.

Financial intermediation

Banks take deposits from customers and then use those funds to lend money to other customers. This process is known as FINANCIAL INTERMEDIATION. The banks act effectively as middlemen providing funds for those that want loans from the deposits made by savers.

The main benefits of financial intermediation are as follows:

- small amounts deposited by savers can be combined to provide larger loan packages to businesses

- short term savings can be transferred into long term borrowings

- search costs are reduced as companies seeking loan finance can approach a bank directly rather than finding individuals to lend to them

- risk is reduced as an individual's savings are not tied up with one individual borrower directly

Assets of banks

When individuals or companies pay money into their accounts with a bank then the bank of course has that money as an asset. However these assets of a retail bank come in a variety of different forms:

- Notes and coin – branches require notes and coins to meet demands for withdrawals by customers

- Balances with the Bank of England. There are two types of such balances – cash ratio deposits and operational deposits. The cash ratio deposit is a requirement of the Bank of England that a certain percentage of a bank's deposits must be held with the Bank of England. Operational deposits are the funds required to meet each bank's obligations under the clearing system for cheque payments

- Bills. The banks will tend to hold very low risk bills. These include the following:
    - Treasury bills – three-month loans issued by the Bank of England on behalf of the government (see later in the chapter)
    - Local authority bills which are similar to Treasury Bills but are issued by local government (see later in the chapter)
    - Commercial bills of exchange which are a promise by one firm to pay another a stated amount on a certain day (see later in the chapter)

- Loans to customers and overdrafts of customers

- Loans to the money markets or other banks.

- Securities.

Liabilities of banks

The liabilities of the banks are the amounts that customers have paid into the bank in the form of their account balances.

Activity 1

What are the main advantages of financial intermediation?

RELATIONSHIP OF THE BANK AND THE CUSTOMER

When money is paid into a bank by an individual or business and an account is opened then that individual or business becomes a customer of the bank.

The legal relationship between the bank and its customer is quite complex and there are indeed potentially four main contractual relationships between the bank and the customer

- the debtor/creditor relationship
- the bailor/bailee relationship
- the principal/agent relationship
- the mortgagor/mortgagee relationship

Debtor/creditor relationship

When the customer deposits money with the bank the bank becomes the debtor and the customer is of course a creditor of the bank. If the customer's account is overdrawn however the bank becomes the creditor and the customer the debtor.

This relationship is essentially a contract between the bank and the customer. There are a number of essential areas in this contract:

- the bank borrows the customer's deposits and undertakes to repay them

- the bank must receive cheques for the customer's account

- the bank will only cease to do business with the customer with reasonable notice

- the bank is not liable to pay until the customer demands payment

- the customer exercises reasonable care when writing cheques

Bailor/bailee relationship

This element of the relationship between customer and bank concerns the bank accepting the customer's property for storage in its safe deposit. The bank will undertake to take reasonable care to safeguard the property against loss or damage and also to re-deliver it only to the customer or someone authorised by the customer.

Principal/agent relationship

An agent is someone who acts on behalf of another party, the principal. Within banking the principal/agent relationship exists where, for example, the customer pays a crossed cheque into the bank. The bank acts as an agent when, as receiving bank, it presents the cheque for payment to the paying bank, and then pays the proceeds into the customer's account.

Mortgagor/mortgagee relationship

If the bank asks the customer to secure a loan with a charge over its assets then the relationship between the two is that of mortgagor and mortgagee. If the customer does not repay the loan then the bank has the right to sell the assets and use the proceeds to pay off the loan.

student notes ✍

Fiduciary relationship

The bank and the customer also have a fiduciary relationship which means that the bank is expected to act with the utmost good faith in its relationship with the customer.

The duties of the bank

Banks have a number of duties to its customers which include the following:

- it must honour a customer's cheques provided that they are correctly made out, there is no legal reason for not honouring it and the customer has enough funds or overdraft limit to cover the amount of the cheque

- the bank must credit cash/cheques that are paid in to the customer's account

- if the customer makes a written request for repayment of funds in its account, for example by writing a cheque, the bank must repay the amount on demand

- the bank must comply with the customer's instructions given by direct debit mandate or standing order

- the bank must provide a statement showing the transactions on the account within a reasonable period and provide details of the balance on the customer's account

- the bank must respect the confidentiality of the customer's affairs unless the bank is required by law, public duty or its own interest to disclose details or where the customer gives his consent for such disclosure

- the bank must tell the customer if there has been an attempt to forge the customer's signature on a cheque

- the bank should use care and skill in its actions

- the bank must provide reasonable notice if it is to close a customer's account.

Customer's duties

The customer also has duties in respect of its dealings with its bank. The two main duties are:

- to draw up cheques carefully so that fraud is not facilitated
- to tell the bank of any known forgeries.

The rights of the bank

The services that the bank provides are of course done as part of its business and as such the bank has certain rights:

- to charge reasonable bank charges and commissions over and above interest

- to use the customer's money in any way provided that it is legal and morally acceptable

- to be repaid overdrawn balances on demand (although the bank will rarely enforce this)

- to be indemnified against possible losses when acting on a customer's behalf.

Activity 2

What are the customer's duties when dealing with the bank?

MONEY MARKETS

The MONEY MARKETS cover a vast array of markets buying and selling different forms of money or marketable securities. MARKETABLE SECURITIES are short term highly liquid investments that are readily convertible into cash. The money markets provide the financial institutions with a means of borrowing and investing to deal with short term fluctuations in their own assets and liabilities.

The main traders in the money markets are banks, the government through the Bank of England, local authorities, brokers and other intermediaries in the market.

Money market financial instruments

There are a variety of different financial instruments that are traded in the money markets. The main types are:

- Bills – short term financial assets that can be converted into cash by selling them in the discount market

- Deposits – money in the bank accounts of banks and other financial intermediaries

- Commercial paper – IOUs issued by large companies which can be either held to maturity or sold to third parties before maturity

- Certificates of deposit (CDs) – a certificate for deposit of £50,000 or more for a fixed term which can be sold earlier than maturity in the CD market (dealt with later in this chapter).

The primary market

A PRIMARY MARKET is where new financial instruments are issued for cash, whereas a SECONDARY MARKET is where existing financial instruments are traded between participants in the market. The Bank of England uses the primary market to smoothe out fluctuations in its weekly cash balances by selling Treasury bills to banks and securities firms if the Bank needs to raise money, or by buying back Treasury bills if the Bank has surplus money.

The local authority market

In this market local government authorities borrow short term funds by issuing local authority bills with a maturity of about one year or shorter.

The inter-bank market

This is a market for very short-term borrowing, often overnight, between the banks. It is used to smooth fluctuations in the banks' receipts and payments. The interest rate charged in this market is the LONDON INTER-BANK OFFERED RATE (LIBOR). The individual banks then use this rate in order to set their own base rate which determines the interest rate that they will offer to their own customers.

Activity 3

What is the primary money market?

DEALING WITH A CASH DEFICIT

As we have seen, preparation of the cash budget or cash flow forecast may highlight a point in the future where the business will be short of funds, ie a CASH DEFICIT. In some cases the senior management of the business may also be able to identify a time when additional finance will be required even before a cash budget is prepared, for example if a Board decision is made to purchase a new property or acquire another business.

For the purposes of Unit 15 it is important that you appreciate:

- the various forms of finance that are available to deal with a cash deficit and

- how to determine the most appropriate type of finance for the particular purpose.

Firstly, therefore, you have to know why the additional finance is required.

Possible reasons for additional finance

There are many reasons why a business may have a cash deficit or need to raise additional finance. The most common reasons are:

- to fund day-to-day working capital

    - to increase stock or sales levels (and therefore debtors)
    - to reduce creditors

- to purchase fixed assets

- to acquire another business

The need to raise the finance may be highlighted by a deficit in the cash budget, by management decisions regarding investment in fixed assets or by the business strategy of growth by acquisition.

Funding working capital

One of the most common reasons for additional finance which is normally highlighted by a deficit in the cash budget is in order to fund the day-to-day working capital of the business. All businesses will have an OPERATING CYCLE which is effectively the period between the payment of money for goods to suppliers and the receipt of money for sales from customers.

If creditors are being paid more quickly than money is being received from debtors then it is likely that at some point the business will require funds to cover the period until the money from debtors is received.

Operating cycle

The operating cycle of a business in days is calculated as follows:

	Days
Stock turnover period	X
Debtors turnover period	X
	X
Less: creditors payment period	(X)
Operating cycle	X

HOW IT WORKS

We will return to the fuel division of SC Fuel and Glass. In the year ending 30 June 2006 the fuel division had total turnover of £7,860,000 and total cost of sales in that year of £4,720,000. At 30 June 2006 the working capital of the fuel division was as follows:

	£000
Stock	440
Debtors	1,120
Creditors	400

The operating cycle for the division can now be calculated:

		Days
Stock turnover period	$\dfrac{440}{4,720} \times 365$	34
Debtors turnover period	$\dfrac{1,120}{7,860} \times 365$	$\dfrac{52}{86}$
Less: creditors payment period	$\dfrac{400}{4,720} \times 365$	(31)
Operating cycle		55

What this shows us is that on average stock is being purchased and held for 34 days before being sold. Once it has been sold it is another 52 days until the money from the sale is received. However the suppliers are being paid 31 days after the purchase of the goods. Therefore there is a difference of 55 days between money going out for payment for the goods and the money being received for the sales themselves.

This period between payment and receipt must be **funded**.

Activity 4

A business has sales for the year of £854,000 and cost of sales of £555,000. At the year end stock is valued at £56,000, debtors total £72,000 and creditors are £48,000. What is the operating cycle of the business in days?

Increasing working capital

After a period of operating, a business may find that it needs an increase in its working capital. This could be due to a number of reasons:

- increase in sales turnover
- increase in debtors

- stock increases
- reduction of creditors

Increase in sales turnover

If sales turnover increases then this will often require increases in both stocks and debtors. The business may be able to gain additional credit from its trade creditors but in the absence of that may have to raise funds to finance this increase.

Care should be taken by any expanding business to ensure that it does not get into an OVERTRADING position. Overtrading is where a business expands more quickly than its funds will allow. The eventual result of overtrading is that the business does not have enough underlying funds in order to pay all of the business debts as they fall due.

Increase in debtors

The additional finance required might be due to an increase in debtors. This could be due to inefficiencies in the credit control of the business or it may be that it has been necessary to increase the credit period and amount offered to customers in order to keep their custom in a competitive market or to increase market share and sales turnover.

Increase in stock

Sometimes additional finance might be required due to an increase in stock levels which is not due to a general increase in turnover. These types of stock increases will normally only be temporary and could be due to any of the following:

- taking advantage of an attractive price by placing a bulk order
- building up stocks in advance of a peak period in a seasonal business
- receipt of a large order from a customer for which supplies must be purchased

Reduction of creditors

In some cases a business may find that it needs to reduce its trade creditors either in order to take advantage of settlement discounts or due to the fact that trade creditors may be pressing the business for quicker payment for their own reasons. This reduction in trade credit will need to be funded by some other source of finance as the taking of credit from suppliers is effectively a source of finance for a business.

In other cases additional finance might be required in the short term to fund payments such as the quarterly VAT payments or the annual corporation tax payment if cash has not been put aside for such purposes.

Purchase of fixed assets

We have seen in the last few paragraphs that there are many reasons why a business may need additional finance in order to fund its working capital and the need for this finance will normally have been highlighted by a budgeted deficit in the cash budget.

However most businesses will need to invest in additional or replacement fixed assets on a fairly regular basis. In many cases a business will not be able to purchase the fixed assets required to maintain or expand operations out of cash and will therefore need to raise finance in order to fund the purchase (alternative methods of funding the purchase of fixed assets will be considered later in the chapter).

Acquisition of another business

Many businesses have a policy of growth by acquisition of other businesses. Other businesses may not generally have such a policy but on occasion a potential acquisition may appear. Such a major amount of expenditure will almost always require funding by some form of external finance.

RAISING ADDITIONAL FINANCE

Once the reasons for the cash deficit or the need for additional finance has been identified the next stage is to determine the form of finance which is required by assessing the various forms of finance that are available and determining which is most appropriate.

The form of finance required

There are many forms of external finance that are available to a business however what is important is that the most appropriate form of finance is sought for the purpose for which the finance is required. We must therefore consider the purpose of the finance and also any internal regulations within the business regarding financing. For example a business may have a policy of ensuring that there is always a cash balance or undrawn overdraft facility of £50,000 available as a back-up.

The forms of finance available will normally be classified according to their timescale or maturity and in general terms the types of finance available can be categorised as:

- short term – anything up to 3 years
- medium term – 3 to 10 years
- long term – over 10 years

We will consider all three of these types of finance but as a general rule the timescale of the finance should match the time scale of the reason for the finance. So if the finance is required for working capital reasons then the finance should be short term, whereas if it is required for longer term investment in fixed assets or another business then the appropriate finance may be medium or long term.

Short term financing

The two main sources of short term financing are an OVERDRAFT or a short term LOAN.

OVERDRAFT FINANCE

Most of us are familiar with the concept of an overdraft, which is a form of short term borrowing from the bank available to both business and personal customers. If a bank is approached for an overdraft then it will normally agree an OVERDRAFT FACILITY. This is the amount by which the business's account is allowed to be overdrawn. It is then up to the customer to determine how much of this overdraft facility is to be used by having an actual overdraft.

HOW IT WORKS

The fuel division of SC Fuel and Glass has an overdraft facility with its bank of £50,000. However for the three months of October, November and December the anticipated cash balances at the end of each month are:

October	£19,260 overdrawn
November	£32,990 in credit
December	£7,660 overdrawn

Therefore the finance is available from the bank up to a total of £50,000 but the business does not anticipate having to borrow all of this money in the near future.

Features of overdraft finance

There are various features of overdraft finance with which you should be familiar:

student notes✍

- overdraft facility and actual overdraft – as we have seen there is a distinction between the overdraft facility offered by the bank and the actual overdraft that the business makes use of

- interest – the interest charged on an overdraft is usually at quite a high margin over and above the bank's base rate. However interest is only charged on the amount of the actual overdraft, calculated on a daily basis, rather than on the total overdraft facility

- commitment fee – in some cases an initial fee will be charged for the granting of the overdraft facility

- repayment – technically an overdraft is repayable on demand to the bank. However in practice it would be rare for a bank to enforce this.

SHORT TERM BANK LOAN

A short term loan with a bank could be arranged rather than an overdraft. This would be a loan for a fixed amount, for an agreed period of time on pre-arranged terms. Such a loan will normally be taken out with formal documentation which will include:

- the term of the loan

- the interest rate

- the way in which the interest is charged (it may be a fixed rate, or vary in line with base rate)

- the repayment date/dates

- any security required for the loan

- any covenants attached to the loan.

We will now briefly consider each of these areas.

Term of the loan

The term of the loan will normally be the subject of negotiations between the customer and the bank. If the purpose of the loan is for the support of working capital or the day-to-day operations of the business then the bank will normally expect to be provided with detailed profit and cash flow projections which will indicate the most appropriate term and timescale for repayment of the loan.

If the loan is required for the purchase of fixed assets then the term of the loan should not normally exceed the useful life of the related fixed assets as the loan will effectively be serviced and repaid out of the profits made by these assets.

Interest

The rate of interest on the loan will normally be set in relation to the bank's base rate which in turn is related to LIBOR. The interest may be VARIABLE RATE INTEREST or FIXED RATE INTEREST. Variable rate interest is where the interest rate charged on the loan amount changes every time the bank's own base rate changes. Fixed rate interest is a set amount that is to be charged for the entire term of the loan.

In general terms if interest rates are expected to rise in the near future a fixed rate of interest would be preferable to a business, but if interest rates are anticipated to fall then a variable rate could be a cheaper option.

Repayment terms

Loans can normally be repaid in three different ways:

- BULLET REPAYMENTS – the full amount of the loan remains outstanding for the entire term of the loan and the full amount is then repaid at the end of this period. Interest is therefore charged on the full loan amount throughout the loan term.

- BALLOON REPAYMENTS – under this method some of the loan principal is repaid during the term of the loan but the majority is repaid at the end of the loan period. Interest will be charged on the loan amount outstanding at any point in time.

- AMORTISING REPAYMENTS – in this case the loan principal is gradually repaid over the term of the loan until there is no principal outstanding at the end of the loan period. Each regular repayment will therefore consist of some loan principal and interest on the amount still outstanding.

Security

In many cases the bank will require the business to provide security for the loan. This may take the form of a FIXED CHARGE or a FLOATING CHARGE over the business's assets.

A fixed charge is where the security is a specific asset or group of assets which the business cannot sell during the term of the loan without the bank's permission. If the business defaults on the loan then the bank can sell the asset in order to repay the outstanding amount.

A floating charge is a charge on a certain group of assets of the business, such as debtors or stock, which will be constantly changing. If the business defaults on the loan then the bank has the right to be repaid from the proceeds of the pledged assets. Usually only a company can give a floating charge, not a sole trader or most forms of partnership.

From the bank's point of view the security that it has for a loan should have an identifiable value which is either stable or increasing, and which can be sold relatively easily and quickly to convert it into cash.

Often a sole trader or partners in a partnership will be required to give personal guarantees for the money loaned. This means that, should the business fail to make payments when due, the individual guarantor will be required to pay from personal assets.

Covenants

In the terms of some loans the bank will insist on certain obligations or restrictions on the business which are known as COVENANTS. Examples of specific loan covenants might include:

- agreement by the business to take out no further loans until this one has been repaid

- agreement by the business to provide regular management accounts and cash flow forecasts to the bank during the term of the loan

- agreement by the business that its total loans must not exceed a set percentage of its capital employed during the term of the loan.

Activity 5

What are the main features of overdraft finance?

Overdraft or bank loan?

As we have seen, for relatively short term borrowing, businesses will tend to have a choice between overdraft finance or a short-term loan. Which is most appropriate?

In general terms the financing method should be matched to the life of the asset for which the financing is required. In most cases therefore an overdraft is most suitable for increased working capital requirements and a loan is more suitable for the purchase of fixed assets or another business.

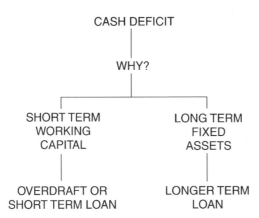

You do need to appreciate the advantages and disadvantages of each of these two main sources of short term finance.

Advantages of a bank overdraft

A bank overdraft as a source of short term funding has a number of advantages:

- flexibility – the full overdraft facility does not need to be used and therefore the precise amount of funding required does not need to be estimated provided that the facility granted is greater than the amount of overdraft anticipated to be required. If necessary an application can be made to the bank to increase an overdraft facility at some point in the future.

- cost – although the interest rate on an overdraft may be higher than the interest rate negotiated for a loan, the overdraft interest paid is calculated daily on the amount of the actual overdraft rather than on a fixed amount for a loan.

- short term – technically an overdraft is repayable on demand and therefore should normally only be used to fund short term working capital requirements. The benefit of this is that when the short term funding requirement is over the overdraft facility is simply not required. There is no necessity to negotiate paying off a loan early or incurring a penalty for early repayment.

Disadvantages of a bank overdraft

However there are also some drawbacks to the use of overdraft finance:

- repayable on demand – technically the overdraft is repayable on demand and if the bank considers that the business performance is not in line with its cash flow forecasts or business plans then the bank could cancel the overdraft facility and require any outstanding amount to be repaid possibly causing major cash flow problems for the business.

- increasing the facility – once an overdraft facility has been agreed with the bank it may be difficult to persuade the bank to increase that facility if additional finance is required

- short term – as the overdraft is repayable on demand it is only really suitable for the financing of short term assets such as investment in additional working capital rather than longer term assets such as fixed assets or acquisition of another business.

- cost - if the full extent of the facility is consistently used, the interest payment will be higher than on a loan of the same amount.

Advantage of loan finance

The main advantage of short term loan finance is that it can be tailored to meet the precise requirements of the business. It can be taken out for a period which matches the assets which it is financing and the repayment terms can be negotiated to match with the cash flows from the asset or the other business cash flows.

Disadvantages of loan finance

The potential disadvantages of short term loan finance include the following:

- cost – if the interest on a loan is fixed rate then this can sometimes be more expensive than interest on an overdraft. Also on a loan the interest charge is based upon the full amount of the loan outstanding whereas with an overdraft interest is only charged on the amount of the overdraft facility actually being used at the current time.

- security – the bank will normally require some form of security for the loan, either a fixed or a floating charge (from a company) or a personal guarantee

- covenants – as we have seen the bank may impose certain restrictions or covenants which will limit the freedom of action of the management of the business

Medium term bank loans

On the whole medium term debt finance should be used to fund the purchase of assets with a 3 to 10 year life such as plant and machinery. However it can also be useful to fund a medium term deficit in working capital.

The terms of such a loan will be similar to those for a short-term loan covering areas such as interest, repayment, security and covenants.

Medium term loans and working capital

As we have seen in most cases a bank loan is most appropriate for the purchase of major assets which will hopefully provide income over the loan period out of which the loan interest and repayments can be made. However in some cases it may be necessary to raise a medium term loan to finance a working capital deficit.

Suppose that a business has consistently had an overdraft of between £50,000 and £70,000 for the last eighteen months. This would appear to be part of the permanent funding capital of the business and would be known as the HARDCORE OVERDRAFT. Overdraft interest tends to be at a higher rate than loan interest as an overdraft is harder to monitor from the bank's perspective and tends to be more volatile. Therefore this company might convert the hardcore overdraft into say a £70,000 5 year loan which will be paid off over the period but which should reduce the amount of overdraft finance required.

Activity 6

What are the main types of conditions that would appear in a loan agreement with a bank?

LEASING OR HIRE PURCHASE

For the purchase of fixed assets such as plant and machinery or motor vehicles there is a further financing option. Rather than purchasing the assets outright the business may find that leasing the asset or purchasing it under a HIRE PURCHASE AGREEMENT is a cheaper option than taking out a bank loan. Many financial intermediaries such as banks and insurance companies provide LEASE FINANCE for a wide range of assets.

There are two types of lease, a FINANCE LEASE and an OPERATING LEASE.

Finance leases

Under a finance lease the lessee has the use of the asset for most, if not all of its useful life. The lessee may even be able to sell the asset at the end of its life with only a proportion of the sale proceeds being returned to the lessor. However the lessee although having use of the asset never actually gains legal title to the asset.

The lessee will normally be responsible for the upkeep and maintenance of the asset and to all intents and purposes owns the asset. The regular finance lease charges will reflect the repayment of the value of the asset and the finance charge to the lessor.

Operating leases

An operating lease is more like short term hire of an asset. This is where the lessor hires out the asset to the lessee for a short period which is normally substantially less than the asset's total life. Once the lease period is over then the lessor will lease the same asset to another lessee. The lessor will tend to be responsible for maintaining the asset and the lessee simply gets the use of the asset for the lease period in return for the lease payments.

An operating lease might be useful if a particular asset was only required by the business for a fairly short period. However if an asset is required for substantially all of its entire useful life then a finance lease would be more appropriate.

Hire purchase agreement

A hire purchase agreement is very similar to a finance lease. The asset is used by the business in return for regular hire purchase charges which cover both the capital cost of the asset and the hire purchase interest. However the difference between hire purchase and a finance lease is that with the final hire purchase payment legal title to the asset then passes to the business.

Activity 7

What is the main difference between a finance lease and a hire purchase agreement?

DEALING WITH A CASH SURPLUS

In some instances the cash budget may highlight a period in time where the business has a CASH SURPLUS, which is money in its current bank account. In most cases money in a current account is not earning any interest or at least a very low rate of interest. It is known as an idle asset. Such cash is effectively not working for the business and should be invested to earn profits for the business.

The cash budget will highlight the anticipated amount of the cash surplus and the anticipated period during which there will be a cash surplus and therefore the business can plan how to invest such funds most effectively.

There are three main factors that should be considered when determining how to invest any surplus funds:

- risk
- return
- liquidity

Risk

RISK is the chance that the business will make a loss on its investment. For example a business invests £20,000 of surplus cash by buying 10,000 shares in another company at £2 per share. It then sells the shares two months later when the cash is required for operational purposes. The share price may have increased to £2.20 per share giving proceeds of £22,000 but there is also the risk that the shares will have decreased in value to say £1.90 per share meaning that only £19,000 is realised and the business has made a loss of £1,000.

When cash is invested there are two main risks. There is the risk that the value of investment will fall (as above) which is the CAPITAL RISK. There is also the risk that the return from the investment will be lower than expected due to changes in market rates of return.

Return

The RETURN on an investment has two potential aspects – the INCOME RETURN and the CAPITAL RETURN. Most investments will pay some form of interest or dividend which is the income return. However most investments will also tend to fluctuate in value over time and this is the capital return (or capital loss).

Liquidity

LIQUIDITY is the term used for the ease and speed with which an investment can be converted into cash. Any investments which are widely traded on a market, such as the money markets, will be very liquid but investments such as a bank deposit account which requires 3 months notice to withdraw the funds would not be a liquid investment.

With investments there tends to be a relationship between each of these three elements of risk, return and liquidity.

Risk and return

As a general rule risk and return are related: the higher the risk of an investment, the higher will be its anticipated return. Most businesses which have surplus funds to invest will want those funds to earn a good profit or return but will not wish to take unnecessary risks. The safety of the value of the asset will also be of great importance.

HOW IT WORKS

The glass division of SC Fuel and Glass has £60,000 to invest for the next month until the money is needed to pay the quarterly VAT bill. It could be paid into an interest bearing deposit account at the bank where it will earn 0.5% interest for the month. Alternatively it could be used to buy shares in another company.

If it is paid into the deposit account then the money bears virtually no risk at all (provided that the bank is creditworthy). One month later the money will be withdrawn and will total:

£60,000 + (60,000 x 0.005) = £60,300

The business has made a profit or return of £300 and the money is available to pay the VAT bill.

If the shares were purchased then it is possible that they would have increased in value to £66,000 in one months time meaning that the glass division has earned a profit of £6,000. However it is also possible, due to the risk of investment in shares, that the shares might have fallen in value to £55,000. This would mean that not only has the glass division made a loss of £5,000 but the full amount of cash is not available to meet the VAT bill.

Activity 8

What is the general relationship between risk and return when considering investments?

Return and liquidity

As we have seen if any surplus cash is invested it is important to ensure that it can be realised, ie converted back into cash, when needed.

The ease of this conversion back into cash will be reflected in the return that the investment gives. If an investment cannot be quickly or easily realised then it will normally give a higher return in compensation for this. If a business has a cash surplus and is certain that it will not need the cash for a particular period of time then it will usually be able to earn a higher return than an investment where the cash can be realised immediately if required.

For example the interest earned on a bank deposit account which requires a month's notice for any withdrawal will be higher than the interest on a deposit account where the funds can be withdrawn at any time.

Risk, return and liquidity

In conclusion therefore when a cash surplus is to be invested the aim will be to earn a good return but without incurring excessive risk of loss and also ensuring that the investment can be realised within the time scale in which the cash is required.

Organisational rules and procedures

In most companies there will be certain regulations and procedures to ensure that the liquidity of the business is safeguarded. Typical of such rules and procedures might be the following:

- a certain amount of cash to be available immediately at any point in time

- investments in certain types of instrument may be limited to a particular financial amount

- surplus funds might only be allowed to be invested in certain specified types of investment

- all investments must be convertible into cash within a certain number of days.

Any such procedures, regulations and limits must be followed at all times.

TYPES OF INVESTMENT

In the previous section we looked at the general considerations that must be taken into account when investing any surplus cash. In this section we will consider the possible types of investment which may be suitable for any cash surplus a business may have.

Bank or building society deposit accounts

One of the safest forms of investment for surplus cash is to pay it into a high street bank or building society deposit account. Retail banks and building societies offer a wide range of such accounts although the interest rate, particularly for small sums, is generally quite low. Online accounts tend to attract a higher interest rate.

There are also higher interest deposit accounts for larger amounts, for example provided that there is always a balance of say £10,000 in the account. Access to the cash is usually immediate and therefore useful if cash requirements are not known for certain.

If the cash is definitely not required in the near future then it could be invested in a deposit account for a fixed term of up to three months at a variable rate of interest which is linked to money market rates. This will give a higher rate of return.

Gilt edged securities

GILT EDGED SECURITIES or GILTS are marketable British Government securities. They are fixed interest securities and they form the major part of the fixed interest market. Gilts are classified according to their redemption dates as follows:

Shorts – lives up to five years eg Treasury 4% 2009

Mediums – lives from five to fifteen years eg Treasury 9% 2012

Longs – lives of more than fifteen years eg Treasury 6% 2028

Undated stocks – no redemption date eg Treasury 2½%

Index linked stocks eg Treasury IL 2½% 2009

Gilts prices

Gilts prices are quoted in the financial press every day and are priced for every £100 of stock.

For example on 5 March 2007 the quoted price of Treasury 4% 2009 was £97.59. This means that £100 of the gilts can be purchased for £97.59.

The gilts will be redeemed in 2009 at their nominal value of £100 and as the maturity date moves closer the gilt price will move towards £100.

HOW IT WORKS

The fuel division of SC Fuel and Glass expects to have approximately £50,000 to invest and is considering an investment in Treasury 4% 2009 stock which are currently priced at £97.59.

At this price the division could purchase £51,234 par value of this stock (£50,000/£97.59 x £100).

Income from gilts

Interest is payable on Treasury stock twice a year at the COUPON RATE, which is the rate quoted in the price of the gilt. So for Treasury 4% 2009 interest for the year is £4 per £100 block of stock and is payable in two instalments of £2.00 each at six month intervals.

Interest yield

The INTEREST YIELD or FLAT RATE YIELD is simply the coupon rate of interest as a percentage of the current price of the gilt. This shows the return on the gilt if it were bought today and held for a year.

HOW IT WORKS

The Treasury 4% 2009 stock which the fuel division is considering investing in is currently priced at £97.59.

$$\text{Interest rate yield} = \frac{£4.00}{£97.59} \times 100 = 4.10\%$$

Activity 9

5% Treasury stock 2008 are currently quoted at £99.68. What is the interest yield on this stock?

Redemption yield

The redemption yield is calculated as:

Interest yield +/– the yield on the gain or loss if held to redemption

The interest yield is calculated as above.

The gain if held to redemption is calculated as:

$$\frac{(\text{redemption price} - \text{current price})}{\text{number of years to redemption}} \times \frac{£100}{\text{current price}}$$

For example, a fictitious gilt might be Treasury 5% 2012 redeemed in 5 years from today's date and currently priced at £95. It will have the following redemption yield

Interest yield = $0.05 \times 100/95 = 0.053 = 5.3\%$

Gain yield $\dfrac{(£100-95)}{5\ years} \times \dfrac{£100}{£95} = 5/5 \times 100/95 = 1.05\%$

The redemption yield will be 6.35% (5.3 + 1.05)

Gilt prices and interest rates

As gilts are marketable securities, their value fluctuates over time. We have already seen that the price of a gilt is partly determined by the period remaining until maturity. The other factor which affects the price of gilts is the current prevailing market rate of interest.

If general interest rates rise then the value of gilts will tend to fall. The reason for this is that with higher general interest rates the gilts stock must also produce a higher return. The coupon rate of interest cannot be altered but if the market value of the stock falls then the same coupon interest will produce a higher yield.

Similarly if interest rates fall then the value of gilts will rise.

This is an important factor in the investment decision and therefore any expected changes in the economic and financial environment should be taken into account when investing any surplus funds.

Local authority stocks

In a similar way to government stocks there are a large number of marketable local authority securities which are available for investment purposes. However local authority stocks are not considered to be quite as secure as central government stocks and the market is not so large which means that local authority stocks have a slightly higher yield than government stocks to compensate.

Certificates of deposit

A CERTIFICATE OF DEPOSIT (CD) is a document issued by a bank or building society which certifies that a certain sum, usually a minimum of £50,000, has been deposited with it to be repaid on a specific date. The term can range from 7 days to five years but is usually for 6 months.

CDs are negotiable instruments which means that they can be bought and sold. Therefore if the holder does not want to wait until the maturity date the CD can be sold in the money market.

CDs offer a good rate of interest, are highly marketable and can be liquidated at any time at the current market rate. The market in CDs is large and active therefore they are an ideal method for investing large cash surpluses.

Bills of exchange

A BILL OF EXCHANGE can be defined as an unconditional order in writing from one person to another requiring the person to whom it is addressed to pay a specified sum of money either on demand (a SIGHT BILL) or at some future date (a TERM BILL). A cheque is a special example of a type of bill of exchange.

Trading in bills of exchange

Most bills of exchange are term bills with a duration or maturity of between two weeks and six months and are of a value of up to £500,000 in any currency. If one company draws a bill on another company this is known as a trade bill. However the market in these is small.

Most bills are BANK BILLS which are bills of exchange drawn and payable by a bank, the most common of these are known as a banker's acceptance. There is an active market in such bills and a company with surplus cash could buy a bill of exchange at a discount and either hold it to maturity or sell it in the market before maturity again at a discount. The difference between the price at which the bill is purchased and the price at which it is sold or it matures is the return to the investor.

Activity 10

What is a certificate of deposit (CD)?

GOVERNMENT MONETARY POLICY

The Knowledge and Understanding requirements for Unit 15 require some background knowledge of government monetary policy. This is a complex area but a brief overview will be given in this section in terms of its relevance to investment and borrowing decisions.

Government monetary policies are the policies that are implemented by the Treasury and the Bank of England in order to deal with the supply of money, interest rates and the availability of credit.

Government market operations

The way in which the government influences the amount of money in the economy is by either restricting or encouraging bank lending. One way of doing this is by the issue of gilts. By selling attractively priced gilts the government takes money away from financial institutions and individuals who pay for these gilts. This takes money out of their bank accounts thereby reducing the banks' asset bases and the amount that the banks can lend.

The use of Treasury Bills by the government also controls bank lending and influences the interest rate. By selling Treasury Bills the government is taking money out of the system and by buying Treasury Bills it can put money back into the system. Through the buying and selling process the government affects the supply and demand levels for investments generally and can influence interest rates.

Interest rate policy

The Bank of England, on behalf of the government, controls the short-term interest rate through its operations in the primary money market. When interest rates are increased this reduces the demand for borrowing. This in turn has the effect of reducing consumer demand as less credit is available and the credit that is available is too costly.

Equally if the Bank of England reduces interest rates this is a boost to the economy as more credit and spending power are available.

Government spending and borrowing

The government spends money on public spending and raises money by taxation. If the government spends more than it raises this will increase the money supply. The excess of government spending over tax revenues is known as the Public Sector Borrowing Requirement (PSBR). The government will wish to control the PSBR and to keep it within certain limits so as not to increase the money supply too much.

If the Government spends less than it raises this will reduce the money supply; the excess of tax revenues over government spending is known as the Public Sector Debt Repayment (PSDR).

PUBLIC SECTOR ACCOUNTING

For those who are used to accruals accounting, it seems difficult to understand a system of accounting that relies solely on cash accounting, and yet for many years until relatively recently this is what the public sector did.

The differences between cash accounting and accruals accounting may be illustrated with a few simple examples.

- **Purchases of fixed assets.** With cash accounting a fixed asset is only recognised when the cash is expended. The results of this are very far reaching

- the fixed asset will be treated as a expense – it will not be capitalised and carried forward in the balance sheet – the organisation does not therefore recognise the value of the assets it has paid for

- perhaps one might say worse of all, the organisation will not provide depreciation (as far as the accounts are concerned the asset does not exist and there is nothing to depreciate). The effect of this is that no depreciation reserve is built up in the accounts ie no assets are set aside to provide for the replacement of the fixed asset.

The result of this is a lack of control over the assets and a lack of resources to maintain the asset base.

- **No attempt to match income with associated expenditure.**

  Consider a simple example where £50,000 cash is received from a customer for a service to be provided in two month's time. The cash is banked and accounted for as income in the normal way but no accrual is set up for let's say the £40,000 of expenses that will be needed to provide the services. The result of this can be very problematic. If another urgent matter arises that requires paying for, it is all too easy to spend the £40,000 on the new urgent matter leaving insufficient funds to provide the service.

- **Public sector pensions.** The pensions of public sector workers are typically unfunded – the public sector pays for these pensions out of current receipts. This is in very sharp contrast to the situation of private sector companies where the law requires pensions to be fully funded by the company. It has been estimated that public sector pensions cost about £20bn per annum which equates to an unrecorded liability of some £500bn

Public sector organisations in the UK have for the most part moved to accrual accounting for example NHS Trusts and Local Authorities. The benefits are

- The adoption of accrual accounting recognises both costs and revenues which gives a fuller picture of the organisation's finances and in particular liabilities.

- Accrual accounting demands better accounting systems and better trained managers who can understand the systems and the financial position that the accounts show.

- Assets are fully recognised when acquired and proper provision for depreciation and maintenance of the asset base is provided.

- Liabilities are fully recognised – not just major liabilities such as pensions but the operating liabilities associated with ongoing projects.

- Expenditure, particularly on the acquisition of major assets that are frequently paid for in stages will be better budgeted and therefore better controlled (eg by strict application of the provisions of SSAP 9)

Capital expenditure may also be less erratic as future commitments on current projects may be fully provided so that managers will not allow huge concentrations of projects to occur in a given year.

Under cash accounting, organisations were frequently allocated a given amount of money to spend in a given year. As the cash could not be carried forward to later years, the organisations frequently spent the allocation on assets/expenditure that was not really needed (otherwise it was lost) rather than carry it forward to projects that would have been more beneficial.

Conceptual framework for not-for profit entities

The IASB and the FASB are currently in a project to produce a new, improved conceptual framework for financial reporting, entitled: The Objective of Financial Reporting and Qualitative Characteristics of Decision-Useful Financial Reporting Information. This project is being undertaken in phases. Phase G is entitled Application to not-for-profit entities in the private and public sector. A monitoring group, including ASB members, set up to advise on this has made the following points:

a) Not-for profit entities have different objectives, different operating environments and other different characteristics from private sector businesses.

b) The following issues exist regarding application of the proposals to not-for-profit entities:

    i)   Insufficient emphasis on accountability/stewardship

    ii)   A need to broaden the definition of users and user groups

    iii) The emphasis on future cash flows is inappropriate to not-for-profit entities

    iv)   Insufficient emphasis on budgeting

Users and user groups

The primary user group for not-for-profit entities is providers of funds. In the case of public bodies, such as government departments, this primary group will consist of taxpayers. In the case of private bodies, such as charities, it will be financial supporters, and also potential future financial supporters. There is also a case for saying that a second primary user group should be recognised, being the recipients of the goods and services provided by the not-for-profit entity.

Cash flow focus

The new framework, like the existing framework, emphasises the need to provide information which will enable users to assess an entity's ability to generate net cash inflows. Not-for-profit entities also need to generate cash flows, but other aspects are generally more significant – for instance, the resources the entity has available to deliver future goods and services, the cost and effectiveness of those it has delivered in the past and the degree to which it is meeting its objectives.

Budgeting

The IASB has decided to leave consideration of whether financial reporting should include forecast information until later in the project. However, for not-for-profit entities, budgets and variance analyses are more important. In some cases, funding is supplied on the basis of a formal, published budget.

Regulatory framework

Regulation of not-for-profit entities, principally local and national governments and governmental agencies, is by the ASB assisted by two specialist advisory committees. These bodies advise the ASB on proposals for Statements of Recommended Practice (SORPs) put forward by specialist bodies developing accounting practice for their sectors.

The ASB gives approval to bodies which wish to develop SORPs. They are developed in accordance with ASB guidelines and the ASB will then give a statement granting approval to the SORP.

These are some SORPs prepared by independent bodies to which the ASB has given its statement:

Authorised Unit Trust Schemes and Authorised Open-Ended Investment Companies
The Investment Management Association

Derivatives
British Bankers Association

Accounting and Reporting by Charities
Charity Commission for England and Wales

Accounting for Further and Higher Education
Universities UK

Code of Practice on Local Authority Accounting in the UK
Chartered Institute of Public Finance and Accountancy

You do not need to remember any of these, but this gives you some idea of the bodies which prepare SORPs. The ASB approval signifies that the SORP complies with current UK accounting standards, the ASB's Statement of Principles and GAAP, apart from any departures arising from the Government's requirements.

Performance measurement – public sector

Not-for-profit and public sector entities produce financial statements in the same way as profit-making entities do but, while they are expected to remain solvent, their performance cannot be measured simply by the bottom line.

A public sector entity is not expected to show a profit or to underspend its budget. In practice, central government and local government departments know that if they underspend the budget, next year's allocation will be correspondingly reduced. This leads to a rash of digging up the roads and other expenditure just before the end of the financial year as councils strive to spend any remaining funds.

Private and public sector entities are judged principally on the basis of what they have achieved, not how much or how little they have spent in achieving it. So how is performance measured?

Public sector entities will have performance measures laid down by government. The emphasis is on economy, efficiency and effectiveness. Departments and local councils have to show how they have spent public money and what level of service they have achieved. Performance measurement will be based on Key Performance Indicators (KPIs). Examples of these for a local council could be:

a) Number of homeless people rehoused
b) % of rubbish collections made on time
c) Number of children in care adopted

Public sector entities use the services of outside contractors for a variety of functions. They then have to be able to show that they have obtained the best possible value for what they have spent on outside services. This principle is usually referred to as Value For Money (VFM). In the UK, local authorities are required to report under a system known as Best Value. They have to show that they applied 'fair competition' in awarding contracts.

Regulation and International Public Sector Accounting Standards Board (IPSASB)

The standards that govern financial reporting in the public sector follow closely the standards that govern the private sector, but may possibly be said to have lagged behind the private sector in the development of standards specifically designed for the needs of the public sector.

The IPSASB in 2004 determined to develop a set of international public sector accounting standards (IPSASs). Many of the current IPSASs are based on the IASs and IFRSs using the IASB Framework.

The IPSASB is developing a new public sector conceptual framework to make explicit the concepts that underpin financial reporting in the public sector.

DEALING WITH CASH

In this chapter so far we have been considering how to raise additional finance if there is a cash deficit and how to invest any cash surplus that a business may have. However some businesses are cash based businesses, usually in the retail trade, and you need to be aware of some of the basic requirements for dealing with amounts of cash taken from customers. There are many businesses in the retail sector or manufacturing businesses with a retail outlet which will necessarily have to deal with potentially large amounts of cash on a daily basis before it can be banked or otherwise invested. However, although in the public sector there are regulations relating to the management of cash balances (for example cash balances cannot be invested without authority, and there can be no speculation with tax payers' money) private entities are not regulated in this way.

Security

Cash is a highly risky asset to be holding on the business premises as it can easily be misappropriated or stolen. For any cash-based business therefore there must be procedures and policies in place which must be followed to ensure that cash and cheques from customers are secure and are banked as quickly as possible and in full. Increasingly customers are choosing to pay by debit card, which means there are fewer transactions involving cash (notes and coin) than there used to be.

Procedures for dealing with cash

Any business dealing with cash must have basic security procedures in place. The main such procedures deal with the following aspects:

- physical safeguards
- checking for valid payment
- reconciliation of cash received
- banking procedures
- recording procedures

Physical safeguards

Any cash or cheques received must be kept safe at all times and must only be accessible to authorised individuals within the organisation. Therefore cash should be kept under lock and key either in a cash box, lockable till or safe. Only authorised individuals should have access to the keys.

Checking for valid payment

Payments received in cash will of course be valid provided that any notes are not forged. However if cheques are accepted as payment then they must be supported by a valid cheque guarantee card and be correctly drawn up, dated and signed. If debit or credit cards are accepted then basic checks should be made on the card and signature and authorisation must be sought for payments which exceed the floor limit.

Reconciliation of cash received

When payments are received in the form of cash, cheques or debit or credit cards then a list of all cash, cheque and card receipts taken during the day must be kept. This list must then be reconciled at the end of each day to the amount of cash in the till, cash box or safe. The list may be manual as each sale is made or may be automatically recorded on the till roll as each sale is rung in.

This reconciliation should not be carried out by the person responsible for making the sales but by some other responsible official. Any discrepancies between the amount of cash recorded as taken during the day and the amount physically left at the end of the day must be investigated.

Banking procedures

Any cash, cheques and debit and credit card vouchers (if the business does not use electronic funds transfer at point of sale, or EFTPOS) should be banked as soon as possible and intact each day. This not only ensures the physical safety of the cash but also that it cannot be used by employees for unauthorised purposes. It also means that once the money is in the bank it is earning the business the maximum amount of interest. All cash should be banked as soon as possible but if it is not possible to bank it until the following day then either the cash must be left in a locked safe overnight or in the bank's overnight safe.

Recording procedures

For security purposes the paying-in slip for the bank should be made out by someone other than the person paying the money into the bank. The total on the paying in slip should also be reconciled to the till records or cash list for the day.

Activity 11

In a retail business where payment is received from customers by cash, cheque and debit/credit card what reconciliation should be carried out at the end of each day?

CHAPTER OVERVIEW

- one of the primary purposes of the banking system is that of financial intermediation

- the assets of the banks take a variety of forms including cash, deposits held with the Bank of England, bills, loans and overdrafts – the liabilities of the bank are its customers' account balances

- there are four potential contractual relationships between a bank and its customer with the most important being the debtor/creditor relationship

- not only do banks have a number of duties to their customers but the customers also have a duty to take care to ensure that fraud is not facilitated

- the money markets are a vast array of markets buying and selling different forms of cash and marketable securities

- once a forecast cash deficit is identified the reason for the deficit must first be determined in order to identify the most appropriate source of finance

- a cash deficit is often caused by working capital problems or by the need to fund an increasing operating cycle – in other cases the cash deficit is due to the need to purchase fixed assets or even acquire another business

- over the short term the two main sources of additional finance are either overdraft finance or a loan

- an overdraft facility may be granted by the bank and the business can then run an overdraft of any amount up to that facility total – interest will be charged only on the amount of the actual overdraft on a daily basis

- if loan finance is taken out the loan agreement will include details of the term of the loan, the interest rate, the repayment pattern, any security and any covenants

KEY WORDS

Primary banks the high street or retail banks

Secondary banks banks other than the primary banks operating in the UK

Financial intermediation the process of banks taking deposits from customers to lend to others

Money markets markets buying and selling different forms of money and marketable securities

Marketable securities short term, highly liquid investments readily convertible into cash

Primary market new financial instruments are issued for cash

Secondary market existing financial instruments are traded between participants in the market.

London Inter-Bank Offered Rate (LIBOR) the interest rate prevailing in the London inter-bank market

Cash deficit shortage of cash

Operating cycle the time period between payment for goods and receipt of the money from sales

Overtrading rapid expansion in business not supported by the capital base of the business

Overdraft the amount by which a customer's bank account is in debit

Overdraft facility the amount of potential overdraft that a bank allows a customer

Loan an amount of money advanced by a bank to its customer

Variable rate interest interest on a loan which changes every time the bank changes its base rate

CHAPTER OVERVIEW cont.

- the choice between an overdraft or a loan will normally depend upon the reason for the deficit – in general a deficit due to working capital shortages will be financed by an overdraft but if the deficit is for the purchase of longer term fixed assets a loan to match the life of the assets would be more appropriate

- an alternative method of financing the purchase of fixed assets is either lease finance or a hire purchase agreement

- if a cash surplus is identified then it should normally be invested to earn profits for the business – when considering potential investments consideration should be given to risk, return and liquidity

- there are many types of investment that would be suitable for surplus cash and these include bank deposit accounts, gilt edged securities, local authority stocks, certificates of deposit and bills of exchange

- government monetary policies are the policies implemented by the Treasury and the Bank of England in order to control the supply of money, interest rates and the availability of credit

- much of government monetary policy is carried out through the issuing or buying of gilts and Treasury Bills in order to control the money supply and interest rates

- in a business where large amounts of cash/cheques/debit and credit card payments are received from customers procedures should be in place to ensure that the cash is physically secure, controlled and paid into the bank as soon as possible

KEY WORDS cont.

Fixed rate interest   an agreed fixed rate of interest for the term of a loan

Bullet repayments   the entire loan is paid off at the end of the loan period with only interest payments during the term of the loan

Balloon repayments   some loan principal is paid off during the term of the loan but most of it at the end of the loan period

Amortising repayments   repayments are made up of interest and principal so that there is no principal remaining at the end of the loan term

Fixed charge   security is a specific asset which cannot be sold without the bank's permission

Floating charge   charge on a group of assets that are constantly changing such as debtors or stock

Covenants   obligations or restrictions placed on the business by the loan provider

Hardcore overdraft   an overdraft which has effectively become a permanent part of the capital of the business

Lease finance   a method of purchasing fixed assets without paying cash up front in full

Hire purchase agreement   payment for a fixed asset in instalments where legal title to the asset passes when the final instalment is made

Finance lease   lease of an asset for substantially the whole of its useful life

Operating lease   short term hire of an asset

Cash surplus   surplus cash held in the business's current account

CHAPTER OVERVIEW cont.

KEY WORDS cont.

Risk   the chance of making a loss

Return   any income and/or capital gain on an investment

Income return   interest or dividend received

Capital return   increase/decrease in market value of an investment

Liquidity   the ease and speed with which an investment can be converted into cash

Gilt edged securities/Gilts   marketable British government securities

Coupon rate   interest rate included in the title of the gilts

Interest yield/flat rate yield   income return on the gilts if held for one year

Redemption yield   return on the gilts if held to maturity

Certificate of deposit   a document issued by a bank which certifies that a certain sum has been deposited with it to be repaid on a specific date – a negotiable instrument and highly marketable

Bill of exchange   unconditional order in writing from one person to another requiring the person to whom it is addressed to pay a specified sum

Sight bill   bill of exchange payable on demand

Term bill   bill of exchange payable at some future date

Bank bill   bill of exchange drawn and payable by a bank

HOW MUCH HAVE YOU LEARNED?

1 Briefly explain the four potential contractual relationships between a bank and its customer.

2 What are the main duties of a bank in relation to its customers?

3 What is LIBOR?

4 A business has sales of £790,000 during the year and cost of sales of £593,000. Stock at the year end was valued at £68,000, debtors were £102,000 and trade creditors were £57,000.

What is the operating cycle (in days) of the business?

5 Compare an overdraft as a source of short term finance to a short term loan with a bank.

6 A Ltd is considering the purchase of shares in B Ltd which will require external finance. What would be the most appropriate source of finance for this purchase, and why?

7 What are the three main repayment patterns of repaying a loan?

8 Explain what is meant by security for a loan and distinguish between a fixed charge and a floating charge.

9 Briefly explain the three factors that should be considered when deciding upon an appropriate form of investment for a cash surplus.

10 Explain the difference between the interest yield and the redemption yield on a gilt-edged security.

11 If there is a general rise in interest rates what effect is this likely to have on the price of gilt-edged securities?

12 What is a bill of exchange? Distinguish between a term bill and a sight bill.

13 If the government spends more than it raises in taxes, what is the deficit known as?

14 What procedures should be put in place in a business with substantial daily receipts of cash and cheques?

chapter 5:
CREDIT CONTROL

chapter coverage 📖

In this chapter we introduce you to the credit control elements of Unit 15. In the next few chapters we will be considering the granting of credit, the monitoring of debtors and the collection of debts. However we start this area of the syllabus with a consideration of the overall role and purpose of credit control. You are also required to have a knowledge of the basic legal issues that affect the granting of credit and dealings with debtors.

The topics to be covered are:

✍ the role of credit control

✍ credit control policy

✍ terms and conditions of credit

✍ payment methods

✍ contract law

✍ Data Protection

KNOWLEDGE AND UNDERSTANDING AND PERFORMANCE CRITERIA COVERAGE

knowledge and understanding

■ legal issues: basic contract; terms and conditions of contracts relating to the granting of credit; Data Protection legislation and credit control information
■ understanding that practice in this area will be determined by an organisation's credit control policies and procedures

THE ROLE OF CREDIT CONTROL

The decision as to whether or not to grant credit to customers is an important commercial decision. The granting of credit to customers means that they will be able to delay payment for goods purchased but this delay is an important marketing aspect of business that will almost always lead to a greater level of sales.

The benefit of offering credit to customers is therefore additional sales and therefore profits. However there are also costs involved in offering credit:

- interest cost – if money is received later from customers then the business is either losing interest as it does not have the money in its bank account or is being charged more interest on any overdraft balance

- bad debts cost – if sales are made for cash then the money is received at the time of the sale. However with a credit sale there is always some risk that the goods will be despatched but never paid for.

Despite these costs of granting credit most businesses will trade on a credit basis with at least some of its customers due to the benefits of additional sales and competitive advantage.

Credit control function

As we have seen there are two main costs involved in trading with customers on credit, the interest cost and the bad debts cost. The role of the credit control function is to minimise these costs.

In a small organisation the credit control function may consist of a single member of the accounting function. However in a larger organisation the credit control function may be an entire department.

There are two main stages in the credit control function:

- the ordering cycle
- the collection cycle

The ordering cycle

The ORDERING CYCLE can be illustrated:

Customer places
order
|
Customer credit
status established
|
Customer offered
credit
|
Goods despatched
|
Goods delivered
|
Invoice despatched

The credit control function will be directly involved with the earlier elements of the ordering cycle – the establishment of the credit status of the customer and the offering of credit to the customer (both of these areas will be dealt with in the next chapter).

Although the credit control function will not normally be involved in the despatch or invoicing of the goods they will need access to the documents involved with these activities.

The collection cycle

The COLLECTION CYCLE starts where the ordering cycle finishes:

Customer receives
invoice
|
Statement sent
to customer
|
Reminder letters
sent
|
Telephone calls
to customer
|
Cash received

These elements form a major part of the credit control function's role and will be dealt with in the final two chapters in this Course Companion.

Activity 1

What are the main elements of the ordering cycle for goods to be sold on credit?

CREDIT CONTROL POLICY

Each business will have its own credit control policies and procedures. These will tend to cover the following areas:

- assessment of credit standing of new customers (see Chapter 6)
- assessment of credit standing of existing customers (see Chapter 6)
- customers exceeding credit limits (see Chapter 6)
- terms and conditions of credit granted (see below)
- payment methods allowed (see below)
- collection procedures (See Chapter 8)

TERMS AND CONDITIONS OF CREDIT GRANTED

The credit terms offered to a customer are part of the contract between the business and the customer (see later in the chapter) and as such should normally be in writing. The TERMS OF CREDIT are the precise agreements with the customer as to how and when payment for the goods should be made. The most basic element of the terms of credit is the time period in which the customer should pay the invoice for the goods. There are a variety of ways of expressing these terms:

- net 10/14/30 days – payment is due 10 or 14 or 30 days after delivery of the goods

- weekly credit – all goods must be paid for by a specified date in the following week

- half monthly credit – all goods delivered in one half of the month must be paid for by a specified date in the following half month

- monthly credit – all goods delivered in one month must be paid for by a specified date in the following month

Settlement discounts

In some cases customers may be offered a SETTLEMENT DISCOUNT or CASH DISCOUNT for payment within a certain period which is shorter than the stated credit period. The details of such discounts will be considered in a later chapter. The terms of such a settlement discount might be expressed as follows:

Net 30 days, 2% discount for payment within 14 days

This means that the basic payment terms are that the invoice should be paid within 30 days of its date but that if payment is made within 14 days of the invoice date a 2% discount can be deducted. It is up to the customer to decide whether or not to take advantage of the settlement discount offered.

Activity 2

If an invoice includes the term "net monthly", what does this mean?

PAYMENT METHODS

In the past the most common method of payment by credit customers has been payment by cheque, however payment may be received from debtors by other methods such as banker's drafts, standing orders, direct debits or various electronic payment methods.

Cheques

A CHEQUE is a written instruction by a bank's customer to pay out a specific sum of money to another person.

Most cheques nowadays are pre-printed with a CHEQUE CROSSING. A crossed cheque has two parallel lines drawn across the face of it which means that the cheque must be paid into a bank account rather than being exchanged for cash. In addition to this most pre-printed cheques have an ACCOUNT PAYEE ONLY CROSSING (A/C Payee only) which means that the cheque can only be paid into the bank account of the person or business named on the cheque as the payee.

When receiving cheques from customers it is important to carry out a few basic checks to ensure that the cheque is valid and will be accepted by the bank when paid in:

- the cheque is correctly made out to the business name otherwise, with an A/c payee only crossing, it cannot be paid into the business bank account

- the words and figures agree otherwise the bank may refuse payment

- the cheque is not wrongly dated because if the date is more than six months ago the bank will not cash it as the cheque will be deemed to be stale

- the cheque is signed

Banker's drafts

A BANKER'S DRAFT is sometimes used for large payments as it is an undertaking by the bank to pay the payee and therefore has the reputation of the bank itself behind it.

Standing orders and direct debits

A STANDING ORDER is an instruction to a bank to pay a fixed amount on fixed dates to another party. It is possible that if some debtors owed the same amount each month then they might set up a standing order to pay your business.

It would however be more common for a debtor to pay by DIRECT DEBIT than standing order as with a direct debit the bank is authorised to make periodic payments at the request of the payee. Therefore if debtors paid by direct debit your business would request payment, say monthly, of the amount due from that debtor and it would be automatically paid by the bank.

BACS

A BACS payment is an electronic payment method whereby banks handle bulk payments for a variety of regular payments such as wages and salaries. Increasingly debtors pay businesses by BACS, in which case the funds will take three days to clear.

CHAPS

CHAPS is an inter-bank payment system which enables large payments to be made on the same day. In the regular course of business it would be fairly unusual to receive payment by this method from a debtor.

Electronic funds transfer (EFT)

Bank EFT systems allow businesses to make regular payments to a number of payees. The bank is supplied with the payee account details and a payment order form for the amount to be paid is completed.

Activity 3

What is the difference between a standing order and a direct debit payment?

CONTRACT LAW

The relationship between a seller of goods and a buyer of goods is a contract and therefore in this section we must consider the basics of contract law.

What is a contract?

A CONTRACT is a legally binding agreement enforceable in a court of law.

As an individual you will enter into contracts every day – when you buy goods in a shop, when you place an order for goods over the telephone, when you employ a plumber to fix a leak. These contracts are usually verbal but contracts can also be in writing. For example if you take out a loan from your bank there will be a written contract.

During your working hours you will also be part of the process of contracts being made between your organisation and its customers and suppliers.

The importance of contract law

The importance of contract law is that if a contract is validly made between two parties then if one party does not satisfactorily carry out their side of the agreement then the other party can take the defaulting party to court for BREACH OF CONTRACT.

How is a contract formed?

For a contract to be formed and to be valid there must be three main elements:

AGREEMENT + VALUE + INTENTION TO CREATE = CONTRACT
LEGAL RELATIONS

AGREEMENT

In legal terms, for there to be a valid agreement there must be a valid offer and a valid acceptance of that offer.

There will be two parties to a contract – the OFFEROR and the OFFEREE. The offeror is the person making the offer and the offeree is the person to whom the offer is made.

The offer

There are a number of important aspects about an offer in contract law:

- it may be verbal or in writing

- it can be made to one specific person, to a specific group of persons such as the employees of an organisation, or even to the whole world, ie anyone who decides to accept the offer

- it must be communicated to the offeree, so if an offer is posted it will not become a valid offer until it reaches the offeree.

HOW IT WORKS

The glass division of SC Fuel and Glass have received a purchase enquiry from a large building contractor concerning the purchase of 1,000 sealed glazed units. For such a large order the glass division is prepared to reduce the price charged to £78 per unit and has sent out a purchase quotation stating this price for the 1,000 units.

This will become a valid offer from SC Fuel and Glass to the building contractor when the building contractor receives the purchase quotation in the post. Therefore obviously it is important that the price quoted is correct as if not the building contractor could legally require SC to sell the unit to them at the price quoted.

Remember also that an offer can be made verbally so if quoting a price to a customer over the telephone ensure that it is the correct price as this will be a valid offer.

An invitation to treat

Care must be taken to distinguish between an offer and an INVITATION TO TREAT. An invitation to treat is an invitation by the seller of goods for the buyer to make an offer to buy them at that price. Example of invitations to treat are advertisements for goods, catalogues and price tickets displayed on goods.

HOW IT WORKS

The glass division of SC Fuel and Glass issues a catalogue to potential and existing customers twice a year showing the different types of double glazed units available and their prices. This is an invitation to treat and not an offer therefore SC is not necessarily tied to the prices quoted in the catalogue. If a customer enquires about purchasing goods from the catalogue then they are making an offer to buy the goods at the catalogue price. It is then up to SC to decide whether or not to accept this offer by selling to the customer at the published price or changing the price if circumstances have changed.

Activity 4

John is in a car showroom and sees a price ticket on a car of £2,395. He offers to buy the car at this price but is informed by the salesman that there was an error on the price ticket which should have read £12,395. Can John insist on buying the car at £2,395? Explain the reason for your answer.

Duration of an offer

If an offer is made then it does not have to remain in place indefinitely. There are a number of ways in which an offer can be brought to an end.

- if there is a set time period for an offer then the offer will lapse at the end of that time period. If there is no express time period set then the offer will lapse after a reasonable period of time

- an offer can be revoked by the offeror at any point in time before it has been accepted – REVOCATION of an offer means that the offer is cancelled

- an offer comes to an end if it is rejected. Care must be taken here as rejection need not only be by the offeree specifically saying no to the offer. An offer is also rejected by a COUNTER-OFFER. For example if an offer is made to sell an item for £1,000 and the offeree replies to say that he will buy it at a price of £900 this is rejection of the original offer to sell

- the offer also comes to an end when a valid ACCEPTANCE is made.

Acceptance of an offer

The ACCEPTANCE of an offer must be an absolute and unqualified acceptance. If not this will amount to a rejection of the offer.

- acceptance can be made verbally or in writing

- acceptance cannot be in the form of silence – for example if an offer is made to "sell my car for £1,000 and I will assume this is a deal if I have not heard from you by Friday" – if the offeree does not reply by Friday there is no valid acceptance and therefore no contract

- if an offer requires a particular form of acceptance (verbal, in writing, by fax) then this is the form in which the acceptance must be made

- if an acceptance is sent by post then the date of the acceptance is the date that the letter was posted (provided that it was properly addressed, stamped and actually put into the post box) not the date on which the acceptance is received by the offeror

- the acceptance must be unqualified – if any additional qualifications or terms are included in an acceptance then this takes the form of a counter-offer which rejects the original offer.

HOW IT WORKS

When SC sent the purchase quotation to the building contractor for the 1,000 sealed double-glazed units for £78 each this was an offer. If the building contractor replies that it will buy the units at this price but they must be delivered tomorrow then this is a counter-offer which rejects SC's original offer. It is then up to SC to determine whether or not to accept this new counter-offer and sell the units to the building contractor under these terms.

VALUE

The second required element of a contract is that of there being some value. The basis of contract law is that we are dealing with a bargain of some sort not just a promise by one of the parties to a contract to do something.

What is required for there to be a valid contract is known in legal terms as CONSIDERATION. Consideration can be thought of as something given, promised or done in exchange for the action of the other party.

In terms of business transactions the consideration given for a sale of goods is either the money paid now or the promise of a debtor to pay at a later date.

The existence of consideration

For there to be a valid contract then consideration must exist and must have some value. To use a legal phrase "consideration cannot be past".

To explain this suppose that Peter helped his neighbour, Andy, with his car when it had broken down with no mention of any payment being required. Three days later Andy promised to pay Peter £50 for his help. If Andy did not pay the £50 Peter would have no recourse in law as the consideration was past and there is therefore no contract.

The value of consideration

Consideration must be sufficient but it need not be adequate.

This means that the consideration must have some monetary value but it need not be the true value of the item or service that is the subject of the contract. Sufficiency of consideration is the legal term used to say that a party's consideration must be something greater than he would do anyway. For example, it would not be valid consideration to agree to drive within the speed limit, in return for money, since people have a legal obligation to drive within the speed limit anyway.

INTENTION TO CREATE LEGAL RELATIONS

Finally for a contract to be valid there must be an intention to create legal relations.

Remember that a contract is a legally binding agreement which means that if one party does not fully play their part in the contract the other party can take them to court for breach of contract. However many agreements that are made are never intended to be legally binding.

In general terms, agreements with friends and family of a social nature are presumed not to have any intention to create legal relations.

In contrast business agreements are presumed to be intended to create legal relations and therefore can be enforced by the law.

BREACH OF CONTRACT

In a number of instances in this chapter we have mentioned one party taking the other to court for BREACH OF CONTRACT. Breach of contract is where one party to the contract does not fulfil his part of the agreement (this area will be covered in more detail in Chapter 8).

HOW IT WORKS

If SC agrees to supply the 1,000 glazed units to the building contractor tomorrow and then fails to do so then they will be in breach of contract and it would be possible for the building contractor to take SC to court to claim damages for any losses due to this breach of contract.

Equally on supply of the units to the building contractor on time SC would expect the building contractor to pay for the goods within the stated credit

student notes✍

period. If the building contractor does not pay then they will be in breach of contract and can in turn be taken to court for damages.

Terms in a contract

In most contracts there are certain terms that must be fulfilled in order for the contract to be carried out. If the terms of a contract are not fulfilled then one party will be in breach of contract. Legally different terms of a contract have different effects.

EXPRESS TERMS are terms that are specifically stated in the contract and are binding on both parties.

CONDITIONS are terms that are fundamental to the contract and if they are broken then the party breaking them will be in breach of contract and can be sued for damages. The injured party can regard the contract as ended.

WARRANTIES are less important terms in a contract. If any of these are not fulfilled then there is breach of contract but the contract remains in force. The injured party can still claim damages from the court for any loss suffered, but he cannot treat the contract as terminated.

IMPLIED TERMS are terms of a contract which are not specifically stated but are implied in such a contract either by trade custom or by the law.

Activity 5

Explain what is meant by consideration within contract law.

DATA PROTECTION

Due to the growth in the use of computer technology the DATA PROTECTION ACT was introduced to make certain restrictions about the use of data about individuals and the use of personal data. It is likely that your organisation will hold data about credit customers and therefore you need to be aware of the broad outlines of the Act. Be aware that the provisions of the Data Protection Act relate to paper-based systems as well as computer systems.

It is important to realise that the Act relates to personal information data held about individuals not about organisations, so will only be relevant to non-corporate customers or to data about individuals who belong to a customer organisation.

Important definitions from the Act

PERSONAL INFORMATION held about a living individual, not only factual information but also expressions of opinion about that individual.

A DATA SUBJECT is an individual who is the subject of personal data.

A DATA CONTROLLER is a person who holds and processes personal information.

Main provisions of the Act

- All data controllers have to notify the Information Commissioner that they are processing personal information. Notification costs £35 and must be renewed annually. It is an offence to process personal data without being registered.

- The register of data controllers maintained by the Information Commissioner is a public register that can be inspected on the Commissioner's website, to find out what processing of personal data is being carried out by a particular data controller.

- All data controllers have to comply with the eight principles of goods practice contained in the Act – see below.

- Any data subject has seven rights under the Act – see below.

Principles of good practice for data controllers

The Act sets out eight principles of good practice which must be followed by data controllers to ensure that personal data is handled properly. These principles state that personal data must be:

- fairly and lawfully processed (see below)

- processed for limited purposes

- adequate, relevant and not excessive

- accurate and up to date

- not kept for longer than necessary

- processed in line with the data subject's rights

- kept securely

- not transferred to countries outside the EU unless such data is adequately protected in those countries.

Personal information will be deemed to be fairly processed if at least one of the following conditions apply:

- the individual has consented to the processing

- processing is necessary for the performance of a contract with the individual

- processing is required under a legal obligation (other than one imposed by the contract)

- processing is necessary to protect the vital interests of the individual

- processing is necessary to carry out public functions, eg administration of justice

- processing is necessary in order to pursue the legitimate interests of the data controller or third parties (unless it could unjustifiably prejudice the interests of the individual)

Sensitive personal information on a data subject includes details of racial or ethnic origin, political opinions, religious or other beliefs, trade union membership, physical or mental health condition, sex life, criminal proceedings or convictions.

For sensitive personal information to be considered fairly processed, at least one of several extra conditions must be met. These include:

- having the explicit consent of the individuals

- being required by law to process the data for employment purposes

- needing to process the information in order to protect the vital interests of the individual or another person

- dealing with the administration of justice or legal proceedings

Data subjects' rights under the Act

Data subjects have seven rights under the Data Protection Act.

- **The right to subject access** – this allows people to find out what information is held about them on computer and within some manual records.

- **The right to prevent processing** – anyone can ask a data controller not to process data relating to them that causes substantial unwarranted damage or distress to them or anyone else.

- **The right to prevent processing for direct marketing** – anyone can ask a data controller not to process data relating to them for direct marketing purposes.

- **Rights in relation to automated decision-taking** – individuals have a right to object to decisions made only by automatic means, eg there is no human involvement

- **The right to compensation** – an individual can claim compensation from a data controller for damage and distress caused by any breach of the Act. Compensation for distress alone can only be claimed in limited circumstances.

- **The right to rectification, blocking, erasure and destruction** – individuals can apply to the court to order a data controller to rectify, block or destroy personal details if they are inaccurate or contain expression of opinion based on inaccurate data.

- **The right to ask the Commissioner to assess whether the Act has been contravened** – if someone believes their personal information has not been processed in accordance with the Data Protection Act, they can ask the Commissioner to make an assessment. If the Act is found to have been breached and the matter cannot be settled informally, then an enforcement notice may be served on the data controller in question.

CHAPTER OVERVIEW

- the benefit of offering credit to customers is the likely increase in sales. However there are also costs of lost interest and potential bad debts. The role of the credit control function is to minimise these costs

- the credit control function will be involved in the ordering cycle in establishing customer credit status and offering credit terms and throughout the collection cycle

- every business will have its own credit control policies, terms and conditions regarding how and when payment is to be made by credit customers

- payment might be received from credit customers by cheque, banker's draft, standing order, direct debit, BACS, CHAPS or electronic funds transfer

- a contract is a legally binding agreement enforceable in a court of law

- for a valid contract to exist there must be agreement, value and an intention to create legal relations

- for an agreement to exist there must be a valid offer and acceptance

- an invitation to treat is an invitation to make an offer – advertisements, catalogues and price labels in shops are examples

- an offer may lapse, be revoked, be rejected, be rejected by a counter-offer or accepted

- acceptance may be verbal or in writing but cannot be in the form of silence – if it is posted in the mail then it is valid from the date that it is posted

- the acceptance must be unqualified – if a qualification or additional term is introduced then this is deemed to be a counter-offer and the original offer is therefore rejected

KEY WORDS

Ordering cycle the processes from when a customer places an order to the sending out of the sales invoice

Collection cycle the processes from the sending out of the sales invoice to the receipt of cash from a customer

Terms of credit the precise agreements as to how and when a customer is due to pay for goods purchased

Settlement/Cash discount a discount offered for payment within a shorter period than the stated credit terms

Cheque a written instruction by a bank's customer to pay out a specified sum to another person

Cheque crossing two parallel lines across the face of a cheque

Account payee only crossing an instruction to the bank to pay a cheque only into the account of the payee named on the cheque

Banker's draft an undertaking by a bank to pay the payee

Standing order an instruction to the bank to pay a fixed amount at regular intervals to another party

Direct debit a request from the payee for a varying amount to be paid to them on a regular basis

BACS electronic payment method by banks for regular amounts such as wages and salaries

CHAPS an inter-bank system for payment of large amounts on the same day

EFT electronic funds transfer between bank accounts of individuals or businesses

CHAPTER OVERVIEW cont.

- a valid agreement must also be supported by consideration – the consideration must be sufficient but it need not be adequate – the consideration must not be past

- for an agreement to be enforceable in law there must have been an intention to create legal relations when the contract was made – normally in business agreements there is a presumed intention to create legal relations

- if any terms of a contract are not fulfilled then the injured party can sue for damages for breach of contract

- the Data Protection Act 1998 was introduced to ensure that there were certain restrictions about the use of data about individuals

KEY WORDS cont.

Contract a legally binding agreement enforceable in a court of law

Breach of contract if one party does not carry out the terms of the contract then that party is in breach of contract

Offeror the person making an offer in the hope of an acceptance

Offeree the person to whom the offer has been made

Invitation to treat an invitation to another party to make an offer

Revocation of an offer an offer is revoked if the offeror removes the offer before it is accepted

Counter-offer if an acceptance is made by an offeree which contains a new term or condition then this is deemed to be a counter-offer which is a rejection of the original offer and constitutes a new offer, which in turn must be accepted by the original offeror for a contract to be made

Acceptance where the offeree accepts the offer

Consideration something given, promised or done in exchange for the action of the other party

Express terms terms that are specifically stated in the contract

Conditions terms that are fundamental to the contract

Warranties less important terms in the contract

Implied terms terms of a contract that are not specifically stated but are implied by trade custom or law

CHAPTER OVERVIEW cont.

KEY WORDS cont.

Data Protection Act act designed to make certain restrictions about the use of data about individuals and the use of personal data

Personal information information held about an individual

Data subject an individual who is the subject of personal data

Data controller a person who determines the manner in which any personal data is to be processed

HOW MUCH HAVE YOU LEARNED?

1   What are the two main costs of making sales on credit?

2   What are the main elements of the collection cycle which will be part of the role of the credit control function within an organisation?

3   A company sets a credit policy of normal payment within 14 days but a 3% settlement discount for payment within 7 days. How would this policy be expressed on an invoice?

4   What does the account payee only crossing on a cheque mean?

5   What is a BACS payment?

6   What are the three main elements that must exist for a contract to be valid?

7   Alan sees an advertisement in the local newspaper for a car costing £3,000. He answers the advert saying that he would like to buy the car but is told by the seller that there was a printing error and the advertisement should have read £5,000. Can Alan insist on buying the car at £3,000? Explain the reason for your answer.

8   A business sends out a purchase quotation to a customer for goods at a cost of £15,000. The customers replies that he would like to accept the quotation but requires that the goods are delivered the next day. Does the business have to provide the goods at this price of £15,000? Explain the reasons for your answer.

9   Explain what is meant by the following types of terms in a contract:

   i)   express terms
   ii)   conditions
   iii) warranties

10   To what type of information does the Data Protection Act apply?

11   What are the eight principles of good practice of the Data Protection Act regarding the handling of personal information?

chapter 6:
GRANTING CREDIT

chapter coverage 📖

In this chapter we will consider one of the core topics for Unit 15, which is the assessment of a potential customer's credit status and the decision as to whether to grant credit to the customer. We will consider the process from the start to the finish. Initially either a new customer will request credit terms or an existing customer will wish to increase their credit limit or change their credit terms. There will then follow a credit status assessment of the customer which will normally use a variety of information available both internally within the business and from external sources. Once the assessment has been carried out the credit controller must make a decision about whether or not to grant credit on the basis of all of the information and then communicate that decision to the customer.

The topics to be covered are:

✍ assessing the credit status of customers – overview

✍ external sources of information on customers

✍ internal sources of information on customers

✍ financial ratio analysis

✍ making a credit assessment decision

✍ communication of the credit assessment decision

✍ refusal of credit

✍ settlement discounts

Performance criteria – element 15.3

- agree credit terms with customers in accordance with the organisation's policies
- identify and use internal and external sources of information to evaluate the current credit status of customers and potential customers
- open new accounts for those customers with an established credit status
- ensure the reasons for refusing credit are discussed with customers in a tactful manner

knowledge and understanding

- sources of credit status information
- external sources of information: banks, credit agencies and official publications
- discounts for prompt payment
- interpretation and use of credit control information
- understanding that practice in this area will be determined by an organisation's credit control policies and procedures
- an understanding of the organisation's relevant policies and procedures

ASSESSMENT OF CREDIT STATUS

The decision to grant credit to a customer is an extremely important commercial decision. The granting of credit to a customer will normally lead to continued and possibly increasing sales to that customer. However there are also risks involved:

- the customer may extend the period of credit by not paying within the stated credit period and therefore depriving the seller of cash which may be required

- the customer may never pay at all if, for example, they went into liquidation and unsecured creditors received nothing.

Therefore a very important role of the credit controller is to be able to assess the credit status of customers to determine whether or not they should be granted a period of credit, how long that credit period should be and what their credit limit should be. This role applies not only to new customers of the business but also to established customers who may wish to increase their credit limit or renegotiate their credit terms.

What is the credit controller looking for?

When evaluating the credit status of a customer the credit controller is looking for a customer who will pay within the stated credit terms and whose business will remain solvent. Some customers will be low risk as they are safe, liquid businesses. Others will be higher risk due to the nature of the business they are in or the way in which the business is run. Higher risk customers however may also be highly profitable customers.

Therefore the credit controller needs to assess the risk of the customer to determine whether the risk is acceptable for the sake of the additional sales that will be made.

Activity 1

What are the risks of granting credit to a customer?

student notes✎

Assessment process

The process of assessing a customer's credit status and the actions that follow can be illustrated:

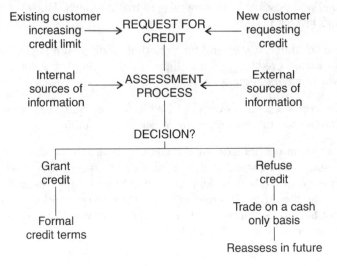

In this chapter we shall look at all of these areas of the credit controller's role.

Sources of information

When assessing the credit status of either an established or a new customer there are a variety of sources of information that the credit controller can draw upon. Some of these sources of information for evaluation of customer credit status are external to the business and others are internal.

Remember that the credit controller is concerned about the customer's ability and tendency to pay within the stated credit terms and also that the customer will remain solvent. No one source of information can guarantee either of these but there are a variety of sources which can be considered and all of the information can be pooled together for a final decision on credit status to be made.

EXTERNAL SOURCES OF INFORMATION

If the credit controller wishes to assess the solvency of the customer and the likelihood of the customer paying within the stated credit period then two of the most obvious potential sources of information are the customer's bank and other suppliers that the customer uses.

Therefore if a new customer approaches the business with an order and a request for credit it is normal practice for the credit controller to ask for a

BANK REFERENCE and normally two TRADE REFERENCES. In order to do this the business will need to ask the new customer for details of their bank and for details of two other suppliers with whom they regularly trade. This may be done in a letter to the potential customer or often by sending the customer a standard CREDIT APPLICATION FORM.

HOW IT WORKS

The fuel division of SC Fuel and Glass have been approached by a new customer, Haven Engineering Ltd. They would like to place regular orders with the fuel division for approximately £15,000 a month and wish to trade on credit with SC.

SC Fuel and Glass have a standard credit application form which the credit controller sends to the finance director of Haven Engineering Ltd.

CREDIT APPLICATION FORM

SC FUEL AND GLASS
CRAWLEY RD
CRAWLEY
CR7 JN9
Tel: 01453 732166 Fax: 01453 732177

Business name   ....

Address   ....

Telephone   ....

E-mail   ....

Amount of credit required   £ .... monthly
                             £ .... in total

You are hereby authorised to contact the parties named below for further information.

Signed .... Position .... Date ....
Signed .... Position .... Date ....

Bank reference

Bank name   ....

Bank address   ....

Account name   ....

Trade references

Name   .... Name   ....
Address .... Address ....

Bank references

Once the potential customer has provided details of their bank and authorised the bank to release the information required then your business can request a reference from the bank.

HOW IT WORKS

SC Fuel and Glass have received the completed credit application form back from Haven Engineering with a request for £15,000 of credit per month. SC Fuel and Glass will now write to Haven Engineering Ltd's bank:

> "Do you consider Haven Engineering Ltd to be good for the figure of £15,000 trade credit per month?"

Bank replies to reference requests

The next stage will be a reply received from the bank which must be interpreted. The banks have two considerations when replying to a request for a reference regarding a customer:

- confidentiality of the customer's affairs

- accusations of negligence from the recipient of the reference of the reference proven to be wrong.

As a consequence bank references tend to all be worded in a similar manner with a well-known "real" meaning. Examples of the most commonly used phrases as a reply to a request for a credit reference and their "real" meaning are as follows:

Bank's reply	Real meaning
The customer's credit for £X is:	
Undoubted	The best type of reference – the customer should be of low risk for the figures stated
Considered good for your purposes	Probably OK and a reasonable risk but not as good as undoubted
Should prove good for your figures	Not quite as certain as the other two and therefore warrants further investigation

Bank's reply	Real meaning
Well constituted business with capital seeming to be fully employed: we do not consider that the directors/owners would undertake a commitment they could not fulfil	Not very hopeful – this probably means the business has cash flow problems and credit should not be extended to them
Unable to speak for your figures	The worst – the bank seems to believe that the business is already overstretched – definitely no credit to be granted

Trade references

Once your business has received details of trade referees from the potential customer then it will be standard practice to send out a letter asking for information from them.

HOW IT WORKS

Haven Engineering Ltd have provided SC with details of two trade referees. The credit controller now completes a standard letter to each of these referees. Here is one of those letters:

SC FUEL AND GLASS
CRAWLEY RD
CRAWLEY
CR7 JN9
Tel: 01453 732166 Fax: 01453 732177

Credit controller
Peterhay Systems
Hove Park Estate
Brighton BR4 7HD

Date:

We have received a request for credit from Haven Engineering Ltd who have quoted yourselves as a referee. We would be grateful if you could answer the following questions, and return this form in the stamped addressed envelope enclosed.

How long has the customer
been trading with you?   ..... years .... mths

Your credit terms with
customer per month   £

Period of credit granted   ....

Payment record   Prompt/occasionally late/slow

Have you ever suspended
credit to the customer?   Yes/No

If yes - when and for how long? ....

....

Any other relevant information ....

....

Thank you for your assistance.

Yours faithfully

Tom Hunt
Credit controller

Problems with trade references

When replies are received from trade referees they should be fairly easy to interpret as the questions asked are fairly direct. However care should be taken not to necessarily take every trade reference at face value.

- Some firms deliberately pay two or three suppliers promptly in order to use them as trade referees whilst delaying payment to their other suppliers

- The trade referee may be connected or influenced in some way by the potential customer, for example it may be a business owned by one of the directors of the customer

- The trade referee given may not be particularly strict themselves regarding credit control therefore their replies might not be typical – the genuine nature of the trade referee should be checked

- Even if the reference is genuine and good it may be that trade with this supplier is on a much smaller basis or different credit terms to that being sought by the customer

Activity 2

What would be the typical response of a credit controller to a bank reference which read "unable to speak for your figures"?

Credit reference agencies

CREDIT REFERENCE AGENCIES are commercial organisations which specialise in providing a variety of information regarding the credit status of companies and individuals. These agencies have large databases of information on companies and individuals and can provide historic information such as financial reports, directors details, payment history, any insolvency proceedings or bankruptcy orders for individuals, bankers' opinions and will sometimes also provide a credit rating.

Examples of credit reference agencies in the UK are Equifax and Experian.

Such credit reference agency reports are a useful source of information for the credit controller but it must be borne in mind that they are a summary of only some of the information about the customer and that they may be based upon out of date historic information.

Companies House

If the potential customer is a company then they must file certain financial information regarding their annual accounts and directors with Companies House. This information can be accessed by anyone but is unlikely to be particularly up to date as companies need not file their annual accounts until some considerable time after their year end.

Publications

More up to date information can often be found about a customer from various media sources. Newspapers such as the *Financial Times* run articles on many companies as do various trade journals for companies in particular lines of business.

Internet

The Internet is a powerful tool for information and by running a search on a company name you may be able to find a number of useful articles and updates.

INTERNAL SOURCES OF INFORMATION

Internal sources of information about an existing customer or potential customer can be both information from employees within the organisation and information that is analysed by employees. In most cases the employees of a business will have little information about potential customers but should have a good level of knowledge of existing customers.

Existing customers

So far in this chapter we have been considering the scenario of a new, potential customer requesting credit facilities. However the credit control function will also have to deal with the situation where existing customers are requesting an increase in their credit limit or other changes to their credit terms. In such cases there will be employees within the organisation who have detailed knowledge of this customer.

Sales staff — The sales staff will deal with customers on a regular basis. They are likely to have opinions as to how well the customer is doing, how efficient they are or any financial difficulties they may be in.

Sales ledger staff — The sales ledger staff deal with the recording and monitoring of invoices and receipts from debtors. They will be able to provide information about the payment history of the customer and the customer's adherence to current credit limits.

Customer visits

Some internal staff, particularly the sales team, are likely to pay fairly regular visits to the customer's premises. From these they should be able to provide feedback as to how prosperous and efficient the customer appears to be.

Financial analysis

One of the most useful sources of internal information however is an analysis of the existing or potential customer's financial statements and the preparation of relevant accounting ratios.

FINANCIAL RATIO ANALYSIS

The purpose of analysing the financial statements for credit control assessment is to find indicators of the customer's performance and position in three main areas:

- profitability
- liquidity
- gearing

In general terms this analysis is only useful if it is carried out over a period of time with analysis of at least the most current three years of financial statements in order to determine any trends in the business performance.

You will have already come across financial ratios in your earlier studies but we will briefly consider the relevant ratios for credit control purposes in the following paragraphs.

Profitability ratios

If credit is to be granted to a new customer or the credit limit of an existing customer increased then one major concern will be the profitability of the customer. If the customer is not profitable in the long term then it will eventually go out of business and this might mean a loss if credit has been granted to the customer.

The main profitability ratios which will give indicators of the customer's long term profitability are:

- GROSS PROFIT MARGIN
- NET PROFIT MARGIN
- RETURN ON CAPITAL EMPLOYED
- NET ASSET TURNOVER

Gross profit margin

$$\frac{\text{Gross profit}}{\text{Sales}} \times 100\%$$

This gives an indication of how profitable the trading activities of the business are. One would expect this to remain fairly constant or be increasing over time.

Net profit margin

$$\frac{\text{Net profit}}{\text{Sales}} \times 100\%$$

The net profit is after all expenses and therefore indicates the overall profitability of the business. The usual profit figure to use is the operating profit. As efficiencies are introduced this ratio should gradually increase over time or at least remain constant.

Return on capital employed (ROCE)

$$\frac{\text{Net profit}}{\text{Capital employed (net assets)}} \times 100\%$$

This is the overall profit indicator showing the profit as a percentage of the capital employed or the net assets of the business. This should be increasing or remaining constant over time.

CAPITAL EMPLOYED is share capital, reserves and long term debt but can also be measured as the net asset total of the business.

Net asset turnover

$$\frac{\text{Sales}}{\text{Capital employed (net assets)}}$$

This ratio, measured as the number of times that sales represent net assets, shows the efficiency of the use of the net assets of the business and together with the net profit margin helps to explain any change in return on capital employed.

Activity 3

A company has a gross profit of £152,000 and operating profit of £76,000. Share capital is £200,000, reserves total £188,000 and there is a long term loan of £100,000. What is the company's return on capital employed?

Liquidity ratios

The purpose of calculating liquidity ratios is to provide indicators of the short and medium term stability and solvency of the business. Can the business pay its debts when they fall due?

Liquidity indicators can be considered in total by calculation of two overall liquidity ratios:

- CURRENT RATIO
- QUICK RATIO or ACID TEST RATIO

Liquidity and working capital management can also be considered by looking at the individual elements of the working capital of the business by calculating various turnover ratios:

- STOCK TURNOVER
- DEBTORS TURNOVER
- CREDITORS TURNOVER

Current ratio

$$\frac{\text{Current assets}}{\text{Current liabilities}}$$

A measure of whether the current assets are enough to pay off the current liabilities. Sometimes stated as ideal at 2:1 but this will depend upon the type of business.

Quick ratio/acid test ratio

$$\frac{\text{Current assets} - \text{stock}}{\text{Current liabilities}}$$

Stock is removed from the current assets in this measure of liquidity as they will tend to take longer to turn into cash than other current assets. Sometimes stated as ideal at 1:1 but again this is dependent upon the type of business.

Stock turnover

$$\frac{\text{Stock}}{\text{Cost of sales}} \times 365 \text{ days}$$

This measures how many days on average stock is being held before being sold. This will depend upon the type of stock but should ideally not be increasing significantly over time.

Debtors turnover

$$\frac{\text{Debtors}}{\text{Sales}} \times 365 \text{ days}$$

This measures how many days on average it takes for debtors to pay. This will depend upon the type of business and the credit terms that are offered. Ideally it should be around the average credit period offered and similar to the time taken to pay creditors.

Creditors turnover

$$\frac{\text{Trade creditors}}{\text{Purchases}} \times 365 \text{ days}$$

This measures how many days on average the business takes to pay its trade creditors. This is of direct relevance as this will give an indication of how long a period of credit the business normally takes from its suppliers.

Very often the purchases figure is not available from financial statements therefore cost of sales is used as an approximation.

Activity 4

A company has sales of £980,000 and cost of sales of £686,000. Stock at the year end is £77,000, debtors are £130,000 and creditors are £89,000. What are the stock turnover, debtors turnover and creditors turnover figures in days?

Gearing ratios

When assessing a customer's credit status the credit controller will also be concerned with the longer term stability of the business. One area of concern here will be the amount of debt in the business's capital structure and its ability to service this debt by paying the periodic interest charges. The two main measures of this longer term position are:

- GEARING RATIO
- INTEREST COVER

Gearing ratio

$$\frac{\text{Long term debt}}{\text{Capital employed}} \times 100\%$$

The gearing ratio is a measure of the proportion of interest bearing debt to the total capital of the business. This is often stated as ideal at 50% or less as the higher the figure the more risky the company might be seen to be.

Interest cover

$$\frac{\text{Profit before interest}}{\text{Interest payable}}$$

The interest cover is calculated as the number of times that the interest could have been paid; it represents the margin of safety between the profits earned and the interest that must be paid to service the debt capital.

MAKING A CREDIT ASSESSMENT

So far in this chapter we have considered a number of internal and external sources of information available to the credit controller in his attempt to assess the current credit status of an existing or potential customer. It is likely that the credit controller will consider most if not all of these sources of information and then must use the information gathered to make a decision about the customer's credit status.

This may be a clear cut decision where the bank reference is good, the trade references are sound and the analysis of the financial statements indicate a profitable and liquid business. This business would appear to be low risk and should be granted credit.

At the other end of the scale the bank and trade references may be poor and assessment of the financial statements indicate problems with profitability and liquidity. This is a high risk business and trade should probably only be carried out on a cash basis.

student notes✍

Conflicting information

However in many scenarios the situation may not be as clear cut. The bank reference may be reasonable and the trade references viewed as sound but the analysis of the financial statements may indicate areas of concern. Or the financial statements may appear sound but the trade references are for much lower amounts of credit than the customer is asking for.

In circumstances such as these the credit controller must assess the conflicting information and determine the best course of action.

HOW IT WORKS

Tom Hunt, the credit controller at SC Fuel and Glass, is considering the request for £15,000 a month of credit facilities for Haven Engineering Ltd. The following references have now been received:

Bank reference

Haven Engineering Ltd – should prove good for your figures.

Trade references

SC FUEL AND GLASS
CRAWLEY RD
CRAWLEY
CR7 JN9
Tel: 01453 732166 Fax: 01453 732177

Credit controller
Peterhay Systems
Hove Park Estate
Brighton BR4 7HD

Date:

We have received a request for credit from Haven Engineering Ltd who have quoted yourselves as a referee. We would be grateful if you could answer the following questions and return in the stamped addressed envelope enclosed.

How long has the customer
been trading with you?   ....3.... years   ....4....mths

Your credit terms with
customer per month   £ 10,000

Period of credit granted   .... 30 days...........................

Payment record   Prompt/occasionally late/slow

Have you ever suspended
credit to the customer?   Yes/No

If yes – when and for how long?...
....

Any other relevant information ....
....

Thank you for your assistance.

Yours faithfully

Tom Hunt
Credit controller

SC FUEL AND GLASS
CRAWLEY RD
CRAWLEY
CR7 JN9
Tel: 01453 732166 Fax: 01453 732177

Credit controller
Harvard Group Ltd
24/26 Fenwick Way
Dorchester DO3 6HD

Date:

We have received a request for credit from Haven Engineering Ltd who have quoted yourselves as a referee. We would be grateful if you could answer the following questions and return in the stamped addressed envelope enclosed.

How long has the customer
been trading with you?   ...5... years   ...8...mths

Your credit terms with
customer per month   £ 10,000

Period of credit granted   30 days

Payment record   Prompt/occasionally late/slow

Have you ever suspended
credit to the customer?   Yes/No

If yes – when and for how long?...........2002 for six months.......

....

Any other relevant information ....

....
..

Thank you for your assistance.

Yours faithfully

Tom Hunt
Credit controller

Tom Hunt has also received summarised financial accounts for Haven Engineering Ltd for the three years ending 31 December 2003, 2004 and 2005.

Summarised profit and loss accounts

Year ending 31 December

	2003 £000	2004 £000	2005 £000
Sales	3,150	3,220	3,330
Cost of sales	2,048	2,061	2,115
Gross profit	1,102	1,159	1,215
Operating expenses	645	676	732
Operating profit	457	483	483
Interest payable	95	100	120
Profit before tax	362	383	363
Tax	91	96	91
Profit after tax	271	287	272

Summarised balance sheets

As at 31 December

	2003 £000	2004 £000	2005 £000
Fixed assets	3,339	3,727	4,112
Current assets:			
Stock	292	328	353
Debtors	639	670	684
Cash at bank	2	2	2
	933	1,000	1,039
Creditors: falling due within one year			
Trade creditors	494	474	463
Other creditors	158	146	109
	652	620	572
Net current assets	281	380	467
Total assets less current liabilities	3,620	4,107	4,579
Long term loans	1,600	1,800	2,000
	2,020	2,307	2,579
Ordinary share capital	1,000	1,000	1,000
Retained profits	1,020	1,307	1,579
	2,020	2,307	2,579

As credit controller Tom Hunt must now assess the information available about Haven Engineering Ltd.

Bank reference

The bank reference is not the most positive that might have been given and therefore indicates that consideration should be given to the liquidity and profitability of the company in particular.

Trade references

Both trade references indicate that Haven Engineering Ltd is a slow payer and therefore again consideration should be given to information in the financial statements to try to determine whether this is due to liquidity problems, general inefficiency or a determined policy of the company.

Credit was suspended by Harvard Group Ltd in 2002 for six months although presumably not since. Finally it must be noted that both referees only have a credit limit with Haven Engineering Ltd of £10,000 compared to the £15,000 of credit being requested by the company.

Financial statement analysis

	2003	2004	2005
Financial ratios:			
Profitability			
Gross profit margin	35%	36%	36.5%
Net profit margin	14.5%	15%	14.5%
Return on capital employed	12.6%	11.8%	10.5%
Asset turnover	0.87	0.78	0.73
Liquidity			
Current ratio	1.43:1	1.61:1	1.82:1
Quick ratio	0.98:1	1.08:1	1.20:1
Stock turnover	52 days	58 days	61 days
Debtors turnover	74 days	76 days	75 days
Creditors turnover	88 days	84 days	80 days
Gearing			
Gearing ratio	44%	44%	44%
Interest cover	4.8 times	4.8 times	4.0 times

From the analysis of the financial ratios a number of points can be made about Haven Engineering Ltd.

Profitability

In terms of profitability the gross profit margin has increased in each of the three years although the net profit margin is fairly constant. Return on capital employed has fallen over the three years due to the decrease in net asset turnover. There has clearly been large investment in fixed assets over the period and as yet this does not appear to have led to largely increased turnover or profits.

Liquidity

The current ratio could be said to be rather low however it has been increasing in each of the three years. The quick ratio however appears healthy and is also improving. The stock turnover period is quite high and has increased by 9 days over the period therefore there is a lot of capital tied up in the stock holdings.

Perhaps of more concern are the debtor and creditor turnover periods. Debtors turnover has remained fairly constant but at around 75 days is a long period. This might account for the length of time that Haven Engineering Ltd takes to pay its own creditors which, although improving, still stands at 80 days, which is 50 days longer than SC's credit terms of 30 days.

Gearing

Although there have been annual small increases in the amount of long term loans the gearing level has remained constant at 44%. Interest cover is also healthy at 4 times or over.

Conclusion

From the evidence from the bank reference, trade references and the financial statements there would appear to be a problem with Haven Engineering regarding the period of time which they take before paying their creditors. The company appears to be profitable and despite the length of time their own debtors take to pay there would not appear to be too serious a liquidity problem. Therefore the late paying of creditors could be a deliberate policy.

It is recommended that only £10,000 of credit is granted to Haven Engineering Ltd initially with an agreement that payment is to be strictly within 30 days of the invoice date. This period of credit should perhaps be limited to a 6 month period during which the receipts from Haven Engineering Ltd should be monitored closely. Haven Engineering Ltd should be made aware that if payments are not received promptly credit facilities will be withdrawn and only cash trading will be available.

COMMUNICATION OF CREDIT ASSESSMENT DECISION

Once a decision has been taken to grant credit to a customer then the precise details of the credit limit and all terms and conditions of trading and payment must be communicated to the new customer in a letter.

HOW IT WORKS

It has been agreed at SC Fuel and Glass that Haven Engineering Ltd should be offered a trial period of credit of 6 months due to their apparently slow creditor payment policy. During this period all receipts will be monitored carefully and if payment is not received within 30 days of the invoice date then the credit facility will be withdrawn.

Tom Hunt has now drafted the letter that will be sent to Haven Engineering Ltd agreeing these terms and conditions.

SC FUEL AND GLASS
CRAWLEY RD
CRAWLEY
CR7 JN9
Tel: 01453 732166 Fax: 01453 732177

Finance Director
Haven Engineering Ltd
Fairstop Park
Havant HV4 7BN

Date:

Dear Sir

Re: Request for credit facilities

Thank you for your enquiry regarding the provision of credit facilities to you of £15,000 on 30 day terms. We have taken up your bank and trade references and examined your last three years of financial statements.

Although your references are satisfactory we have some concerns about your creditor payment policy which appears to be excessively long. Although your profitability and liquidity generally appear sound we would not normally extend credit on the type of timescale on which you appear to pay your creditors.

However due to your bank and trade references we would be happy to offer you a credit facility for 6 months at the end of which period the movement on your account would be reviewed and the position re-assessed. The credit limit that we could offer you would initially be £10,000 and the payment terms would be strictly 30 days from the invoice date.

Thank you for your interest in our company and we look forward to trading with you on the basis set out above.

Yours faithfully

Tom Hunt
Credit controller

Opening a new customer account

Once a decision has been made to grant credit to a customer then a file on that customer and an account in the sales ledger must be set up. For this to take place the following information will be required:

- the business name of the customer

- the contact name and title within the customer's business

- business address and telephone number

- the credit limit agreed upon

- the payment terms agreed

- any other terms such as settlement discounts offered (see later in this chapter)

REFUSAL OF CREDIT

In many cases once the credit controller has carried out checks on a new potential customer such as bank references, trade references, credit agency reports and analysis of financial statements then a decision will be made to grant the customer credit, the terms of payment will be communicated to the new customer and an account set up for the customer in the sales ledger.

However in some cases the credit controller may decide that it is not possible to trade with a new potential customer on credit terms.

Reasons for refusal of credit

Refusing to grant credit to a new customer is a big decision for the credit controller as the business will not wish to lose this potential customer's business but the credit controller will have taken a view that the risk of non-payment from the customer is too high for credit terms to be granted.

Refusal of credit however does not necessarily mean that the potential customer's business is bad or is likely not to survive; it simply means that on the evidence available to the credit controller the risk of non-payment is too high for the company to take the risk.

There are a variety of reasons why a decision might be made not to grant credit to a new customer. They could include the following:

- a non-committal or poor bank reference

- poor trade references

- concerns about the validity of any trade references submitted

- adverse press comment about the potential customer

- poor credit agency report

- indications of business weakness from analysis of the financial statements

- lack of historical financial statements due to being a recently started company

The credit controller will consider all of the evidence available about a potential customer and the reason for the refusal of credit may be due to a single factor noted above or a combination of factors.

Communication of refusal of credit

If credit is not to be granted to a potential customer then this must be communicated to the customer in a tactful and diplomatic manner. The reasons for the refusal of credit must be politely explained and any future actions required from the potential customer should also be made quite clear. The credit controller, whilst not wishing to grant credit to the customer at the current time, will also not necessarily want to lose the potential business of this customer.

Trading on cash terms

In almost all cases where credit is to be refused to a potential customer the company should make it quite clear that they would be happy to trade with the customer on cash terms. This may be acceptable to the customer, even if it is not the desired outcome, and the business will not be lost.

Future re-assessment of creditworthiness

In some cases, although the granting of credit to the new customer has been refused now, it may be that the credit controller wishes to encourage the customer to apply for credit terms in the future. For example with a newly formed company there may be little external information on which the credit controller can rely at the current time but if financial statements and references can be provided in the future then the decision as to whether or not to trade on credit terms in future can be re-assessed.

Communication method

In most cases it may be most appropriate to communicate the reasons for the refusal of credit initially in a letter. However in such a letter the credit controller may suggest that a further telephone call might be appropriate in order to discuss the matter and any future actions that may be necessary.

HOW IT WORKS

In the last week Tom Hunt has also been assessing requests for credit from two other potential new customers.

Glowform Ltd have requested to trade with the fuel division on credit and would like a £5,000 credit limit and 60 days credit. Tom requested two trade references and a bank reference and financial statements for the last three years. Glowform Ltd have provided a bank reference which states that the "the company appears to be well constituted but we cannot necessarily speak for your figures due to the length of time that the company has been in operation." The company has also provided one trade reference which is satisfactory from a company which allows Glowform Ltd £3,000 of credit on 30 day terms. However the company has only been in operation for just over a year and has as yet not been able to provide you with any financial statements.

Joseph Partners have requested 30 days of credit and a credit limit of £6,000. They have provided their balance sheet at their last year end which was four months ago, and the profit and loss account for the year to that date. The financial statements indicate fairly low levels of profitability but there is nothing to compare the figures to. The bank reference is satisfactory but of the two trade references one has only been trading with Joseph Partners for two months.

student notes✍

The two letters which Tom Hunt has drafted to these businesses are shown below.

SC FUEL AND GLASS
CRAWLEY RD
CRAWLEY
CR7 JN9
Tel: 01453 732166 Fax: 01453 732177

Finance Director
Glowform Ltd

Date:

Dear Sir

Re: Request for credit facilities

Thank you for your enquiry regarding the provision of credit facilities of £5,000 of credit on 60 day terms. We have taken up your trade and bank references of which you kindly sent details.

We have some concerns about offering credit at this early stage of your business as there are as yet no financial statements for your business that we can examine. Therefore at this stage I am unable to confirm that we can provide you with credit facilities immediately.

We would of course be delighted to trade with you on cash terms until we have had an opportunity to examine your first year's trading figures. Therefore please send us a copy of your first year financial statements when they are available and in the meantime contact us if you would like to start trading on a cash basis.

Thank you for your interest in our company.

Yours faithfully

Tom Hunt
Credit controller

> **SC FUEL AND GLASS**
> **CRAWLEY RD**
> **CRAWLEY**
> **CR7 JN9**
> Tel: 01453 732166 Fax: 01453 732177
>
> Finance Partner
> Joseph Partners
>
> Date:
>
> Dear Sir
>
> **Re: Request for credit facilities**
>
> Thank you for your enquiry regarding the provision of credit facilities of £6,000 on 30 day terms. We have taken up your trade references and examined your latest set of financial statements.
>
> We have some concerns about your level of profitability and would like the opportunity to examine your balance sheets and profit and loss accounts for the two previous years. As one of your trade references has only been trading with you for two months we would also request details of a further supplier that we could contact for a trade reference.
>
> At this stage I am unable to confirm that we can provide you with a credit facility but we will reconsider the situation when we receive your financial statements and additional trade reference.
>
> Thank you for your interest in our company and in the meantime we would of course be delighted to trade with you on a cash terms basis.
>
> Yours faithfully
>
> Tom Hunt
> Credit controller

Activity 5

What potential reasons could there be for not agreeing to trade on credit with a new customer?

SETTLEMENT DISCOUNTS

When offering to trade with a customer on credit terms a credit limit must be set and the terms of payment communicated to the customer. These terms, such as net 30 days, must be clearly stated to the customer in writing and on all invoices, statements etc sent to the customer.

One of the terms of trading on credit that could be offered to a customer is that of a SETTLEMENT DISCOUNT. A settlement or cash discount is an incentive to the customer to pay their outstanding invoices earlier by offering a percentage discount off the invoice total if the customer pays within a certain period which is shorter than the stated, normal credit terms.

Benefits of a settlement discount

The benefit to a business of offering a settlement discount to credit customers is that if the customers take up the discount then the money will be received earlier. This means that it can be either invested to earn interest or can be used to reduce any overdraft balance therefore reducing the amount of interest paid.

Costs of a settlement discount

The cost of a settlement discount if the customer takes it up is that the discount will be deducted from the face value of the invoice and therefore less money will be received by the business although of course it will be received sooner.

It is possible to approximate the ANNUAL COST OF OFFERING A SETTLEMENT DISOUNT to customers by using the following formula:

$$\frac{d}{100 - d} \times \frac{365}{N - D} \times 100\%$$

where   d = discount percentage given
         N = normal payment term
         D = discount payment term

HOW IT WORKS

The fuel division of SC Fuel and Glass is considering offering a settlement discount of 2% for payment within 14 days, whereas the average credit terms are payment within 60 days.

The annual cost of the discount can be estimated:

Annual cost

$$\frac{2}{100 - 2} \times \frac{365}{60 - 14} \times 100\% = 16\%$$

As it would cost 16% per annum to offer this discount it would most probably be cheaper to borrow from the bank to raise any funds required, at a rate of say 7 or 8%.

Activity 6

A business currently trades on 30 day credit terms but is considering offering a settlement discount of 1% for payment within 10 days of the invoice date. What is the approximate annual cost of this settlement discount?

CHAPTER OVERVIEW

- when evaluating a customer's credit status the concerns will be that the customer will pay within the stated credit terms and that their business will remain solvent

- when either a potential new customer requests credit or an existing customer requests an increase in credit limit the credit controller will make use of internal and external information about the customer in order to determine whether or not the request should be granted

- external sources of information are most commonly a bank reference and two trade references

- in some cases a credit controller will use the services of a credit reference agency for information about a potential customer and a possible credit rating

- other sources of external information are Companies House records, official publications and the Internet

- when considering requests from existing customers it is likely that staff within the business will have internal information about the customer and may possibly have made visits to the customers premises

- the most common form of internal analysis of both existing and potential new customers is financial ratio analysis of their financial accounts, preferably for the last three years or more

- once all of the relevant information has been gathered about a customer then a decision must be made as to whether or not to grant them credit – in many cases the information may be conflicting with some sources suggesting that credit should be granted and other sources not proving so healthy

- once a decision has been made as to whether or not to grant credit to a customer this decision must be communicated to the customer normally by letter

KEY WORDS

Bank reference a bank's opinion of its customer's business position and credit status

Trade reference a reference from one of a business's current suppliers regarding their payment record

Credit application form a form sent to a prospective new customer asking for details including bank and trade reference details

Credit reference agency commercial organisation providing background information and credit status information about companies and individuals

Gross profit margin measure of the profit from trading activities compared to sales

Net profit margin measure of the overall profit compared to sales

Return on capital employed measure of the overall profit compared to total capital employed

Capital employed share capital, reserves and long-term debt; also measured as the net asset total of the business

Net asset turnover measure of the amount of sales compared to total capital employed

Current ratio current assets as a ratio to current liabilities

Quick/acid test ratio current assets minus stocks as a ratio to current liabilities

Stock turnover the average number of days which stock is held for

Debtors turnover the average number of days before debtors pay the amounts owed

Creditors turnover the average number of days credit taken from trade creditors

Gearing ratio the total long term debt capital as a percentage of the total capital employed

CHAPTER OVERVIEW cont.

- where credit is to be granted to a new customer the details of the credit limit and terms of payment must be made quite clear and a new account for that customer must be opened within the sales ledger

- in some cases it might be decided to refuse credit to a customer in which case this must be communicated to the customer in a tactful and diplomatic manner

- in some cases a customer may be offered a chance for future re-assessment of their credit status and in the meantime an offer for trading on cash terms will be made

- in agreeing credit terms with a customer it may be that the customer is offered a settlement discount for payment earlier than the agreed credit period – although this has a benefit to the seller in that the cash is received sooner it also has a cost in that less is received due to the discount

KEY WORDS cont.

Interest cover the number of times the annual interest payment is covered by profits earned

Settlement discount discount offered to customers for payment of the due amount earlier than the normal credit terms

Annual cost of offering settlement discount

$$\frac{d}{100-d} \times \frac{365}{N-D} \times 100\%$$

HOW MUCH HAVE YOU LEARNED?

1 If a potential new customer approaches your business with a request for credit facilities what would be the process that would be followed by the credit controller?

2 You are the credit controller for AKA Ltd and you are considering a request from Kelvin & Sons who wish to trade on credit with your company. You are considering offering them a credit limit of £10,000 with payment terms of payment within 30 days of the invoice date.

You have written to Kelvin & Sons' bank, Southern Bank, asking for a reference having specified that you are considering a credit limit of £10,000. The bank's reply is given below.

"Should prove good for your figures"

What if any conclusions could you draw from the bank reference?

3 You are the credit controller for a company and you are considering a request from Caterham Ltd who wish to trade on credit with your company. Caterham Ltd asked for a credit limit of £15,000 with payment terms of payment within 30 days of the invoice date. You have a standard form for trade references and Caterham Ltd have provided you with the name and address of another supplier of theirs, SK Traders, to whom you have sent the standard trade reference form. The reply you receive is given below.

Trade reference

> We have received a request for credit from Caterham Ltd who have quoted yourselves as a referee. We would be grateful if you could answer the following questions and return in the stamped addressed envelope enclosed.
>
> How long has the customer
> been trading with you?   ..4.. years . 2... mths
>
> Your credit terms with
> customer per month   £ 8,000
>
> Period of credit granted   .... 30 days............................
>
> Payment record   Prompt/occasionally late/slow
>
> Have you ever suspended
> credit to the customer?   Yes/No
>
> If yes – when and for how long? ....
>
> ....
>
> Any other relevant information ....
>
> ....
>
> Thank you for your assistance.

What, if any, conclusions could you draw from the trade reference?

4 What services does a credit reference agency typically provide?

5 What information could be provided by Companies House about a company that was requesting credit from your business?

6 You are the credit controller for a business and you have been approached by Franklin Ltd who wish to place an order with your business and wish to trade on credit. They would like a credit limit of £5,000 per month. Franklin Ltd have provided you with their last two years profit and loss accounts and balance sheets.

Profit and loss account for the year ended 31 March

	2006 £000	2005 £000
Turnover	1,000	940
Cost of sales	(780)	(740)
Gross profit	220	200
Operating expenses	(100)	(90)
Operating profit	120	110
Interest payable	(30)	(20)
Profit before tax	90	90
Taxation	(23)	(23)
Profit after tax	67	67
Dividends	(20)	(20)
Retained profit for the year	47	47

Balance sheets at 31 March

	2006 £000	2005 £000
Fixed assets	1,335	1,199
Current assets		
Stocks	110	90
Debtors	140	150
	250	240
Current liabilities		
Trade creditors	160	161
Bank overdraft	300	200
	460	361
Net assets	1,125	1,078
Share capital	800	800
Profit and loss	325	278
	1,125	1,078

Prepare a memo in which you compute three key accounting ratios (for both years) which will assist in making a recommendation on whether to extend credit or not.

7 You are the credit manager for Acorn Enterprises and your name is Jo Wilkie. You have been assessing the financial statements for Little Partners who have requested £8,000 of credit on 60 day terms. You also have received a satisfactory bank reference and trade references.

Your analysis of the 2005 and 2004 financial statements show the following picture:

	2005	2004
Gross profit margin	30%	28%
Net profit margin	4%	3%
Interest cover	1.5 times	0.9 times
Current ratio	1.3 times	0.8 times

You are to draft a suitable letter to Little Partners dealing with their request for credit facilities.

8   You are the credit controller for a business and you received a request from Dawn Ltd for credit of £5,000 from your company on a 30 day basis. Two trade references have been provided but no bank reference. You have also been provided with the last set of published financial statements which include the previous year's comparative figures. The trade references appeared satisfactory although one is from Johannesson Partners and it has been noted that the managing director of Dawn Ltd is Mr F Johannesson. Analysis of the financial statements has indicated a decrease in profitability during the last year, a high level of gearing and low liquidity ratios.

Draft a letter to the finance director of Dawn Ltd on the basis that credit is to be currently refused but may be extended once the most recent financial statements have been examined.

9   Your company currently has an average credit period of 45 days but is considering offering a 2% settlement discount for payment within 10 days. What is the approximate annual cost of this discount?

chapter 7:
MANAGEMENT OF DEBTORS

———— chapter coverage 📖 ————

If a business is to extend credit to its customers then these debtors must be monitored and managed in order to reduce the risks of trading on credit. In this chapter we consider how credit customer transactions and balances should be monitored and how debtors should be managed to ensure that monies are received in full and on time.

The topics covered are:

✍ placing of orders and credit limits

✍ aged debtor analysis

✍ measurement of average credit period taken

✍ bad and doubtful debts

✍ debt collection policy

✍ debt collection process

KNOWLEDGE AND UNDERSTANDING AND PERFORMANCE CRITERIA COVERAGE

Performance criteria – element 15.4

- monitor information relating to the current state of debtors' accounts regularly and take appropriate action
- send information regarding significant outstanding accounts and potential bad debts promptly to relevant individuals within the organisation
- ensure discussions and negotiations with debtors are conducted courteously and achieve the desired outcome

knowledge and understanding

- legal and administrative procedures for the collection of debts
- methods of analysing information on debtors: age analysis of debtors; average periods of credit given and received; incidence of bad and doubtful debts

TRANSACTIONS WITH CREDIT CUSTOMERS

Once it has been agreed with a customer that they may trade on credit terms with the business we have already seen that an account will be set up for that customer in the sales ledger. You will appreciate from your earlier double entry bookkeeping studies that the entries in this account will be invoices and credit notes sent to the customer and receipts received from the customer.

One of the roles of the credit control team will be to monitor the transactions on each debtors account and in particular the balance on the account on a regular basis.

Placing an order

The first step in the monitoring of a credit customer's activities is at the initial stage of each transaction when the customer places an order for more goods. When the initial agreement was made with the customer to trade on credit terms a CREDIT LIMIT will have been set by the credit controller for that customer.

The credit limit is the maximum amount that should be outstanding on the customer's account in the sales ledger at any point in time. The credit limit that is set is not an arbitrary amount, it will have been considered in the light of the credit risk of the customer and it is therefore important that the credit limit is adhered to.

Therefore when a customer places an order the first stage is to check that the value of the order does not take the customer's account over their credit limit. If the value of the order does mean that the customer's balance exceeds the credit limit then this must be discussed with the customer. Although the business will not wish to lose the sale it is important that the credit limit is not exceeded and therefore discussions with the customer will be required to explain that the new order can only be processed once money has been received for earlier invoices therefore leaving the account balance with the new order value below the credit limit.

HOW IT WORKS

One of SC Fuel and Glass's customers is Nerrington Engineering. On 14 July 2006 the balance on their account in the sales ledger is £4,484.04, which is made up as follows:

		£
26/04/06	Invoice 203741	1,350.67
28/05/06	Invoice 203882	994.60
06/06/06	Credit note 016452	(103.25)
14/06/06	Invoice 203903	1,226.57
28/06/06	Invoice 203911	1,015.45
		4,484.04

On this date Nerrington have placed an order for an additional £1,245.60 of fuel however this will take their account balance over their credit limit of £5,000. Tom Hunt, the credit controller for the fuel division, therefore makes a telephone call to the accountant at Nerrington to explain the situation. It is agreed that Nerrington will draw a cheque for £2,242.02 which will pay off invoices 203741 and 203882 less the credit note. Once this cheque has been received it is agreed that the new order will be processed and the fuel delivered.

Activity 1

Why is it important that the credit limit set for a customer should not be exceeded?

Review of customer accounts

As well as checking that each order does not mean that the customer's balance exceeds their credit limit, each customer's account should be monitored on a regular basis. This review should be looking for debts that are not being paid within the stated credit terms and old debts that have not been paid at all.

Accuracy of customer accounts

In order for this review of customer accounts to be meaningful it is important that the customer accounts are kept up to date and accurate. This means that invoices and credit notes must be processed and posted promptly to the customer's account and that receipts of monies from debtors must also be accurately and promptly recorded in the customer's account so that the correct balance and position can be seen at any point in time.

AGED DEBTOR ANALYSIS

One particularly useful method of reviewing customer account balances is by producing an AGED DEBTOR ANALYSIS. This can either be done manually or more commonly nowadays by computer.

An aged debtor analysis splits the total balance on a debtor's account into amounts which have been outstanding for particular periods of time, for example:

- current – up to 30 days
- 31 to 60 days
- 61 to 90 days
- over 90 days

HOW IT WORKS

We will return to the account of Nerrington Engineering in the sales ledger of SC Fuel and Glass. At 30 June 2006 the account balance is made up as follows:

		£
26/04/06	Invoice 203741	1,350.67
28/05/06	Invoice 203882	994.60
06/06/06	Credit note 016452	(103.25)
14/06/06	Invoice 203903	1,226.57
28/06/06	Invoice 203911	1,015.45
		4,484.04

The precise age of each of the outstanding invoices however can be shown more clearly if an aged debt analysis is prepared.

Aged debt analysis – 30 June 2006

	Total £	Credit limit £	Current <30 days £	31–60 days £	61–90 days £	> 90 days £
Nerrington Engineering	4,484.04	5,000	2,138.77	994.60	1,350.67	–

Note that the 'current' portion is made up of Invoices 203903 and 203911 less the credit note which were all issued in June.

Using the aged debtor analysis

The regular review of the aged debtor analysis should highlight the following potential problems:

- credit limit exceeded
- slow payers
- recent debts cleared but older outstanding amounts
- old amounts outstanding but no current trading

Credit limit exceeded

As we have already seen when an order is placed by a credit customer the first step is to check whether this would mean that the customer's credit limit would be exceeded. However this will not always take place or on occasions when the order is placed the customer's account is not up to date so that it appears that the credit limit would not be exceeded and therefore the sale is agreed.

However if review of the aged debtor analysis indicates that a customer's credit limit has been exceeded then this must be investigated.

If a customer is highlighted in the aged debtor analysis as having exceeded their credit limit then normally the customer should be told that no further sales will be made to them until at least some of the outstanding balances have been repaid. However in some circumstances liaison between the sales ledger and the sales department may result in an increase in the customer's credit limit if they have a good payment record and are simply increasing their trade with our company rather than just delaying paying the amounts due. The types of checks that would be carried out before an increase in an existing customer's credit limit were considered in the previous chapter.

Activity 2

If an invoice to a customer was not promptly recorded in the customer's sales ledger account what effect might this have next time the customer placed an order?

Slow payers

Some businesses can be identified from the aged debtor listing as being slow payers as they always have amounts outstanding for say 31 – 60 days and 61 – 90 days as well as current amounts. If the credit terms are 30 days from the invoice date then all amounts other than current amounts will be overdue.

In these cases consideration should be given to methods of encouraging the customer to pay earlier. This could be in the form of a reminder letter or telephone call (see later in the chapter) or perhaps the offer of a settlement discount for earlier payment.

Recent debts cleared but older amount outstanding

If a customer is generally a regular payer and fairly recent debts have been cleared but there is still an outstanding older amount then this will normally indicate either a query over the amount outstanding or a problem with the recording of invoices, credit notes or payments received.

If there appears to be no communication with the debtor about a queried invoice that would account for the old debt outstanding then the invoice postings, credit note postings and payments received from that debtor should be checked to ensure that there have been no errors which have resulted in the recording of this outstanding amount. If there appear to be no errors then the debtor should be contacted in order to find out what the problem is concerning payment of this particular amount.

Old amounts outstanding and no current trading

This situation would be of some concern for the credit control team. It would appear that the debtor is no longer buying from the business but still owes money from previous purchases. In this case the debtor should be contacted immediately and payment sought. If no contact can be made with the debtor or there is a genuine problem with payment, such as bankruptcy or liquidation, consideration should be given to writing off the debt as bad (see later in the chapter).

HOW IT WORKS

Given below is an extract from the aged debtor analysis of the fuel division of SC Fuel and Glass at 30 June 2006.

Aged debtor analysis – 30 June 2006

	Total £	Credit limit £	Current <30 days £	31–60 days £	61–90 days £	> 90 days £
Pentagon Ltd	7,357.68	10,000	4,268.79	3,088.89		
White & Co	1,363.56	2,000	1,135.46		228.10	
Nantwich Ltd	3,745.24	5,000	732.34	1,983.36	1,029.54	
Bella Partners	4,836.47	4,000	2,295.36	2,541.11		
Manfred Paul	832.56	1,000				832.56

The position of each debtor must be considered and any necessary action taken.

Pentagon Ltd — when the credit agreement with Pentagon Ltd is checked it is noted that this long standing customer is allowed 60 days of credit from the invoice date therefore there are no amounts overdue

White & Co — the credit terms for this business are 30 days from the invoice date therefore the amount over 60 days of £228.10 is certainly overdue. However with no other overdue amounts this might indicate that there is a query regarding this figure and the customer's correspondence file should be checked. If there appears to be no queried amount then there might have been an error in the posting to the account which must also be checked

Nantwich Ltd   the credit terms for this business are 30 days from the invoice date therefore the vast majority of the debt is outstanding. This company appears to be a slow payer and consideration should be given to encouraging them to pay within the stated credit period

Bella Partners   credit terms of 30 days therefore over half the debt is overdue. The customer has also exceeded their credit limit and the reason for this should be investigated. It may be decided to stop any further supplies to the customer until the overdue amounts are paid

Manfred Paul   This is of great concern as there has been no current trading but there is an old amount outstanding. The customer should be contacted immediately with a view to collection of the amount due.

Activity 3

The aged debtor analysis for a business shows that a customer has £736.50 owing from the current period and £104.00 due from the 61 – 90 day period. What course of action should be taken concerning this debtor?

Measurement of overdue debt

A further use that can be made of the aged debtor analysis is to measure the amount of overdue debt as a percentage of the entire debt which will give an indication of the efficiency of the credit control team. This can either be done for individual customers or for debtors in total.

HOW IT WORKS

The entries for Nantwich Ltd in the SC Fuel and Glass aged debt analysis are reproduced below.

	Total £	Credit limit £	Current <30 days £	31–60 days £	61–90 days £	> 90 days £
Nantwich Ltd	3,745.24	5,000	732.34	1,983.36	1,029.54	

The overdue amount as a percentage of the total debt can be calculated:

$$= \frac{1{,}983.36 + 1{,}029.54}{3{,}745.24} \times 100\%$$

$$= 80\%$$

Such a figure might highlight Nantwich Ltd as a slow payer and potential problem customer which may deserve the attentions of the credit controller.

Measuring the average period of credit

A business will have its own credit control policies and will set credit terms for each of its credit customers. However it is business reality that not all, and possibly not very many, customers will stick to their credit terms. Therefore it is useful for a business to be able to determine the average period of credit taken by its customers in total. If these figures are compared over time then any improvement or deterioration of credit control procedures can be identified.

There are three main methods of calculating an AVERAGE PERIOD OF CREDIT:

- debtors turnover
- the count-back method
- the partial month method.

HOW IT WORKS

The aged debtor analysis totals for the glass division of SC Fuel and Glass at 30 June 2006 are given below:

	Total £000	Credit limit £000	Current <30 days £000	31–60 days £000	61–90 days £000	> 90 days £000
Total	1,885	2,500	968	589	269	59

Sales for the year to 30 June 2006 totalled £12,480,000 and credit terms are payment within 30 days of the invoice.

Debtors turnover

This is the number of days sales outstanding as debtors at the end of the year and we considered its calculation in the previous chapter:

$$\text{Debtors turnover} = \frac{1,885,000}{12,480,000} \times 365 \text{ days}$$

$$= 55 \text{ days}$$

The count-back method

This method assumes that debtors represent the most current sales. Sales for the glass division for the previous months have been investigated and were as follows:

	£000
Before April	9,112
April	1,056
May	1,128
June	1,184
	12,480

	£000
Total debtors at end of June	1,885
Less: June sales	(1,184)
May sales not yet received	701

Days outstanding	Days
June	30
May unpaid $\dfrac{701}{1,128}$ x 31 days	19
Debtors days outstanding	49

Partial month method

Under this method the unpaid portion of each month's sales is identified and converted into days outstanding. Each month's figures are then aggregated.

	Sales (a) £000	Unpaid amount (b) £000	(c) Days	b/a x c
Before April	9,112	59	274	1.8
April	1,056	269	30	7.6
May	1,128	589	31	16.2
June	1,184	968	30	24.5
	12,480	1,885	365	50.1

Each method has given us a different average credit period due to the different assumptions and calculations made:

Debtors turnover	55 days
Count back	49 days
Partial month	50 days

However whichever method is used it is quite clear that the average period of credit taken by the glass division's customers is significantly greater than the 30 days credit period granted to credit customers.

student notes✍

Activity 4

A business made sales in July and August of £800,000 and £900,000 respectively. At the end of August debtors totalled £1,350,000. What is the average period of credit taken using the count back method?

BAD AND DOUBTFUL DEBTS

The aged debt analysis can also be used to identify debts which might be BAD DEBTS or DOUBTFUL DEBTS.

A bad debt is one where it is almost certain that the monies will not be received. A doubtful debt is one where there is some doubt over the eventual receipt of the money but it is not such a clear case as a bad debt. The reason for the distinction between the two is that in the financial accounting records a bad debt is written off (and no longer appear in the ledger or on the balance sheet) whereas a doubtful debt is provided against (so it still appears in the ledger, and on the balance sheet where it is netted off against the provision).

Identification of bad and doubtful debts

As the people dealing with the accounts of debtors and analysing the aged debtors the credit control team are in a position to be able to assess potential bad debts. They should ensure that when doing this they use all available information. This might include the following:

- evidence of long outstanding debts from the aged debtor analysis

- a one off outstanding debt when more recent debts have been cleared

- correspondence with debtors

- outstanding older debts and no current business with the customer

- a sudden or unexpected change in payment patterns

- request for an extension of credit terms

- press comment

- information from the sales team

When considering the aged debtor analysis earlier in this chapter we saw that the pattern of the ageing of debts for individual debtors can give a clue as to any problems with each individual debtor. Such potential problems must then be investigated and the outcome might be that a bad or doubtful debt is identified.

HOW IT WORKS

Given again is the extract from the fuel division's aged debtor analysis at 30 June 2006.

Aged debtor analysis – 30 June 2006

	Total £	Credit limit £	Current <30 days £	31–60 days £	61–90 days £	> 90 days £
Pentagon Ltd	7,357.68	10,000	4,268.79	3,088.89		
White & Co	1,363.56	2,000	1,135.46		228.10	
Nantwich Ltd	3,745.24	5,000	732.34	1,983.36	1,029.54	
Bella Partners	4,836.47	4,000	2,295.36	2,541.11		
Manfred Paul	832.56	1,000				832.56

The two debts which we might wish to consider are the old debts owing by White & Co and by Manfred Paul.

Upon investigation it is discovered that the amount of £228.10 is in dispute with White & Co as they have no record of having received this delivery of fuel. SC's despatch team are still trying to find evidence that the fuel was despatched but as yet they can find no delivery note to support the invoice that was sent out. This could be viewed as a doubtful debt as there is certainly some doubt as to whether this was in fact a valid sale or not.

Manfred Paul was an individual customer with whom SC has traded periodically. Upon contacting Manfred Paul it has been discovered that he has been declared bankrupt and has no funds to pay his creditors. This debt will probably be declared a bad debt.

Information about potential bad and doubtful debts

If a member of the credit control team discovers that a debt is highly likely to be classified as bad or doubtful then it will probably not be that person's responsibility to write the debt off or provide against it. This will normally be the role of a more senior member of the accounting function. Therefore it is important that all information about potential bad or doubtful debts is communicated clearly to the relevant person within the accounting function as this will have an impact on the preparation of the financial statements for the business.

Incidence of bad debts

It is part of business life that some debts will be declared bad debts and written off.

It can be argued that a high level of bad debts in an organisation is an indicator of poor credit control, although there could obviously be other reasons such as the general economic climate. A high level of bad debts could be an indication of:

- sales being made to high risk customers
- poor assessment of creditworthiness
- lack of useful information for checking on creditworthiness
- weak sales ledger accounting
- poor follow up procedures for outstanding debts

So in order to have some form of control over amounts being written off it may be useful to calculate an indicator concerning the incidence of bad debts as these are the ones where it is fairly certain the business will never receive its money and therefore a loss is made on the sale.

Therefore a bad debts ratio can be calculated as:

$$\frac{\text{Bad debts}}{\text{Credit sales}} \times 100\%$$

If there is a significant increase in this ratio then there would appear to be credit control problems particularly with the initial screening of customers for credit status.

HOW IT WORKS

The sales of the glass division of SC Fuel and Glass for the year ending 30 June 2006, was £12,480,000. During the year £320,000 of debts were identified as bad debts and were written off.

$$\text{Bad debt ratio} = \frac{£320,000}{£12,480,000} \times 100\%$$

$$= 2.6\%$$

Activity 5

What is the distinction between a bad debt and a doubtful debt, and why is this distinction important?

DEBT COLLECTION POLICY

As we have seen when credit is extended to a customer the credit terms will be made clear. However many customers will not adhere strictly to those credit terms and will effectively make use of what they might view as free credit by taking as long as possible to pay what is due.

Most businesses will therefore have some sort of policy regarding the collection of debts and the processes that will take place to chase up any outstanding amounts.

DEBT COLLECTION PROCESS

The debt collection process starts with the sending out of the sales invoice on which the credit terms should be clearly stated. Thereafter a variety of reminders are sent to the customer to encourage them to pay within the credit terms and for those overdue debts a further series of reminders.

A typical debt collection process can be illustrated:

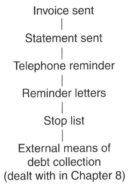

Invoice sent
|
Statement sent
|
Telephone reminder
|
Reminder letters
|
Stop list
|
External means of
debt collection
(dealt with in Chapter 8)

Sales invoice

Once a sale has been made the first communication with the customer is to send out the sales invoice. This should be sent promptly as soon as the goods or services have been provided and should clearly state the payment period agreed.

Statements

Most businesses will then send a monthly STATEMENT to the customer showing the balance at the end of that month and how that is made up ie, invoices, credit notes, payments received. The statement may include a remittance advice which is encouraging the customer to pay the amounts due and which also indicates which invoices are being covered by this payment.

Telephone calls

An OVERDUE DEBT is one which has not been paid within the stated credit period and once a debt has become overdue it is common practice to make a telephone call to the customer to enquire about the situation, determine whether or not there is a query over the amount due and agree when the debt will be paid.

When making this type of telephone call particular attention should be paid to the following matters:

- discussion with the customer should always be courteous

- the precise amount of the debt should be pointed out and the fact that it is overdue

- it should be established whether there is any query with regard to the debt and if so any appropriate action should be agreed to resolve the query

- if there is no query then a date for payment of the debt should be established

Reminder letters

If there has been no response to any telephone calls requesting payment of the overdue amount then this will be followed up with a REMINDER LETTER.

This first reminder letter is designed to point out the facts, the amount outstanding and as a reminder or encouragement to pay the amount due very soon. As with all letters to customers it must be courteous and succinct as well as firm.

The reminder letter will be sent out when the debts are a certain amount overdue. The timescale of the reminder letter will depend upon the organisation's policy towards debt collection but might be sent out 7 days after a debt becomes overdue. Therefore if an invoice is sent to a customer with 30 day credit terms then the first reminder letter will be sent out 37 days after the invoice was sent out.

The first reminder letter will normally be sent to the person with day to day responsibility for payment of creditors.

An example of a typical first reminder letter is given below:

> Date
>
> Dear Sir
>
> **Account No: 385635/A**
>
> I do not appear to have received payment of the invoices detailed below. I trust that this is an oversight and that you will arrange for immediate payment to be made. If you are withholding payment for any reason, please contact me urgently and I will be pleased to assist you.
>
> | Invoice No | Terms | Due date | Amount £ |
> |---|---|---|---|
> | | | | |
>
> If you have already made payment please advise me and accept my apology for having troubled you.
>
> Yours faithfully
>
> Credit controller

Practice in this area will vary between organisations and some organisations will send out an initial reminder letter before a telephone call is made to the customer.

Final reminder letter

If there is no response from the initial reminder letter then there will tend to be little point in sending a second reminder letter. However at this stage another telephone call might be useful to clear up any misunderstanding and to assess whether further action is required.

The options for the business at this point are generally:

- to put the debt into the hands of a debt collector (see next chapter)

- to take the debtor to court for payment (see next chapter)

- to suspend any further sales to the company until payment is received by placing the customer on a STOP LIST

Whatever action is to be taken a final reminder letter must be sent to the customer detailing this action if payment is not received. This final reminder letter will normally be sent to a senior member of the management team such as the chief accountant or finance director.

Typical letters are shown below.

Debt collection letter

Date

Dear Sir

Account No: 385635/A

Further to our invoices detailed below and the reminder letter dated 14 July 2006 I do not appear to have received payment. If you are withholding payment for any reason, please contact me urgently and I will be pleased to assist you.

Invoice No	Terms	Due date	Amount £

I regret that unless payment is received within the next seven days I will have no alternative but to put the collection of the amounts due into the hands of a third party.

If you have already made the payment please advise me and accept my apology for having troubled you.

Yours faithfully

Credit controller

Court proceedings letter

Date

Dear Sir

Account No: 385635/A
Total amount outstanding £1,138.30

Despite the previous reminders and telephone calls we have still not received your payment in settlement of the above account total. You have promised payment on a number of occasions but no payment has been received to date.

We regret that due to the above we have no alternative but to consider the Small Claim procedure in the County Court in order to recover the sum outstanding. Prior to us taking such action we would however wish to give you one final opportunity to make payment. We will therefore delay submission of the claim to the County Court for a period of seven days from the date of this letter in the hope that the account is settled. We will not enter into any further correspondence regarding this matter other than through the County Court.

Please note that if we are forced to take legal action you may become liable for the costs of such action which if successful may affect your future credit rating.

Yours faithfully

Credit controller

Stop list letter

Date

Dear Sir

Account No: 385635/A

Further to our invoices detailed below, I do not appear to have received payment. I trust that this is an oversight and that you will arrange for immediate payment to be made. If you are withholding payment for any reason, please contact me urgently and I will be pleased to assist you.

Invoice No	Terms	Due date	Amount £

I regret that unless payment is received within the next seven days I will have no alternative but to stop any further sales on credit to you until the amount owing is cleared in full. If you have already made payment please advise me and accept my apology for having troubled you. Please note that if we are forced to take legal action you may become liable for the costs of such action which if successful may affect your future credit rating.

Yours faithfully

Credit controller

HOW IT WORKS

The glass division of SC Fuel and Glass has the following written policy for debt collection.

Debt collection policy

1   Invoices should be sent out on the same day as goods are delivered

2   An aged analysis of debtors should be produced monthly

3   Statements are sent to credit customers on the first working day of each month

4   A reminder letter is sent when a debt is 7 days overdue

5   A telephone call to chase payment must be made when a debt is 14 days overdue

6   When the debt is 30 days overdue the customer will be placed on the stop list and a letter sent confirming this. A meeting should then

be arranged with the customer in order to discuss the account position

7   When the debt is 60 days overdue it will be placed in the hands of a debt collector or legal proceedings will be commenced based upon the decision of the Financial Controller.

An invoice was sent to Yarrow Ltd, for £8,570 on 1 June on 30 day credit terms. This debt is still outstanding at 30 June. The process that would follow providing that the money was not received would be:

- 7 July – first reminder letter sent

- 14 July – telephone reminder

- 30 July – placed on stop list and final reminder letter sent. Meeting arranged to resolve the payment problem

- 30 August – decision taken regarding final treatment of overdue amount

Activity 6

What factors are important when planning to make a telephone call to a customer regarding an overdue amount?

CHAPTER OVERVIEW

- one of the roles of the credit control team is to monitor the transactions and balances on credit customers accounts

- when an order is placed by a customer it should be checked that the value of this order will not lead to the customer exceeding their agreed credit limit

- an aged debtor analysis is a useful tool in monitoring credit customers accounts and can be used to identify credit limits exceeded, slow payers, problem amounts and potential bad and doubtful debts

- the overall average period of credit taken by debtors can be measured by calculating debtors turnover based upon annual sales, using the count back method or using the partial month method

- the credit control team should be aware of factors that might indicate a possible bad debt or doubtful debt and the appropriate member of the accounting function should be immediately informed of all the circumstances if such a debt is identified

- the debt collection process starts with the sending out of sales invoices and statements – if payment is not received within the stated credit period this will be followed by telephone reminders, reminder letters and eventually action such as cessation of trading, use of debt collectors or legal proceedings

- most businesses will have a written debt collection policy which must be followed

KEY WORDS

Credit limit the maximum amount that should be outstanding on a customer's sales ledger account at any point in time

Aged debtor analysis an analysis of each individual debtor's balance split into amounts that have been outstanding for particular periods of time

Average period of credit the number of days on average that credit sales are outstanding

Bad debts debts where it is almost certain that the monies due will not be received

Doubtful debts debts where there is some doubt over whether the monies due will eventually be received

Statement analysis of the amount due by a customer and the transactions on their account for the last period which is periodically sent to the customer

Overdue debt a debt which has not been paid within the stated credit period

Reminder letter a letter sent to a customer encouraging payment of an overdue debt

Stop list a list of customers to whom goods should not be sold on credit

HOW MUCH HAVE YOU LEARNED?

1 Why is it important that customer accounts in the sales ledger are kept accurately up to date?

2 A customer of a business has an outstanding balance on its sales ledger account of £17,685 at 31 July. This balance is made up as follows:

		£
22 May	Inv 093106	2,184
3 June	Inv 093182	3,785
21 June	Inv 093265	4,839
2 July	Credit note 04623	(536)
5 July	Inv 093321	3,146
20 July	Inv 093346	4,267
		17,685

The customer's name is Fording Ltd and the company has a credit limit of £20,000.

Complete the aged debtor analysis given below for this customer as at 31 July.

	Total £	Credit limit £	Current <30 days £	31–60 days £	61–90 days £	> 90 days £

3 What types of problems with debtors accounts might be highlighted by analysis of an aged debtor listing?

4 Given below are extracts from an aged debtor analysis for a company at 30 September:

	Total £	Credit limit £	Current <30 days £	31–60 days £	61–90 days £	> 90 days £
Kerry & Co	5,389	8,000	4,999		390	
Marshall Ltd	16,378	15,000	16,378			
Leyton Ltd	5,377	10,000	1,854	1,757	1,766	

Credit terms are that payment is due within 30 days of the invoice date.

For each customer state what the aged debtor listing might indicate about that customer and what if any action might be required.

5 Given below are the totals of the aged debtor listing for a business at 31 July.

	Total £	Credit limit £	Current <30 days £	31–60 days £	61–90 days £	> 90 days £
Total	436,790	550,000	203,200	164,800	68,790	

The sales for the year ending 31 July totalled £2,530,000 and were made up as follows:

	£
Before May	1,898,300
May	215,700
June	206,000
July	210,000
	2,530,000

Calculate the average period of credit taken in days using each of the following methods:

- debtors turnover based on annual total sales
- the count back method
- the partial month method

6   What information available to the credit control team might indicate the existence of a bad or doubtful debt?

7   A company has a policy of granting credit terms of 30 days from the invoice date. Once an invoice is 7 days overdue a telephone call is made to the customer to enquire about the debt. Once an invoice is 14 days overdue a reminder letter is sent to the customer. Once an invoice is 30 days overdue the customer is placed on the stop list and a letter is sent informing them of this.

Given below is an extract from the company's aged debtor listing at 30 June.

	Total £	Credit limit £	Current <30 days £	31–60 days £	61–90 days £	> 90 days £
Travis Ltd	4,678	5,000		4,678		
Muse Ltd	3,557	5,000	2,669	888		
Keane Ltd	6,248	8,000	5,145		1,103	

- the balance owing by Travis Ltd is made up of invoice number 467824 dated 15 May

- invoice number 467899 to Muse Ltd for £2,669 was dated 2 June and invoice number 467831 for £888 was dated 23 May

- invoice number 467781 for £1,103 was dated 22 April

For each customer determine what action if any is necessary according to the credit collection policy and draft any letters that might be necessary to send to these customers.

chapter 8:
COLLECTION OF DEBTS

chapter coverage 📖

In this final chapter of the Course Companion element of Unit 15 we will consider the alternative methods of collecting debts from credit customers other than through the normal activities of the credit control team or sales ledger team. As a last resort if a debt remains unpaid then there are legal proceedings that can be brought for breach of contract. Finally in this chapter a basic understanding of bankruptcy for an individual and insolvency for a company is required which will help in determining whether in realistic terms a debt should be written off as bad or at the very least provided for as a doubtful debt.

The topics covered are:

✍ methods of debt collection

✍ legal remedies for breach of contract

✍ bankruptcy and insolvency

✍ bad and doubtful debts

Performance criteria – element 15.4

- use debt recovery methods appropriate to the circumstances of individual cases and in accordance with the organisation's procedures

- base recommendations to write off bad and doubtful debts on a realistic analysis of all known factors

knowledge and understanding – accounting principles and theory

- legal issues: remedies for breach of contract
- legal and administrative procedures for the collection of debts
- the effect of bankruptcy and insolvency on organisations
- methods of collection
- factoring arrangements
- debt insurance
- evaluation of different collection methods
- an understanding of the organisation's relevant policies and procedures

METHODS OF DEBT COLLECTION

As we have seen in the previous chapters, with good credit control procedures, ranging from the credit assessment process to the monitoring of debtors, monies will be received from credit customers. This may sometimes require encouragement such as reminder letters or telephone calls but the money should eventually be received. However there will be some cases in which either the debt is never collected and has to be written off as a bad debt or the business has to resort to legal procedures to obtain payment.

Before we consider these matters there are other methods that a business can use to minimise the possibility of either the loss of the debt or resorting to legal procedures. There are a variety of different methods of collecting the debts that are due and we will consider the costs and benefits of each of these. The methods available include:

- debt collection agencies
- factoring
- invoice discounting
- debt insurance

Debt collection agencies

DEBT COLLECTION AGENCIES or CREDIT COLLECTION AGENCIES are commercial organisations that specialise in the collection of debts. Most collection agencies are paid by results and will charge a percentage of the debts collected for the business although some will require an advance subscription for their services.

The collection agency will use appropriate methods for collecting the debts. These may be:

- collection by telephone and letter
- collection by personal visits
- negotiation of a payment plan with the debtor

Collection agencies are an effective method of collecting debts that are proving difficult in the normal course of trading and as collection agencies tend to be viewed as a normal business service they are unlikely to have an adverse effect on the relationship between the business and its customer. However the collection agency does of course charge a fee for its services.

Factoring services

FACTORING is a financing service provided by specialist financial institutions, often subsidiaries of major banks, whereby money can be advanced to a company on the basis of the security of their debtors. A factor will normally provide three main services and a company can take advantage of some or all of these:

- provision of finance
- administration of the sales ledger
- insurance against bad debts.

Provision of finance by a factor

When sales on credit are made by a business, then there will be a period of time elapsing before the money for those sales is received from the business's debtors. Many businesses may find that they require the cash sooner than the debtors are prepared to pay, for example to pay suppliers or reduce an overdraft. This is particularly the case for fast growing companies.

The factor will therefore advance a certain percentage of the book value of the debtors, often about 80%, as an immediate payment. The debts are then collected by the factor and the remaining 20% less a fee handed over to the business when the debts are received by the factor.

There is obviously a charge for this service and this will tend to be in two parts:

- a service charge or commission charge
- an interest charge on amounts outstanding

One further hidden cost of factoring can be a loss of customer confidence or goodwill as they will be aware that the business has factored its debts which may have a negative impact on future relations with the customer. Many customers will still view the use of a factor as an indication that a business is in financial difficulty despite the increasing use of factoring within business.

HOW IT WORKS

Suppose that the fuel division of SC Fuel and Glass were considering the use of factor finance in order to pay its suppliers earlier in order to take advantage of settlement discounts offered. The book value of the fuel division's debts receivable is currently £700,000. The factor has agreed to advance 80% of this amount to the fuel division therefore the fuel division receives £560,000 (80% x £700,000) immediately from the factor.

The factor will then collect the debts on behalf of SC from its customers and will pay over the remaining £140,000 when this has been done less the commission and interest charges that the factor will charge.

Administration of the sales ledger by a factor

 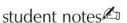

Many factoring arrangements go further than simply providing finance on the security of the debtors and will take over the entire administration of the sales ledger. This will tend to include the following:

- assessment of credit status
- sending out sales invoices
- recording sales invoices and receipts
- sending out statements
- sending out reminders
- collecting payments from debtors

The benefit to the business is a cost-saving from not having to run its own sales ledger and also it benefits from the expertise of the factor in this area. However a fee will of course be charged for this service normally based upon a percentage of turnover.

Insurance against bad debts

If a factor has total control over all aspects of credit management of the sales ledger then they may be prepared to offer a WITHOUT RECOURSE FACTORING ARRANGEMENT. This means that the factor has no right to claim against the business if a debtor does not pay. Effectively the factor is bearing the risk of any bad debts and of course will charge a higher fee for accepting this additional risk.

In other circumstances the business will retain the risk of bad debts and this is known as WITH RECOURSE FACTORING.

Activity 1

What are the three main services provided by a factor?

Advantages and disadvantages of factoring

The benefits and costs of factoring can be summarised:

Advantages	Disadvantages
advance of cash which may not be available from other sources	cost – commission and interest
specialist debt administration skills of the factor	potential loss of customer goodwill
specialist debt collection skills of the factor	higher costs for credit insurance

Advantages	Disadvantages
saving in in-house sales ledger costs	problems of reverting to in house debt collection in future
reduction in bad debts cost	
frees up management time	

Activity 2

Why might the use of factor finance adversely affect customer goodwill?

Invoice discounting

It was mentioned above that one of the costs of factoring is the potential loss of customer goodwill if it is known that the business is using a factor to collect its debts. The reason for this is that some customers may infer cash flow problems from the use of a factor which may not give them confidence to continue trading with the business.

One alternative therefore is INVOICE DISCOUNTING which is a service much related to factoring. Invoice discounting is where the debts of a business are purchased by the provider of the service at a discount to their face value. The discounter simply provides cash up front to the business at the discounted amount rather than any involvement in the business's sales ledger. Under a confidential invoice discounting agreement the business's customers will only be aware of the arrangement if they do not pay their debt.

The discount at which the debts are purchased will tend to be quite high and therefore invoice discounting, being an expensive source of finance, is normally only used for a one-off exceptional cash requirement.

Activity 3

Distinguish between invoice discounting and factoring arrangements.

Debt insurance

DEBT INSURANCE is insurance cover taken out against the incurring of bad debts. It has nothing to do with advances of money or collection of debts as with factoring but is simply an insurance policy to cover debts which go bad and are never received from the customer. Such insurance, also known as credit insurance, is available from a number of sources and there are several types of policy available.

Types of debt insurance policy

The most common policy is a WHOLE TURNOVER POLICY. This type of policy can operate in one of two ways:

- the entire sales ledger can be covered but the amount paid out for any bad debt claim would only be normally about 80% of the claim

- alternatively approximately 80% of the debtors can be insured for their entire amount and any claim on these debtors would be paid in full.

Either way under this type of policy only a proportion of bad debts will be covered for loss.

A further type of policy is an ANNUAL AGGREGATE EXCESS POLICY where bad debts are insured in total above an agreed limit or excess in a similar way to household or car insurance policies.

Finally it is possible to purchase insurance for a specific debtor account rather than debtors in total.

The cost of insurance will differ depending upon the insurer and the type of policy but premiums will tend to be 1 – 2% of the amounts insured.

LEGAL REMEDIES

If all other attempts to recover a debt fail then a business may need to resort to the law in order to claim the money due to them.

Remember from an earlier chapter that an agreement between a seller and a buyer of goods will be a contract provided that there is:

- valid agreement
- consideration
- intention to create legal relations

Therefore if the seller of the goods or services provides those goods or services but the buyer does not pay for them then the buyer is in BREACH OF CONTRACT.

Remedies for breach of contract

A breach of contract arises where one party to the contract does not carry out their side of the bargain eg a credit customer who does not pay. There are a number of remedies available to the injured party for breach of contract which include:

- action for the price – a court action to recover the agreed price of the goods/services

- monetary damages – compensation for loss

- termination – one party refusing to carry on with the contract

- specific performance – a court order that one of the parties must fulfil their obligations

- quantum meruit – payment ordered for the part of the contract performed

- injunction – one party to the contract being ordered by the court not to do something

In terms of a debtor not having paid for goods or services provided, the most appropriate remedy would normally be an action for the price.

Activity 4

What are the three essential elements for there to be a valid contract?

Bringing a dispute to court

If it is decided that the only course of action to recover money owed by a debtor is that of legal action then the first step is to instruct a solicitor. The solicitor will require details of the goods or services provided, the date the liability arose, the exact name and trading status of the debtor, any background information such as disputes in the past and a copy of any invoices that are unpaid.

In some cases the threat of legal action will be enough and even after the solicitor has got involved there can be a negotiated settlement between the business and their debtor as the debtor may not want to run the risk of going to court and any costs that might be incurred. However in other situations the case will be taken to court.

Which court?

If the claim is for less than £5,000 then the claim will be made in the small claims division of the County Court, under what is known as the small claims track. Any other claims for less than £15,000 will normally be dealt with the County Court under the fast track procedure, whereby the case is heard speedily. Claims involving greater amounts will be heard under the multi-track procedure, in either the County Court or the High Court, depending on the complexity of the case.

Procedure

Once the appropriate court has received all of the paperwork for the claim it will issue a summons to the debtor requiring an acknowledgement of service of the summons. If the debtor does not reply then the judgement will go against him.

The debtor may also admit the claim and perhaps offer to pay by instalments. If the business does not accept this then the court will determine a suitable method of paying off the debt.

Activity 5

An action is to be brought against a trade debtor for unpaid amounts of £10,000. In which court would this action normally be brought?

Methods of receiving payment under a court order

Once there has been a court order that the money due must be paid there are a number of methods of achieving this:

- attachment of earnings order – the business will be paid the amount owing directly by the debtor's employer as a certain amount is deducted from their weekly/monthly pay. However this is only viable for a debtor who is an individual and is in stable, consistent work

- third-party debt order (garnishee order) – this allows the business to be paid directly by a third party who owes the debtor money

- warrant of execution – a court bailiff seizes and sells the debtor's goods on behalf of the business

- administrative order – the debtor makes regular, agreed payments into court to pay off the debt

- receiver – a receiver is appointed to receive money that will become owing to the debtor, eg rents

- charge – a legal charge is taken on property or financial assets, so the creditor is paid when the assets are sold

- bankruptcy notice – see next section

- liquidation – see next section.

HOW IT WORKS

SC Fuel and Glass is owed £2,800 by one of its hauliers, Terence Frame & Sons. The claim was taken to the Small Claims Court and Terence Frame & Sons were ordered to pay the full amount due. This was done by a garnishee order, whereby a third party, Cranford Garages Ltd who owed Terence Frame & Sons £4,000 themselves paid over an amount of £2,800 to SC Fuel and Glass.

BANKRUPTCY AND INSOLVENCY

BANKRUPTCY arises where an individual cannot pay their debts and is declared bankrupt and INSOLVENCY is where a company cannot pay their debts as they fall due.

When assessing bad debts it is likely that if an individual debtor is bankrupt or a company debtor is insolvent then the business will receive little or nothing of the debt due. It is also important to be aware of the bankruptcy and insolvency legal issues as it may be that the use of bankruptcy or insolvency legislation becomes the only course available for a business in order to receive payment or at least part-payment of a debt.

Petition for bankruptcy

Before a petition for bankruptcy against an individual is issued a creditor for a debt of at least £750 must issue a STATUTORY DEMAND for payment of the amount due within a certain period of time. This may result in the debtor offering a settlement. If however there is no settlement offer from the debtor a petition for bankruptcy will be received from the court.

Consequences of a petition for bankruptcy

The consequences of a petition for bankruptcy against a debtor are:

- if the debtor pays money to any other creditors or disposes of any property then these transactions are void

- any other legal proceedings relating to the debtor's property or debts are suspended

- an interim receiver is appointed to protect the estate

Consequences of a bankruptcy order

The consequences of a bankruptcy order are:

- the official receiver takes control of the assets of the business

- a statement of the assets and liabilities is drawn up – this is known as a STATEMENT OF AFFAIRS

- the receiver summons a meeting of creditors within 12 weeks of the bankruptcy order

- the creditors appoint a trustee in bankruptcy

- the assets of the business are realised and distribution is made to the various creditors

- the creditor who presented the petition does not gain any priority for payment over other creditors

Order of distribution of assets

The assets of the bankrupt will be distributed in the following order:

- bankruptcy costs

- (secured) creditors

- preferential creditors such as employees, pension schemes, HM Revenue & Customs

- unsecured creditors such as trade creditors

- the bankrupt's spouse

- the bankrupt

As an unsecured trade creditor a business with debts due from a bankrupt should submit a written claim to the trustee detailing how the debt is made up. This may also need to be substantiated with documentary evidence.

Activity 6

What is the difference between bankruptcy and insolvency?

Insolvency

The process of insolvency for a company that cannot pay its debts as they fall due is similar to that of a bankrupt individual. Again if a creditor for £750 or more serves the company with a written demand and after three weeks the company fails to pay then the Insolvency Act 1986 will term the company unable to pay its debts.

There are then a number of possible options the main ones being:

- liquidation
- administration

Liquidation

In a liquidation the company is dissolved and the assets are realised with debts being paid out of the proceeds and any excess being returned to the shareholders. This process is carried out by a liquidator on behalf of the shareholders and/or creditors. The liquidator's job is simply to ensure that the creditors are paid and once this is done the company can be wound up.

Payment of creditors

In order for a creditor to claim payment in a liquidation it will need to provide evidence that there is a proper liability of the company which will often be by a formal procedure known as proof of debts.

Once this has been accepted the order in which the assets of a company are applied is:

- secured creditors with fixed charges
- costs of winding up the company
- preferential unsecured debts such as employees
- secured creditors with floating charges
- unsecured creditors such as trade creditors
- deferred debts such as unpaid dividends to shareholders

Administration

An alternative to a liquidation is that the shareholders, directors or creditors can present a petition to the court for an administration order. The effect of this is that the company continues to operate but an insolvency practitioner is put in control of it, with the purpose of trying to save the company from insolvency as a going concern or at least achieve a better result than a liquidation.

Activity 7

What is the role of an insolvency practitioner under an administration order?

BAD AND DOUBTFUL DEBTS

We considered the topic of bad and doubtful debts in the previous chapter. However it must again be considered here in the light of the legal and administrative issues that have been considered in this chapter. We have seen that there are a number of methods of collecting debts rather than in the normal course of business and these may be successful in the collection of debts which would otherwise have been classified as bad debts. We have also seen that potential bad debts can be insured against although it is necessary to ensure that the cost of the insurance does not exceed the threat of the bad debt.

We have also considered the legal methods of getting payment of a debt through the courts in an action for the price due to a breach of contract and the situation of an individual being declared bankrupt or a company being declared insolvent.

If an action for the price fails then it is certain that the debt must be written off as a bad debt as the courts have decided that this is not a valid debt of the business. If an individual customer is declared bankrupt or a company debtor goes into liquidation or administration the situation is not so clear cut. The process of liquidation or administration may take some little while and whilst unsecured trade creditors are some way down the list of order of payments in such cases it is possible that the debtor may be able to pay all or at least some of the debt due to the business.

The key factor is that the appropriate person within the accounting function must be kept aware of the details of the situation. As the credit control team are likely to be some of the first to hear of a customer's bankruptcy or liquidation it is important that all key facts are reported to the accounting personnel clearly and promptly and that any recommendations to write off the debt or to provide against it are based upon a realistic analysis of all of the factors involved.

CHAPTER OVERVIEW

- if amounts due from credit customers cannot be recovered in the normal course of business there are a variety of other alternatives

- a debt collection agency will use appropriate methods for collecting debts on a business's behalf without normally affecting customer goodwill – a fee will be charged for the agency's services

- a factoring agreement can be for the provision of finance, the administration of the sales ledger and with a without recourse agreement for protection against bad debts

- the fees charged by a factor will depend upon the level of service provided but it can also affect customer goodwill – the benefits of factoring include an advance of cash, specialist services of the factor and a reduction in sales ledger and management time and costs

- invoice discounting is similar to factoring although as it will be anonymous will not tend to affect customer goodwill

- debt insurance is not a method of collecting debts but of insuring against the risk of bad debts

- an agreement between a seller and a buyer of goods/services will normally be a contract and therefore if the buyer does not pay for the goods/services they will be in breach of contract and can be taken to an appropriate court for a remedy – usually an action for the price

- if the court agrees that the debtor must pay the amount due this can be done by an attachment of earnings order, a garnishee order, a warrant of execution or in extreme cases a bankruptcy notice or liquidation

KEY WORDS

Debt/Credit collection agencies commercial organisations that specialise in the collection of debts

Factoring a service whereby a factor advances money on the security of a business's debts and may also provide other services such as administration of the sales ledger

Without recourse factoring a factoring arrangement where the factor bears all the risk of bad debts

With recourse factoring a factoring arrangement where the business retains the risk of bad debts

Invoice discounting a service whereby sales invoices are purchased for cash immediately at a discount to their face value

Debt insurance insurance cover for bad debts either for the majority of the sales ledger or for specific sales ledger accounts

Whole turnover policy insurance for the whole sales ledger for say 80% of bad debts or for 80% of the sales ledger for all bad debts

Annual aggregate excess policy bad debts are insured for an amount above an agreed limit or excess

Breach of contract where one party to a contract does not carry out their side of the bargain

Bankruptcy where an individual cannot pay their debts

Insolvency where a company cannot pay their debts

CHAPTER OVERVIEW cont.

- if an individual customer is declared bankrupt or a company debtor goes into liquidation or administration the unsecured creditors such as trade creditors are unlikely to receive all of the amounts due but may receive some of the outstanding amount

- all information about potential bad or doubtful debts, particularly relating to court proceedings, bankruptcy or insolvency must be reported to the appropriate accounting personnel with a realistic analysis of all of the factors involved

---

KEY WORDS cont.

Statutory demand final demand for payment which must be issued before a petition for bankruptcy can be made

Statement of affairs a statement of the bankrupt's assets and liabilities

---

HOW MUCH HAVE YOU LEARNED?

1   Explain what is meant by without recourse factoring and with recourse factoring. Which is likely to be the more expensive service?

2   What are the main benefits and costs of using a factoring service for sales ledger administration and collection of debts?

3   Explain two types of debt insurance policy that a business could take out.

4   What are the legal remedies available for a breach of contract?

5   Briefly explain three methods of achieving payment from a debtor under a court order.

6   What are the consequences of a bankruptcy order against an individual?

7   What is the order of distribution of the assets of a company which is in liquidation?

ANSWERS TO CHAPTER ACTIVITIES

CHAPTER 1 Monitoring cash receipts and payments

1 Setting up a provision for doubtful debts – charge to profit but no cash effect
   Accrual of electricity bill – charge to profit but no immediate cash effect

2 i)   cash transaction
   ii)   cash transaction
   iii) credit transaction
   iv)   credit transaction

3 Exceptional receipt – insurance claim received for damaged stock
   Exceptional payment – hire of machinery due to breakdown of own machinery

4 A receipts and payments cash budget is prepared by totalling the cash receipts for the period and totalling the cash payments for the period. The net of these two amounts is the net cash movement for the period and this is applied to the opening forecast cash balance in order to find the closing forecast cash balance.

   A profit and loss account and balance sheet cash flow forecast is based upon a forecast profit and loss account for a period together with forecast balance sheets at the start and end of the period. The cash flow forecast starts with the forecast net operating profit and adjustments are then made for non-cash flows such as depreciation and profit/loss on sale of fixed assets. There are then adjustments for increases/decreases in debtors, creditors and stocks which gives the net cash flow from operating activities. Finally the cash flows from capital expenditure and sales and from financing activities are included to find the net cash flow for the period.

5 Favourable variance

6 An adverse variance is subtracted from the budgeted cash balance in order to reconcile to the actual cash balance.

7 Discretionary payment – training costs
   Non-discretionary payment – corporation tax

CHAPTER 2 Preparing cash budgets

1 November receipts

	£
October sales (400,000 x 40%)	160,000
September sales (360,000 x 35%)	126,000
August sales (320,000 x 25%)	80,000
	366,000

2 October payments

	£
September purchases (260,000 x 75% x 60%)	117,000
August purchases (240,000 x 75% x 40%)	72,000
	189,000

3 October receipts

	£
October sales (150,000 x 10% x 97.5%)	14,625
September sales (100,000 x 50%)	50,000
August sales (120,000 x 40%)	48,000
	112,625

4 Cash budget – November

	£
Cash receipts:	
Cash sales	64,000
Credit sales November (238,000 x 40% x 98%)	93,296
October (216,000 x 60%)	129,600
Total cash receipts	286,896
Cash payments:	
Purchases on credit	144,000
Wages and salaries	80,000
Overheads (65,000 – 15,000)	50,000
Dividend	20,000
Total cash payments	294,000
Net cash flow	(7,104)
Opening balance	(10,200)
Closing balance	(17,304)

5 Production budget – August

	Units
Sales	45,000
Less: opening stock of finished goods	(4,000)
Add: closing stock of finished goods	6,000
Production quantity	47,000

Purchases budget – units – July (for August production)

	Kgs
For production (47,000 x 5)	235,000
Less: opening stock of raw materials	(40,000)
Add: closing stock of raw materials	30,000
Purchases	225,000

Purchases payment – August

	£
225,000 kgs x £7.50	1,687,500

6

	£
Budgeted operating profit	269,600
Adjustments for non-cash flows:	
Add: depreciation	31,500
loss of sale of fixed assets	14,200
Working capital adjustments:	
Increase in stocks	(5,400)
Increase in debtors	(6,700)
Increase in creditors	4,200
Net cash flow from operating activities	307,400

CHAPTER 3 Further aspects of cash budgeting

1

	£000	*Three month moving average* £000
January	129	
February	138	134
March	135	138
April	142	142
May	150	148
June	153	150
July	148	151
August	151	154
September	162	159
October	165	166
November	172	167
December	164	

2

		£000	Four quarter moving average £000	Centred moving average £000
2004	Q1	305		
	Q2	300		
			334.25	
	Q3	352		337.4
			340.50	
	Q4	380		343.9
			347.25	
2005	Q1	330		349.4
			351.50	
	Q2	327		352.8
			354.00	
	Q3	369		354.6
			355.25	
	Q4	390		355.8
			356.25	
2006	Q1	335		357.3
			358.25	
	Q2	331		359.5
			360.75	
	Q3	377		
	Q4	400		

3

		£000	Trend (from previous activity) £000	Seasonal variation £000
2004	Q1	305		
	Q2	300		
	Q3	352	337.4	+ 14.6
	Q4	380	343.9	+ 36.1
2005	Q1	330	349.4	− 19.4
	Q2	327	352.8	− 25.8
	Q3	369	354.6	+ 14.4
	Q4	390	355.8	+ 34.2
2006	Q1	335	357.3	− 22.3
	Q2	331	359.5	− 28.5
	Q3	377		
	Q4	400		

Average seasonal variation:

	Q1	Q2	Q3	Q4
2004			+ 14.6	+ 36.1
2005	– 19.4	– 25.8	+ 14.4	+ 34.2
2006	– 22.3	– 28.5		
	– 41.7	– 54.3	+ 29.0	+ 70.3
Average	– 20.9	– 27.2	+ 14.5	+ 35.2
Adjustment	– 0.4	– 0.4	– 0.4	– 0.4
	– 21.3	– 27.6	+ 14.1	+ 34.8

4

			£000	Trend (from earlier activity) £000	Seasonal variation %
2004	Q1		305		
	Q2		300		
	Q3		352	337.4	104.3
	Q4		380	343.9	110.5
2005	Q1		330	349.4	94.4
	Q2		327	352.8	92.7
	Q3		369	354.6	104.1
	Q4		390	355.8	109.6
2006	Q1		335	357.3	93.7
	Q2		331	359.5	92.1
	Q3		377		
	Q4		400		

Average seasonal variation:

	Q1 %	Q2 %	Q3 %	Q4 %
2004			104.3	110.5
2005	94.4	92.7	104.1	109.6
2006	93.7	92.1		
	188.1	184.8	208.4	220.1
Average	94.1	92.4	104.2	110.1
Adjustment	– 0.2	– 0.2	– 0.2	– 0.2
	93.9	92.2	104.0	109.9

5 Increase in trend

$$= 359.5 – 337.4$$
$$= 22.1$$

Average increase in trend $= \dfrac{22.1}{7}$

$$= 3.2 \text{ per quarter}$$

Additive model

2007 Q1 (359.5 + (3 x 3.2) – 21.3) = 347.8
     Q2 (359.5 + (4 x 3.2) – 27.6) = 344.7
     Q3 (359.5 + (5 x 3.2) + 14.1) = 389.6
     Q4 (359.5 + (6 x 3.2) + 34.8) = 413.5

Multiplicative model

2007 Q1 (359.5 + (3 x 3.2)) x 93.9%   = 346.6
     Q2 (359.5 + (4 x 3.2)) x 92.2%   = 343.3
     Q3 (359.5 + (5 x 3.2)) x 104.0% = 390.5
     Q4 (359.5 + (6 x 3.2)) x 109.9% = 416.2

6 October 43,000 x £95   = £4,085,000
   November 40,000 x £95 x 1.05   = £3,990,000

7 October 100,000 x 15.80 x 1.012   = £1,598,960
   November 100,000 x 15.80 x 1.012 x 1.012 = £1,618,147

8 May 200,000 x 195.9/195.3   = £200,614
   June 200,000 x 196.4/195.3   = £201,126

CHAPTER 4 Managing cash balances

1 The main advantages of financial intermediation are:

- small amounts deposited by savers can be combined to provide larger loan packages to businesses

- short term savings can be transferred into long term borrowings

- search costs are reduced as companies seeking loan finance can approach a bank directly rather than finding individuals to lend to them

- risk is reduced as an individual's savings are not tied up with one individual borrower directly

2 A customer's duties when dealing with its bank are:

- to draw up cheques carefully so that fraud is not facilitated
- to tell the bank of any forgeries known

3 The primary money market is made up of the banks, securities firms and the Bank of England. It is used by the Bank of England to smooth out fluctuations in cash balances by buying or selling Treasury bills.

4
		Days
Stock turnover 56,000/555,000 x 365		37
Debtors turnover 72,000/854,000 x 365		31
		68
Creditors turnover 48,000/555,000 x 365		(32)
Operating cycle		36

5 The main features of overdraft finance are:

- overdraft facility and actual overdraft – there is a distinction between the overdraft facility offered by the bank and the actual overdraft that the business makes use of

- interest – the interest charged on an overdraft is usually at quite a high margin over and above the bank's base rate. However interest is only charged on the amount of the actual overdraft, calculated on a daily basis, rather than on the total overdraft facility

- commitment fee – in some cases an initial fee will be charged for the granting of the overdraft facility

- repayment – technically an overdraft is repayable on demand to the bank. However in practice it would be rare for a bank to enforce this.

6 The main types of conditions that would appear in a loan agreement with a bank will concern the following:

- the term of the loan
- the interest rate
- the way in which interest is charged
- the repayment schedule
- any security required
- any covenants stipulated

7 The main difference between a finance lease and a hire purchase agreement is that under a finance lease the lessee never becomes the legal owner of the asset whereas under a hire purchase agreement the legal title to the asset passes when the final hire purchase instalment is made.

8 The general relationship between risk and return in the context of investments is that the higher the risk of the investment the higher the expected return. The lower the risk of the investment the lower the return.

9 Interest yield $= \dfrac{5.00}{99.68} \times 100$

$= 5.02\%$

10 A Certificate of Deposit (CD) is a document issued by a bank or building society which certifies that a certain sum has been deposited with it to be repaid on a specific date. CDs are negotiable instruments and can be bought or sold in an active market at any time until their maturity date.

11 A reconciliation should be made of the total of the list of receipts during the day to the actual amount of cash, cheques and credit card vouchers at the end of the day.

CHAPTER 5 Credit control

1 The ordering cycle involves the following:

- customer places an order
- customer credit status is established
- customer is offered credit
- goods are despatched
- goods are delivered
- invoice is despatched

2 "Net monthly" means that the invoice must be paid in full within a month of the invoice date.

3 A standing order is an instruction from the payer to its bank to pay a certain set amount to the payee on a regular basis. A direct debit however is a request from the payee for an amount which will vary each time a payment is due.

4 John cannot insist on purchasing the car at the lower price as the price ticket is an invitation to treat rather than an offer. John makes the offer to buy the car for £2,395 but this is rejected by the salesman.

5 Consideration is the value element of a contract. Consideration is something given, done or promised in exchange for the action of the other party.

CHAPTER 6 Granting credit

1 There are two main risks in granting credit to a customer:

- the customer will exceed the stated credit period therefore depriving the seller of the use of the cash

- the customer may never pay at all, a bad debt

2 A bank reference stating "unable to speak for your figures" is one of the worst type of bank references and would indicate that the customer is a high risk customer and credit would probably not be granted.

3 Return on capital employed $= \dfrac{76,000}{488,000} \times 100$

$= 15.6\%$

4 Stock turnover $= \dfrac{77,000}{686,000} \times 365$

$= 41$ days

Debtors turnover $= \dfrac{130,000}{980,000} \times 365$

$= 48$ days

Creditors turnover $= \dfrac{89{,}000}{686{,}000} \times 365$

$= 47$ days

5   Reasons for not agreeing to trade on credit with a customer might include the following:

- a non-committal or poor bank reference
- poor trade references
- concerns about the validity of any trade references submitted
- adverse press comment about the potential customer
- poor credit agency report
- indications of business weakness from analysis of the financial statements
- lack of historical financial statements due to being a recently started company

6   Cost of discount $= \dfrac{1}{100-1} \times \dfrac{365}{30-10} \times 100$

$= 18.4\%$

CHAPTER 7   Management of debtors

1   The credit limit that is set for a credit customer will have been set by the credit controller as part of his assessment of the risk of the customer. Therefore if this credit limit is exceeded it is potentially increasing the risk that the business faces from these sales on credit.

2   If an invoice is not promptly recorded in the customer's sales ledger account then this may mean that the next time that the customer places an order the balance on his account is too low. When the credit limit is checked to ensure that it is not exceeded by the new order value therefore the sale might be authorised even though in actual fact the new order might take the customer over their credit limit.

3   As the debtor has current amounts due but no 30 to 61 day amounts due it could be assumed that he was a regular payer and therefore that the £104 due from 61 to 90 days was an amount that was being queried. The best course of action would be to check the customer's correspondence file to determine whether this amount was being queried and also to check that the amount was in fact due from this customer and that there were no errors in posting to the customer's account. Then a telephone call would be made to the customer to enquire why this overdue amount has not been paid.

4

	£
Total debtors	1,350,000
August sales	(900,000)
July sales not yet paid	450,000

	Days
Average period of credit	
August	31
July $\dfrac{450{,}000}{800{,}000} \times 31$	17
	48

237

5   A bad debt is one where it is almost certain that the money is not going to be received whereas a doubtful debt is one where there is some doubt over whether the money will be received but no certainty. The importance of the distinction between a bad and a doubtful debt is in their respective accounting treatments. A bad debt is written off from the financial statements whereas a provision is set up for a doubtful debt.

6   When making a telephone call to discuss an overdue debt with a customer the following factors are of particular importance:

■   discussion with the customer should always be courteous

■   the precise amount of the debt should be pointed out and the fact that it is overdue

■   it should be established whether there is any query with regard to the debt and if so any appropriate action should be agreed to resolve the query

■   if there is no query then a date for payment of the debt should be established

CHAPTER 8   Collection of debts

1   The three main services provided by a factor are:

■   provision of finance
■   administration of the sales ledger
■   insurance against bad debts

2   Some customers may view the use of a factor by a business as a sign that the business is in financial or cash flow difficulty and therefore may re-consider whether to carry on trading with them.

3   Invoice discounting is simply the provision of finance to a business by the purchase of its invoices at a discount. There is no involvement with the business's sales ledger. However under a factoring agreement the factor will normally run the sales ledger and collect the debts as well as providing finance in the form of an advance based upon a percentage of the face value of the debtors.

4   The three essential elements for there to be a valid contract are:

■   valid agreement
■   consideration
■   intention to create legal relations

5   The County Court.

6   Bankruptcy is where an individual is unable to pay their debts whereas insolvency is where a company is unable to pay its debts.

7   The role of an insolvency practitioner under an administration order is to try to save the company or at the very least to achieve a better result for the creditors than a liquidation.

HOW MUCH HAVE YOU LEARNED? – ANSWERS

CHAPTER 1 Monitoring cash receipts and payments

1 Although it is important that a business makes a profit in the long run, it can be argued that it is also crucial that a business also has a healthy cash balance. If a business cannot meet its payments when they fall due then it may not be able to continue in existence even if it is profitable.

2 Differences between profit and cash:

Accruals concept –	in the calculation of profit, income and expenses are included in the period in which they are earned or incurred rather than the period in which the cash is received or paid
Non-cash expenses –	depreciation and increases in provisions are charges to profit but there is no cash flow related to the expense
Capital receipts/payments –	receipts such as issues of share capital or additional capital from a sole trader have no effect on profit. Dividend or drawings payments affect cash but not the profit of the business.
Capital expenditure –	purchases of fixed assets are a large drain on cash balances but profit is only reduced by the annual depreciation charge
Sale of fixed assets –	when a fixed asset is sold the full amount of the proceeds is added to the cash balance but only the profit or loss on the sale is included in the calculation of profit

3 i) Cash receipts from credit customers
Cash sales
Payments to credit suppliers
Wages payments
Payments for expenses

ii) Receipt of government grant
Payment of legal claim

4

		£
Net operating profit		X
Adjustments for:		
i) depreciation		X
ii) profit on sale of fixed asset		(X)
iii) increase in stocks		(X)
iv) increase in debtors		(X)
v) increase in creditors		X
Net cash flow from operating activities		X

5 i) Credit sales receipts   £25,000 adverse
   Credit suppliers   £13,000 adverse
   Capital expenditure   £40,000 adverse

  ii) Improve credit collection to speed up receipt of money from debtors
   Lengthen the period of credit taken from suppliers
   Postpone the purchase of fixed assets

6 Reconciliation of budgeted cash balance to actual cash balance

	£
Budgeted cash balance at 31 May	45,200
Additional cash sales receipts (45,000 – 43,000)	2,000
Shortfall in credit sales receipts (256,000 – 231,000)	(25,000)
Additional payments to credit suppliers (189,000 – 176,000)	(13,000)
Additional overheads (44,500 – 43,200)	(1,300)
Capital expenditure	(40,000)
Lower opening cash balance (53,400 – 52,100)	(1,300)
Actual cash balance	(33,400)

7 Possible actions for improving cash position

- improve credit collection and speed up receipts from credit customers
- sell fixed asset earlier or arrange for cash to be received earlier
- increase credit period taken from suppliers by paying later
- delay capital expenditure in April and May
- finance capital expenditure differently eg lease or HP finance
- delay training courses
- negotiate credit terms for repairs and maintenance costs

CHAPTER 2 Preparing cash budgets

1 Forecast cash receipts

	January £	February £	March £
Cash sales (10% of sales figure)	70,000	73,000	76,000
Credit sales 40% x 720,000	288,000		
40% x 700,000		280,000	
40% x 730,000			292,000
45% x 750,000	337,500		
45% x 720,000		324,000	
45% x 700,000			315,000
	695,500	677,000	683,000

2 Forecast cash payments

Purchases

	October £	November £	December £	January £	February £
75% of sales	592,500	562,500	540,000	525,000	547,500

Cash payments

	January £	February £	March £
October purchases			
592,500 x 15%	88,875		
November purchases			
562,500 x 65%	365,625		
562,500 x 15%		84,375	
December purchases			
540,000 x 20% x 98%	105,840		
540,000 x 65%		351,000	
540,000 x 15%			81,000
January purchases			
525,000 x 20% x 98%		102,900	
525,000 x 65%			341,250
February purchases			
547,500 x 20% x 98%			107,310
	560,340	538,275	529,560

3 Cash budget for the quarter ending 31 December

	October £	November £	December £
Cash receipts:			
Sales proceeds from equipment		4,000	
Sales (W1)	331,200	373,500	411,200
Total receipts	331,200	377,500	411,200
Cash payments:			
Purchases (W2)	206,000	226,000	249,000
Wages	42,000	42,000	42,000
General overheads (W3)	25,000	29,800	31,000
Selling expenses (W4)	18,000	20,000	22,500
New equipment		40,000	
Overdraft interest	500	103	–
Total payments	291,500	357,903	344,500
Net cash flow for the month	39,700	19,597	66,700
Opening balance	(50,000)	(10,300)	9,297
Closing balance	(10,300)	9,297	75,997

WORKINGS

Working 1 – sales receipts

		October £	November £	December £
July sales –	340,000 x 8%	27,200		
August sales –	300,000 x 40%	120,000		
	300,000 x 8%		24,000	
September sales –	360,000 x 30%	108,000		
	360,000 x 40%		144,000	
	360,000 x 8%			28,800
October sales –	400,000 x 20% x 95%	76,000		
	400,000 x 30%		120,000	
	400,000 x 40%			160,000
November sales –	450,000 x 20% x 95%		85,500	
	450,000 x 30%			135,000
December sales –	460,000 x 20% x 95%			87,400
		331,200	373,500	411,200

Working 2 – purchases payments

		October £	November £	December £
August purchases –	200,000 x 70%	140,000		
September purchases –	220,000 x 30%	66,000		
	220,000 x 70%		154,000	
October purchases –	240,000 x 30%		72,000	
	240,000 x 70%			168,000
November purchases –	270,000 x 30%			81,000
		206,000	226,000	249,000

Working 3 – gencral overheads

	October £	November £	December £
September overheads			
(30,000 – 5,000) x 20%	5,000		
October overheads			
(30,000 – 5,000) x 80%	20,000		
(30,000 – 5,000) x 20%		5,000	
November overheads			
(36,000 – 5,000) x 80%		24,800	
(36,000 – 5,000) x 20%			6,200
December overheads			
(36,000 – 5,000) x 80%			24,800
	25,000	29,800	31,000

Working 4 – selling expenses

	October £	November £	December £
September sales – 360,000 x 5%	18,000		
October sales – 400,000 x 5%		20,000	
November sales – 450,000 x 5%			22,500

4 Cash flow forecast for the quarter ending 31 December

	October £	November £	December £
Cash receipts:			
Sales (W1)	427,200	417,600	429,600
Cash payments:			
Purchases (W2)	168,960	169,440	177,360
Wages (W3)	100,500	109,500	111,000
Production overheads (W4)	65,280	71,520	70,080
General overheads	52,000	52,000	58,000
Total payments	386,740	402,460	416,440
Net cash flow for the month	40,460	15,140	13,160
Opening balance	20,000	60,460	75,600
Closing balance	60,460	75,600	88,760

WORKINGS

Working 1 – sales receipts

	October £	November £	December £
August sales 7,000 x £60 x 40%	168,000		
September sales 7,200 x £60 x 60%	259,200		
7,200 x £60 x 40%		172,800	
October sales 6,800 x £60 x 60%		244,800	
6,800 x £60 x 40%			163,200
November sales 7,400 x £60 x 60%			266,400
	427,200	417,600	429,600

Working 2 – purchases payments

Production budget – units

	September Units	October Units	November Units	December Units
Sales	7,200	6,800	7,400	7,500
Less: opening stock	(800)	(800)	(700)	(600)
Add: closing stock	800	700	600	500
	7,200	6,700	7,300	7,400

Purchases budget – kgs

	September kgs	October kgs	November kgs	December kgs
Required for production				
(7,200 x 4kg)	28,800			
(6,700 x 4kg)		26,800		
(7,300 x 4kg)			29,200	
(7,400 x 4kg)				29,600
Less: opening stock	(7,000)	(7,000)	(7,400)	(8,000)
Add: closing stock	7,000	7,400	8,000	7,600
	28,800	27,200	29,800	29,200

Purchases – £

	September £	October £	November £	December £
28,800 x £6	172,800			
27,200 x £6		163,200		
29,800 x £6			178,800	
29,200 x £6				175,200

Payments – £

	October £	November £	December £
September purchases			
172,800 x 60%	103,680		
October purchases			
163,200 x 40%	65,280		
163,200 x 60%		97,920	
November purchases			
178,800 x 40%		71,520	
178,800 x 60%			107,280
December purchases			
175,200 x 40%			70,080
	168,960	169,440	177,360

Working 3 – wages payments

Production budget – units

	September Units	October Units	November Units	December Units
Sales	7,200	6,800	7,400	7,500
Less: opening stock	(800)	(800)	(700)	(600)
Add: closing stock	800	700	600	500
	7,200	6,700	7,300	7,400

Wages payments

	October £	November £	December £
6,700 x 2 hours x £7.50	100,500		
7,300 x 2 hours x £7.50		109,500	
7,400 x 2 hours x £7.50			111,000

Working 4 – production overheads

	October £	November £	December £
27,200 x £6	163,200		
29,800 x £6		178,800	
29,200 x £6			175,200
Production overhead – 40% of materials purchases	65,280	71,520	70,080

5   Cash flow forecast for the quarter ending 31 December

	£000
Operating profit	122
Adjustments for non-cash flows:	
Depreciation	64
Adjustments for working capital:	
Increase in stock	(3)
Increase in debtors	(15)
Increase in creditors	29
Net cash flow from operating activities	197
Non-operating cash flows	
Interest paid	(12)
Taxation paid	(40)
Dividend paid	(22)
Payments to acquire fixed assets (W1)	(398)
Long term loan	100
Issue of share capital (W2)	150
Decrease in cash	(25)

WORKINGS

Working 1 – payments to acquire fixed assets

Fixed assets at NBV			
	£000		£000
Opening balance	488	Depreciation	64
Additions (bal fig)	398	Closing balance	822
	886		886

Working 2 – issue of share capital

	£000
Increase in share capital (500 – 400)	100
Increase in share premium	50
Cash received	150

CHAPTER 3 Further aspects of cash budgeting

1

		Takings £	5 day moving average £
Week 1	Tues	560	
	Wed	600	
	Thurs	630	720
	Fri	880	716
	Sat	930	714
Week 2	Tues	540	716
	Wed	590	710
	Thurs	640	712
	Fri	850	714
	Sat	940	708
Week 3	Tues	550	700
	Wed	560	704
	Thurs	600	710
	Fri	870	
	Sat	970	

2 i)

		Costs £	4 quarter moving average £	Centred moving average £
2004	Q1	265,400		
	Q2	259,800		
			247,800	
	Q3	230,400		246,963
			246,125	
	Q4	235,600		245,438
			244,750	
2005	Q1	258,700		244,488
			244,225	
	Q2	254,300		243,575
			242,925	
	Q3	228,300		242,538
			242,150	
	Q4	230,400		241,763
			241,375	
2006	Q1	255,600		241,000
			240,625	
	Q2	251,200		240,275
			239,925	
	Q3	225,300		
	Q4	227,600		

As the trend line is decreasing this indicates that factory costs are generally getting lower over the three year period.

ii)

		Costs £	Centred moving average (trend) £	Seasonal variation £
2004	Q1	265,400		
	Q2	259,800		
	Q3	230,400	246,963	− 16,563
	Q4	235,600	245,438	− 9,838
2005	Q1	258,700	244,488	+ 14,212
	Q2	254,300	243,575	+ 10,725
	Q3	228,300	242,538	− 14,238
	Q4	230,400	241,763	− 11,363
2006	Q1	255,600	241,000	+ 14,600
	Q2	251,200	240,275	+ 10,925
	Q3	225,300		
	Q4	227,600		

Average seasonal variation

	Q1 £	Q2 £	Q3 £	Q4 £
2004			− 16,563	− 9,838
2005	+ 14,212	+ 10,725	− 14,238	− 11,363
2006	+ 14,600	+ 10,925		
	+ 28,812	+ 21,650	− 30,801	− 21,201
Average	+ 14,406	+ 10,825	− 15,400	− 10,600
Adjustment	+ 193	+ 192	+ 192	+ 192
	+ 14,599	+ 11,017	− 15,208	− 10,408

iii) The trend has decreased from £246,963 to £240,275 over a period of 7 quarter decreases. Therefore an average quarterly decrease of:

$$\frac{£246,963 - 240,275}{7} = £955$$

2007	Q1	£240,275 − (3 x 955) + 14,599 =	£252,009
	Q2	£240,275 − (4 x 955) + 11,017 =	£247,472
	Q3	£240,275 − (5 x 955) − 15,208 =	£220,292
	Q4	£240,275 − (6 x 955) − 10,408 =	£224,137

3 i), ii)

		5 day moving Production Units	Seasonal average (trend) Units	variation %
Week 1	Mon	1,400		
	Tues	1,600		
	Wed	1,800	1,630	110.4
	Thurs	1,800	1,626	110.7
	Fri	1,550	1,630	95.1
Week 2	Mon	1,380	1,636	84.4
	Tues	1,620	1,638	98.9
	Wed	1,830	1,628	112.4
	Thurs	1,810	1,642	110.2
	Fri	1,500	1,648	91.0
Week 3	Mon	1,450	1,652	87.8
	Tues	1,650	1,658	99.5
	Wed	1,850	1,672	110.6
	Thurs	1,840		
	Fri	1,570		

Average seasonal variation

	Mon %	Tues %	Wed %	Thurs %	Fri %
Week 1			110.4	110.7	95.1
Week 2	84.4	98.9	112.4	110.2	91.0
Week 3	87.8	99.5	110.6		
	172.2	198.4	333.4	220.9	186.1
Average	86.1	99.2	111.1	110.5	93.1
Adjustment	–	–	–	–	–
	86.1	99.2	111.1	110.5	93.1

iii) Increase in trend 1,672 – 1,630 = 42
Number of increases = 10
Average increase = 4 units per day

Week 4	Mon	$(1,672 + (3 \times 4)) \times 86.1\%$	=	1,450 units
	Tues	$(1,672 + (4 \times 4)) \times 99.2\%$	=	1,675 units
	Wed	$(1,672 + (5 \times 4)) \times 111.1\%$	=	1,880 units
	Thurs	$(1,672 + (6 \times 4)) \times 110.5\%$	=	1,874 units
	Fri	$(1,672 + (7 \times 4)) \times 93.1\%$	=	1,583 units

4 The problems of using time series analysis for cash budgeting purposes include the following:

- only with a large amount of historic data available will the results be reliable. The further into the future the forecast the less reliable will be the results

- there is an assumption that the trend and seasonal variations from the past will continue into the future

- cyclical and random variations are ignored.

5

	January £	February £	March £
Cash receipts:			
Sales:			
December sales (4,800 x £35)	168,000		
January sales (5,000 x £35 x 1.08)		189,000	
February sales (5,600 x £35 x 1.08)			211,680
	168,000	189,000	211,680
Cash payments:			
Purchases			
January purchases (5,200 x £20)	104,000		
February purchases (5,800 x £20 x 1.05)		121,800	
March purchases (5,500 x £20 x 1.05)			115,500
	104,000	121,800	115,500

6   December cash payment is November overheads.
November overheads:
$$£160,000 \times 1.075 = £162,800$$
$$£162,800 \times 1.075 = £165,649$$

7
October	£10.80 x 151.6/148.5	=	£11.03
November	£10.80 x 154.2/148.5	=	£11.21
December	£10.80 x 158.7/148.5	=	£11.54

8 i) No discounts taken

	October £	November £	December £
August purchases (330,000 x 30%)	99,000		
September purchases (380,000 x 70%)	266,000		
(380,000 x 30%)		114,000	
October purchases (400,000 x 70%)		280,000	
(400,000 x 30%)			120,000
November purchases (440,000 x 70%)			308,000
Total payment	365,000	394,000	428,000

ii) **Discounts taken**

	October £	November £	December £
August purchases			
(330,000 x 30%)	99,000		
September purchases			
(380,000 x 70%)	266,000		
(380,000 x 30%)		114,000	
October purchases			
(400,000 x 40% x 97%)	155,200		
(400,000 x 40%)		160,000	
(400,000 x 20%)			80,000
November purchases			
(440,000 x 40% x 97%)		170,720	
(440,000 x 40%)			176,000
December purchases			
(390,000 x 40% x 97%)			151,320
Total payment	520,200	444,720	407,320

9 Step 1 Set up the basic spreadsheet

	A	B	C	D
		Jan	Feb	Mar
		£000	£000	£000
1	Sales	489.6		
2	**Cash receipts**			
3	Cash sales	48.96		
4	One month after sale	216.0		
5	Two months after sale	211.77	216.0	
6	Total receipts	476.73		
7	**Cash payments**			
8	Purchases	342.72		
9	Overheads	80.64		
10	Fixed assets			
11	Tax			
12	Dividends			40.0
13	Total payments	423.36		
14	Net cash flow	53.37		
15	Opening balance	45.0		
16	Closing balance	98.37		
17				
18	Sales growth rate	1.02		
19	Overheads growth rate	1.008		
20	Cost of sales	0.7		
21	Cash sales	0.1		
22	Debtors within one month	0.45		
23	Debtors within two months	0.45		

Step 2 Calculate the formulae for each figure:

February sales		= +B1 * B18
March sales		=+C1 * B18
Cash sales	January	=+B1 * B21
	February	=+C1 * B21
	March	=+D1 * B21

Receipts one month after sale
February	=+B1 * B22
March	=+C1 * B22

Receipts two months after sale
March	=+B1 * B23

Total receipts
January	=+B3 + B4 + B5
February	=+C3 + C4 + C5
March	=+D3 + D4 + D5

Purchases
January	=+B1 * B20
February	=+C1 * B20
March	=+D1 * B20

Overheads
February	=+B9 * B19
March	=+C9 * B19

Total payments
January	=+B8 + B9 + B10 + B11 + B12
February	=+C8 + C9 + C10 + C11 + C12
March	=+D8 + D9 + D10 + D11 + D12

Net monthly cash flow
January	=+B6 – B13
February	=+C6 – C13
March	=+D6 – D13

Opening cash balance
February	=+B16
March	=+C16

Closing cash balance
January	=+B14 + B15
February	=+C14 + C15
March	=+D14 + D15

Step 3 Enter the formulae in the correct cells in the spreadsheet

	A	B	C	D
		Jan	Feb	Mar
		£000	£000	£000
1	Sales	489.6	=+B1*B18	=+C1*B18
2	**Cash receipts**			
3	Cash sales	=+B1*B21	=+C1*B21	=+D1*B21
4	One month after sale	216.0	=+B1*B22	=+C1*B22
5	Two months after sale	211.77	216.0	=+B1*B23
6	Total receipts	=+B3+B4+B5	=+C3+C4+C5	=+D3+D4+D5
7	**Cash payments**			
8	Purchases	=+B1*B20	=+C1*B20	=+D1*B20
9	Overheads	80.64	=+B9*B19	=+C9*B19
10	Fixed assets			
11	Tax			
12	Dividends			40.0
13	Total payments	=+B8+B9+B10 +B11+B12	=+C8+C9+C10 +C11+C12	=+D8+D9+D10 +D11+D12
14	Net cash flow	=+B6-B13	+C6-C13	=+D6-D13
15	Opening balance	45.0	+B16	=+C16
16	Closing balance	=+B14+B15	=+C14+C15	=+D14+D15
17				
18	Sales growth rate	1.02		
19	Overheads growth rate	1.008		
20	Cost of sales	0.7		
21	Cash sales	0.1		
22	Debtors within one month	0.45		
23	Debtors within two months	0.45		

CHAPTER 4 Managing cash balances

1 Debtor/creditor relationship

When the customer deposits his money with the bank then the bank becomes the debtor and the customer is of course a creditor of the bank. If the customer's account is overdrawn however the bank becomes the creditor and the customer the debtor.

This relationship is a contract between the bank and the customer and there are a number of essential areas in this contract:

- the bank borrows the customer's deposits and undertakes to repay them
- the bank must receive cheques for the customer's account
- the bank will only cease to do business with the customer with reasonable notice
- the bank is not liable to pay until the customer demands payment
- the customer exercises reasonable care when writing cheques

Bailor/bailee relationship

This element of the relationship concerns the bank accepting the customer's property for storage in its safe deposit. The bank will undertake to take reasonable care to safeguard the property against loss or damage and also to re-deliver it only to the customer or someone authorised by the customer.

Principal/agent relationship

An agent is someone who acts on behalf of another party, the principal. Within banking the principal/agent relationship exists where for example the customer pays a crossed cheque into the bank. The bank then acts as an agent when presenting the cheque for payment and paying the proceeds into the customer's account.

Mortgagor/mortgagee relationship

If the bank asks the customer to secure a loan with a charge over its assets then the relationship between the two is that of mortgagor and mortgagee. If the customer does not repay the loan then the bank has the right to sell the asset and use the proceeds to pay off the loan.

2 The main duties of a bank in relation to its customers are as follows:

- the bank must honour the customer's cheques provided that they are correctly made out, there is no legal reason for not honouring it and the customer has enough funds or overdraft limit to cover the amount of the cheque

- the bank must credit cash/cheques that are paid in to the customer's account

- if the customer makes a written request for repayment of funds in its account, for example by writing a cheque, the bank must repay the amount on demand

- the bank must comply with the customer's instructions given by direct debit mandate or standing order

- the bank must provide a statement showing the transactions on the account within a reasonable period and provide details of the balance on the customer's account

- the bank must respect the confidentiality of the customer's affairs unless the bank is required by law, public duty or its own interest to disclose details or where the customer gives his consent for such disclosure

3 LIBOR stands for the London Inter-bank Offered Rate which is the interest rate prevailing in the inter-bank market.

4

	Days
Stock turnover 68,000/593,000 x 365	42
Debtors turnover 102,000/790,000 x 365	47
	89
Creditors turnover 57,000/593,000 x 365	(35)
Operating cycle	54

5 Once an overdraft facility has been agreed with the bank then it is at the company's own discretion as to how much use to make of that facility and the interest charged is only on the actual amount of the overdraft. In contrast if a loan is negotiated with the bank then the full amount of the loan will be received and interest will be charged on the full outstanding amount.

The term of a loan will have been agreed in advance with the bank and therefore can be guaranteed for the time scale required by the business whereas an overdraft is technically repayable on demand. As a loan is for a fixed amount of time, if the finance is not needed for as long as was initially thought the business still has to pay for the loan (or incur a penalty charge for early repayment) whereas with an overdraft the facility would simply not be used.

A bank loan will often require security, sometimes required for an overdraft, and also may have covenants attached to it which restrict the freedom of action of the managers of the business.

6 A medium-term loan from a bank would probably be the most appropriate source of finance for the purchase of the shares in B Ltd. Provided that the intention is to keep the shares for some time and to therefore benefit from income from those shares in that period then the loan would match the time scale of the investment in the company and the income could be used to service the loan.

7 The three main repayment patterns of repaying a loan are:

Bullet repayments – the full amount of the loan remains outstanding for the entire term of the loan and the full amount is then repaid at the end of this period. Interest is therefore charged on the full loan amount throughout the loan term.

Balloon repayments – under this method some of the loan principal is repaid during the term of the loan but the majority is repaid at the end of the loan period. Interest will be charged on the loan amount outstanding at any point in time.

Amortising repayments – in this case the loan principal is gradually repaid over the term of the loan until there is no principal outstanding at the end of the loan period. Each regular repayment will therefore consist of some loan principal and interest on the amount still outstanding.

8 Security for a loan takes the form of the bank having a charge over assets of the business taking out the loan. This means that if the business defaults on the loan the bank can sell the asset over which it has a charge in order to pay off the outstanding amount of the loan.

A fixed charge is where the security is a specific asset or group of assets which the business cannot sell during the loan term without the bank's permission.

A floating charge is where the security is on a certain group of assets such as debtors or stock which by their nature will be constantly changing. The business is allowed to buy and sell these assets and the bank has a right to be repaid out of the assets the business has at the time of default.

9 The three factors to be considered when deciding upon an appropriate form of investment are risk, return and liquidity.

Risk is the chance that the investment will fall in value and the business will make a loss. The return on the investment is both any income in the form of dividend or interest or in the form of capital gain. Liquidity is the ease and speed with which the investment can be converted into cash.

10 The interest yield shows the income return on the gilt if it were purchased today and held for a year. However the redemption yield gives an overall return on the gilt if it were held to maturity.

11 If interest rates rise then the price of gilts will be expected to fall in order to maintain an adequate return on the investment.

12 A bill of exchange is an unconditional order in writing from one person to another requiring the person to whom it is addressed to pay a specified sum of money either on demand or at some future date.

If the bill is payable on demand this is known as a sight bill. If the bill is payable at some specified future date this is known as a term bill.

13 Public Sector Borrowing Requirement

14 The following procedures should be put into place in a business that has substantial cash and cheque receipts from customers:

Physical safeguards

Any cash or cheques received must be kept safe at all times and must only be accessible to authorised individuals within the organisation. Therefore cash should be kept under lock and key either in a cash box, lockable till or safe. Only authorised individuals should have access to the keys.

Checking for valid payment

Payments received in cash will of course be valid provided that any notes are not forged. However if cheques are accepted as payment then they must be supported by a valid cheque guarantee card and be correctly drawn up, dated and signed. If debit or credit cards are accepted then basic checks should be made on the card and signature and authorisation must be sought for payments which exceed the floor limit.

Reconciliation of cash received

When payments are received in the form of cash, cheques or debit and credit cards then a list of all cash, cheque and card receipts taken during the day must be kept. This list must then be reconciled at the end of each day to the amount of cash in the till, cash box or safe. The list may be manual as each sale is made or may be automatically recorded on the till roll as each sale is rung in.

This reconciliation should not be carried out by the person responsible for making the sales but by some other responsible official. Any discrepancies between the amount of cash recorded as taken during the day and the amount physically left at the end of the day must be investigated.

Banking procedures

Any cash, cheques and card vouchers should be banked as soon as possible and intact each day. This not only ensures the physical safety of the cash but also that it cannot be used by employees for unauthorised purposes. It also means that once the money is in the bank it is earning the business the maximum amount of interest. All cash should be banked as soon as possible but if it is not possible to bank it until the following day then either the cash must be left in a locked safe overnight or in the bank's overnight safe.

Recording procedures

For security purposes the paying-in slip for the bank should be made out by someone other than the person paying the money into the bank. The total on the paying in slip should also be reconciled to the till records or cash list for the day.

CHAPTER 5 Credit control

1   The two main costs of making sales on credit are:

- lost interest – as the receipt of money is delayed the money is not earning interest in a bank account nor reducing interest on any overdraft balance

- bad debts – the receipt from the debtor is not certain therefore there is always a risk that the amount due will never be received.

2   The main elements of the collection cycle are:

- customer receives invoice
- statement is sent to customer
- telephone reminders to customer
- reminder letters sent to customer
- cash eventually received

3   Net 14 days   3% discount for payment within 7 days

4   An account payee only crossing means that the cheque can only be paid into the bank account of the payee named on the cheque.

5   A BACS payment is a form of electronic payment method where the bank pays regular, bulk amounts directly into other bank accounts.

6   The three main elements of a contract are agreement, value and intention to create legal relations.

7   Alan cannot insist on purchasing the car for £3,000 as the advertisement is an invitation to treat not an offer. When Alan answers the advertisement he is making an offer to purchase the car for £3,000 which can be accepted or rejected by the seller.

8   The business does not have to supply the goods at £15,000 as the additional term of delivery the next day is a counter-offer which rejects the original offer.

9   i)   Express terms are terms which are specifically stated in the contract and are binding on both parties.

   ii)   Conditions are terms that are fundamental to the contract and if they are broken there is a breach of contract. The injured party can sue for breach of contract and consider the contract terminated.

   iii) Warranties are less important terms in a contract. If they are not fulfilled there is a breach of contract. The injured party can still claim damages for any loss suffered but may not consider the contract to be terminated.

10 The Data Protection Act applies to both paper based systems and computer systems and protects personal information. Personal information is information held about living individuals.

11 The eight principles of good information of the Data Protection Act are that personal information must be:

- fairly and lawfully processed
- processed for limited purposes
- adequate, relevant and not excessive
- accurate and up to date
- not kept for longer than necessary
- processed in line with the data subject's rights
- kept securely
- not transferred to countries outside the EU unless such data is adequately protected in those countries.

CHAPTER 6 Granting credit

1 The process to be followed after an application for credit from a new potential customer would be as follows:

- analysis of external information ie, bank reference, trade references, credit agency report
- analysis of internal information such as ratio analysis of recent financial statements
- make a decision regarding credit status
- communicate the decision to the customer

2 This is not the very highest quality reference that could be received from a bank but it is fairly positive and in the absence of any other negative information should make the credit controller reasonably confident about extending credit to Kelvin & Sons.

3 The information provided in the trade reference looks fairly positive in that SK Traders offer monthly payment terms which are only occasionally overrun. However the amount of credit they offer is only £8,000 whereas Caterham Ltd have applied to you for credit of £15,000.

In conjunction with perhaps another trade reference and other internal and external information about Caterham Ltd this trade reference may give you some confidence in the company.

4 Credit reference agencies can provide a variety of information about companies and individuals which can include the following:

- historic financial statements
- directors details
- payment history
- details of any insolvency proceedings or bankruptcy orders
- bankers' opinions
- credit rating

5 Companies House can provide copies of the information that must be filed there annually by companies such as their annual financial statements.

6

MEMO

To:
From:
Date:
Subject: **Franklin Ltd request for credit**

The financial statements for Franklin Ltd have been analysed for the purpose of aiding in the decision as to whether or not to extend credit to the company. The following three ratios are key to this analysis:

	2006	2005
Gross profit margin	22.0%	21.3%
Interest cover	4 times	5.5 times
Creditors turnover period	75 days	79 days

Gross profit margin

The gross profit margin has increased slightly over the two years which bodes well for the overall profitability of the business if such increases continue.

Interest cover

Interest cover has reduced as the overdraft interest has increased but it is still fairly safe at 4 times interest payable.

Creditors turnover

Although the turnover period has reduced from 79 days to 75 days this is still a very long period of credit particularly considering that most credit periods are 30 to 60 days.

Note only three ratios were required but others that could have been usefully used are:

	2006	2005
Net profit margin	12.0%	11.7%
Return on capital employed	10.7%	10.2%
Current ratio	0.5 to 1	0.7 to 1
Quick ratio	0.3 to 1	0.4 to 1

7

ACORN ENTERPRISES

Finance Partner
Little Partners

Date

Dear Sir

Re: Request for credit facilities

Thank you for your enquiry regarding the provision of credit facilities to yourselves for £8,000 of credit on 60 day terms. We have taken up your bank and trade references and examined your latest set of financial statements.

Although your references are satisfactory we have some concerns about your profitability and liquidity. Clearly your overall profitability and liquidity position have improved since 2004 but their levels are still lower than we would normally accept in order to grant a credit facility.

However due to your bank and trade references we would be happy to offer you a credit facility for 6 months at the end of which period the movement on your account would be reviewed and the position re-assessed. The credit limit that we could offer you would initially be £3,000 and the payment terms would be strictly 30 days from the invoice date.

Thank you for your interest in our company and we look forward to trading with you on the basis set out above.

Yours faithfully

Jo Wilkie
Credit manager

8

ACORN ENTERPRISES

Finance Director
Dawn Ltd

Date

Dear Sir

Re: Request for credit facilities

Thank you for your enquiry regarding the provision of credit facilities to yourselves for £5,000 of credit on 30 day terms. We have taken up your trade references and examined your latest set of financial statements.

We are unfortunately concerned about your levels of profitability, gearing and liquidity in the most recent year and also have some concerns about one of the trade references from Johannesson Partners.

On balance we are not in a position to grant your request of trade credit at the current time although we would of course be delighted to trade with you on a cash basis. If you do not wish to trade on this basis and would like to enquire about credit terms in the future then we would be delighted to examine your current year's financial statements when they are available.

Thank you for your interest shown in our business.

Yours faithfully
Credit controller

---

9 Cost of discount $= \dfrac{2}{100-2} \times \dfrac{365}{45-10} \times 100$

$= 21.3\%$

CHAPTER 7 Management of debtors

1 If customer accounts in the sales ledger are not kept accurately up to date then a number of errors could be made when dealing with customers:

- orders may be taken which take the customer over their credit limit
- incorrect information might be given to a customer who enquires about their balance
- the monthly statement sent to the customer may be incorrect
- problem items may not be highlighted by the aged debtor listing.

2

	Total Total £	Credit limit £	Current <30 days £	31–60 days £	61–90 days £	> 90 days £
Fording Ltd	17,685	20,000	6,877	8,624	2,184	

3 The problems with debtors accounts which may be highlighted by an aged debtors listing include:

- credit limits exceeded
- slow payers
- amounts in dispute
- potential bad or doubtful debts

4 Kerry & Co – the vast majority of this customer's debt is current with a relatively small amount outstanding in 61 to 90 days. This might indicate that there was some dispute or error about this outstanding amount which should be investigated.

Marshall Ltd – this customer has exceeded their credit limit which should be investigated. However the balance is all current and if this is a valued and reliable customer it may be considered necessary to increase their credit limit to facilitate higher levels of trading.

Leyton Ltd – this customer would appear to be a persistently late payer with approximately one third of their total debt spread over each month for the last three months. The credit controller will need to re-affirm the credit terms of 30 days with the customer and possibly offer some incentive for earlier payment such as a settlement discount.

5 Debtors turnover

$$= \frac{436{,}790}{2{,}530{,}000} \times 365$$

$$= \quad 63 \text{ days}$$

Count back method

	£
Debtors	436,790
July sales	(210,000)
	226,790
June sales	(206,000)
May sales not yet received	20,790

Average period of credit	Days
July	31
June	30
May $\dfrac{20{,}790}{215{,}700} \times 31$	3
	64

Partial month method

	Sales £	Unpaid amount £	Days	b/a x c
	(a)	(b)	(c)	
May	215,700	68,790	31	9.9
June	206,000	164,800	30	24.0
July	210,000	203,200	31	30.0
				63.9

6 Information that might be available to the credit control team which might indicate a bad or doubtful debt includes:

- evidence of long outstanding debts from the aged debt analysis
- a one off outstanding debt when more recent debts have been cleared
- correspondence with debtors
- outstanding older debts and no current business with the customer
- a sudden or unexpected change in payment patterns
- request for an extension of credit terms
- press comment
- information from the sales team

7 **Travis Ltd**
This amount is 14 days overdue and therefore a reminder letter must be sent to the customer.

Purchase ledger manager
Travis Ltd

30 June

Dear Sir

I do not appear to have received payment of the invoice detailed below. I trust that this is an oversight and that you will arrange for immediate payment to be made. If you are withholding payment for any reason, please contact me urgently and I will be pleased to assist you.

Invoice No	Terms	Due date	Amount £
467824	30 days	15 June	4,678.00

If you have already made payment please advise me and accept my apology for having troubled you.

Yours faithfully

Credit Controller

Muse Ltd
The invoice number 467831 for £888 is 7 days overdue and therefore a telephone call is necessary to the purchase ledger manager explaining that the amount is overdue, determining whether there is any query with the amount and agreeing a date for payment of the overdue amount.

Keane Ltd
Invoice number 467781 for £1,103 is more than 30 days overdue and therefore Keane Ltd will be put on the stop list and no more sales on credit will be made to the company until the overdue amount is received. A letter would be sent to the Financial Controller of Keane Ltd.

Financial Controller
Keane Ltd

Date

Dear Sir

Further to our invoice detailed below, I do not appear to have received payment. I trust that this is an oversight and that you will arrange for immediate payment to be made. If you are withholding payment for any reason, please contact me urgently and I will be pleased to assist you.

Invoice No	Terms	Due date	Amount £
467781	30 days	22 May	1,103.00

I regret that unless payment is received within the next seven days I will have no alternative but to stop any further sales on credit to you until the amount owing is cleared in full. If you have already made payment please advise me and accept my apology for having troubled you.

Yours faithfully

Credit Controller

CHAPTER 8 Collection of debts

1 Without recourse factoring is where the factor, having checked the credit status of the debtors, assumes all of the risk of bad debts with no recourse to the business if debtors do not pay. In contrast a with recourse factoring agreement is one where the business bears the risk of bad debts as the factor has recourse to the business if customers do not pay.

Due to the additional risk it is likely that a without recourse factoring agreement would be more expensive.

2   **Benefits**

- advance of cash which may not be available from other sources
- specialist debt administration skills of the factor
- specialist debt collection skills of the factor
- saving in in-house sales ledger costs
- reduction in bad debts cost
- frees up management time

Costs

- commission charge
- interest
- potential loss of customer goodwill and confidence
- problems of reverting back to in-house sales ledger administration in the future

3 Any two of the following:

- a whole turnover policy is where either the whole sales ledger is covered but the amount paid out for any bad debt is only say 80% of the claim or 80% of the sales ledger is covered for an entire claim

- an annual aggregate excess policy is where bad debts are insured in total above an agreed limit or excess

- a specific debtor policy is where only specific sales ledger customers are insured for the bad debts risk

4 The legal remedies available for a breach of contract are:

- action for the price – a court action to recover the agreed price of the goods/services
- monetary damages – compensation for loss
- termination – one party refusing to carry on with the contract
- specific performance – a court order that one of the parties must fulfil their obligations
- quantum meruit – payment ordered for the part of the contract performed
- injunction – one party to the contract being ordered by the court not to do something

5 Methods of achieving payment from a debtor under a court order include:

- attachment of earnings order – the business will be paid the amount owing directly by the debtor's employer as a certain amount is deducted from their weekly/monthly pay. However this is only viable for a debtor who is an individual and is in stable, consistent work

- third-party debt order – this allows the business to be paid directly by a third party who owes the debtor money, often by means of appointing a receiver

- warrant of execution – a court bailiff seizes and sells the debtor's goods on behalf of the business

- administrative order – the debtor makes regular, agreed payments into court to pay off the debt

Note that only three methods were required.

6 The consequences of a bankruptcy order against an individual are:

- the official receiver takes control of the assets of the business
- a statement of the assets and liabilities is drawn up – this is known as a statement of affairs
- the receiver summons a meeting of creditors within 12 weeks of the bankruptcy order
- the creditors appoint a trustee in bankruptcy
- the assets of the business are realised and distribution is made to the various creditors

7 The order of distribution of the assets of a company in a liquidation are:

- secured creditors with fixed charges
- costs of winding up the company
- preferential unsecured debts such as employees
- secured creditors with floating charges
- unsecured creditors such as trade creditors
- deferred debts such as unpaid dividends to shareholders

REVISION COMPANION UNIT 15

chapter 1:
MONITORING CASH RECEIPTS AND PAYMENTS

1 Explain the difference between profit and cash flow.

2 You work in a small business which installs fire alarms. As the only member of the accounts department, you report directly to the proprietor, Mr Blaze. One day, you find the following long note from Mr Blaze on your table.

'I've been to the bank and asked them to lend me some money. I've always had money in the bank, but because the loan is to acquire some new equipment, the bank wants a full set of accounts. The manager asked for profit and loss accounts and a cash flow statement. He then started jabbering on in jargon I didn't understand: something about *cash cycle times*, as he said they were relevant. He asked me if I would be able to repay the loan out of *operating cash flow*. I asked him if that meant petty cash. I also said we were a profitable business. But then he said he needed some ideas as to how *liquid* we are. I said we were a solid company, we've been trading for many years. He said I'd better chat to an accountant. Please help!'

Task

Draft a memorandum to Mr Blaze to clear up his confusion.

3 Give FIVE examples of types of reasons why there might be a difference between the profit that a business makes and its cash balance.

4 Give THREE examples of regular cash receipts and TWO examples of irregular cash receipts.

5 Give THREE examples of regular cash payments and TWO examples of irregular cash payments.

6 Explain the differing impact upon a business's cash flow of:

a) Payments to employees for wages
b) Purchase of plant and machinery

7 Explain how a cash flow forecast can be prepared using an opening and closing budgeted balance sheet and a budgeted profit and loss account.

8 Given below is the cash budget for the month of June for a business together with the actual cash flows for the month of June.

Cash budget June

	Budget £	Actual £
Receipts:		
Cash sales receipts	101,000	94,000
Credit sales receipts	487,000	475,000
Total receipts	588,000	569,000
Payments:		
Credit suppliers	(303,000)	(294,000)
Wages	(155,000)	(162,000)
Variable expenses	(98,600)	(99,400)
Fixed expenses	(40,000)	(40,000)
Capital expenditure	–	(45,000)
Total payments	(596,600)	(640,400)
Net cash flow for the month	(8,600)	(71,400)
Bank b/f	20,300	20,300
Bank c/f	11,700	(51,100)

i) Compare the actual cash flows to the budgeted cash flows and identify any variances indicating whether they are favourable or adverse variances.

ii)   What actions could have been taken to try to avoid the overdraft at the end of June or to reduce it?

9   Given below is the cash budget and actual cash flows for a business for the month of July.

	Budget £	Actual £
Receipts:		
Cash sales	264,000	277,000
Receipts from credit customers	888,000	863,000
Proceeds from sale of fixed assets	–	22,000
Total receipts	1,152,000	1,162,000
Payments:		
Payments to credit suppliers	742,000	777,000
Wages	197,000	197,000
Variable overheads	51,300	58,700
Fixed overheads	66,000	68,000
Purchase of fixed assets	–	46,000
Dividend payment	50,000	50,000
Total payments	1,106,300	1,196,700
Net cash flow	45,700	(34,700)
Opening cash balance	16,200	16,200
Closing cash balance	61,900	(18,500)

i)   Reconcile the budgeted cash balance at 31 July to the actual cash balance at that date.

ii)   What actions could have been taken to avoid the use of overdraft finance by the end of the month?

10   A company has just prepared its cash flow forecast for the three months ending 30 September. The cash flow forecast indicates that there will be a significant overdraft at the end of August and September. What actions might the company take to avoid or reduce this potential overdraft?

1   A business makes 30% of its monthly sales for cash with the remainder being sold on credit. On average 40% of the total sales are received in the month following the sale and the remainder in the second month after the sale. Sales figures are estimated to be as follows.

	£
August	240,000
September	265,000
October	280,000
November	250,000
December	220,000

What are the cash receipts from sales that are received in each of the three months from October to December?

2   A business purchases all of its goods on credit from suppliers. 20% of purchases are offered a discount of 2% for payment in the month of purchase and the business takes advantage of these discounts. A further 45% of purchases are paid for in the month after the purchase and the remainder two months after the purchase. Purchases figures are estimated to be as follows.

	£
August	180,000
September	165,000
October	190,000
November	200,000
December	220,000

What are the cash payments made to suppliers in each of the three months from October to December?

3   A business sells its single product for £50 which produces a gross profit margin of 40%. The product is purchased in the month of sale and is paid for in the month following the purchase.

Estimated sales quantities are as follows.

	Units
July	5,000
August	5,200
September	5,500
October	5,750

What are the cash payments to suppliers in each of the three months from August to October?

4   a)   Louie Ltd has annual sales of £6,000 and a mark up of $33^1/_3$%. Calculate its purchases for the year.

b)   Dewie Ltd has annual purchases of £12,000 and a margin of 20%. Calculate its sales for the year.

c)   Growler Ltd has sales for the year of £16,000 and annual profits of £6,000. Calculate:

i)   its mark up
ii)   its margin

For parts a) to c) assume the companies have no opening and closing stock.

5   A business makes all of its sales on credit with a 3% settlement discount offered for payment within the month of the sale. 25% of sales take up this settlement discount and 70% of sales are paid in the following month. The remainder are bad debts.

Sales figures are as follows.

	£
March	650,000
April	600,000
May	580,000
June	550,000

What are the cash receipts for sales that are received in each of the three months from April to June?

6   Puppy's sales in the year ended 31 December were £300,000 and cost of sales was £200,000. Stocks were £15,000, creditors £12,000 and debtors £20,000 at the start of the year. At the end of the year stocks were £19,000, creditors £14,000 and debtors £25,000.

Task

Calculate the gross profits and the operational cash flows resulting from the year's trading.

7   A manufacturing company is preparing its cash budget for the three months ending 31 July. The goods are produced in the month of sale and the quantity of sales are estimated to be as follows.

	April	May	June	July	August
Unit sales	1,000	1,200	1,300	1,500	1,600

The materials required for the product are 2kg per unit costing £40 per kg and are purchased in the month prior to production and paid for in the following month. At 1 April there are 550 kgs of raw material in stock but these are to be reduced by 50 kgs per month for each of the next four months.

At 1 April there are estimated to be 180 units of the product in stock but the production manager wishes to increase these stock levels by 20 units each month for the foreseeable future.

You are helping to produce the cash budget and you are required to prepare the following:

i)   the production budget for the five month period
ii)   the purchases budget in kgs and £s for May to July
iii) the cash payments to suppliers for May to July

8   A business manufactures and sells a single product each unit of which requires 20 minutes of labour. The wage rate is £8.40 per hour. The sales of the product are anticipated to be:

	April	May	June	July
Sales units	7,200	7,050	6,550	6,150

The product is produced one month prior to sale and wages are paid in the month of production. Stock levels of finished goods are to remain at 1,000 units until the end of May when they will be reduced to 900 units and reduced further to 750 units at the end of June.

What are the cash payments for wages for each of the three months from April to June?

9 A business is about to prepare a cash budget for the quarter ending 30 September. The recent actual and estimated sales figures are as follows.

	£
April (actual)	420,000
May (actual)	400,000
June (estimate)	480,000
July (estimate)	500,000
August (estimate)	520,000
September (estimate)	510,000

All sales are on credit and the payment pattern is as follows.

20% pay in the month of sale after taking a 4% settlement discount
40% pay in the month following the sale
25% pay two months after the month of sale
12% pay three months after the month of sale

There are expected to be 3% bad debts.

The purchases of the business are all on credit and it is estimated that the following purchases will be made.

	£
May	250,000
June	240,000
July	280,000
August	300,000
September	310,000

40% of purchases are paid for in the month after the purchase has been made and the remainder are paid for two months after the month of purchase.

Wages are expected to be £60,000 each month and are paid in the month in which they are incurred. General overheads are anticipated to be a monthly £50,000 for June and July increasing to £55,000 thereafter. 75% of the general overheads are paid in the month in which they are incurred and the remainder in the following month. The general overheads figure includes a depreciation charge of £6,000 each month.

Selling expenses are expected to be 10% of the monthly sales value and are paid for in the month following the sale.

The business has planned to purchase new equipment for £42,000 in August and in the same month to dispose of old equipment with estimated sales proceeds of £7,500.

Overdraft interest is charged at 1% per month based on the overdraft balance at the start of the month. At 1 July it is anticipated that the business will have an overdraft of £82,000.

You are required to prepare the cash budget for the three months ending 30 September.

10   A manufacturing business is to prepare its cash budget for the three months ending 31 December. The business manufactures a single product which requires 3 kg of raw material per unit and 3 hours of labour per unit. Production is in the month of sale. The raw material cost is anticipated to be £9 per kg and the labour force are paid at a rate of £7.20 per hour. Each unit of the product sells for £75.

The forecast sales in units are as follows.

	August	September	October	November	December
Forecast sales – units	5,000	5,100	5,400	5,800	6,000

Sales are on credit with 40% of debtors paying the month after sale and the remainder two months after the sale.

Stocks of completed units are anticipated to be 500 until the start of October but these are to be increased by 100 units each month at the end of October, November and December.

The raw materials required for production are purchased in the month prior to production and 60% are paid for in the following month and the remainder two months after purchase. The anticipated stocks of raw materials are 3,000 kgs until the end of September and the planned stock levels at the end of each month thereafter are as follows:

October	3,200 kgs
November	3,500 kgs
December	4,000 kgs

Wages are paid in the month in which they are incurred.

Production overheads are expected to be £60,000 each month and are paid for in the month in which they are incurred. This figure includes depreciation of £10,000 per month for machinery. General overheads are anticipated to be £72,000 each month in October and November increasing to £80,000 in December and are paid in the month in which they are incurred. The figure for general overheads includes £12,000 of depreciation each month.

The cash balance at 1 October is expected to be £40,000 in credit.

You are required to prepare the cash budget for the three months ending 31 December.

11   Given below is the forecast profit and loss account for a business for the three months ending 31 December together with forecast balance sheets at that date and also at the previous 30 September.

Forecast profit and loss account for three months ending 31 December

	£000
Sales	860
Cost of sales	600
Gross profit	260
Depreciation	20
Overheads	100
Operating profit	140
Interest paid	10
Profit before tax	130
Tax	30
Retained profit	100

Forecast balance sheet

	31 December		30 September	
	£000	£000	£000	£000
Fixed assets		1,050		760
Current assets:				
Stock	100		80	
Debtors	95		65	
Cash	–		10	
	195		155	
Creditors: amounts falling due within one year:				
Trade creditors	100		75	
Bank overdraft	15		–	
Tax	30		40	
	145		115	
Net current assets		50		40
Creditors: amounts falling due after more than one year:				
Long term loan		(200)		–
		900		800
Share capital		600		600
Retained profit		300		200
		900		800

From the forecast profit and loss account and forecast balance sheets prepare a cash flow forecast for the three months ending 31 December.

12 Marquis Marketing Ltd operates in a highly seasonal sector of the retail industry. The company's management is estimating its cash requirements for the third quarter of 2006 for which the following schedule of anticipated inflows and outflows has been produced by the sales and production departments.

Month	Sales £	Purchases £
May	160,000	240,000
June	320,000	60,000
July	80,000	40,000
August	80,000	120,000
September	160,000	180,000
October	220,000	120,000
November	180,000	80,000

Sales are made on two months' credit, whilst suppliers allow one month's credit. Monthly salaries amount to £36,000 and the company's annual rent of £48,000 is paid quarterly in advance.

An overdraft of £112,000 is expected to exist on 30 June.

Tasks

a) Prepare a cash budget for the period July-September 2006.

b) Comment on the cash budget you have prepared with particular reference to the ways in which Marquis Marketing Ltd might control the seasonality of its cash requirements.

13 a) Using the information given below, complete a cash budget for Wilson for the six months January – June 2006.

The actual figures for November and December were:

Month (2005)	Production (units)	Sales (units)
November	7,000	7,000
December	8,000	8,000

The plans for the next six months are shown below.

Month (2006)	Production (units)	Sales (units)
January	10,000	8,000
February	12,000	10,000
March	12,000	12,000
April	14,000	13,000
May	15,000	14,000
June	15,000	16,000

The selling price is £20.50 per unit, with an anticipated price increase to £21.50 per unit from 1 June.

Raw material costs £4 per unit.

Wages and other variable costs are £8 per unit.

Other fixed costs are £1,800 per month rising to £2,200 from 1 May onwards.

Twenty per cent of sales are for cash, the remainder being paid in full 60 days following delivery.

Material purchases are paid one month after delivery and are held in stock for one month before entering production.

Wages and variable and fixed costs are paid in the month of production.

A new machine costing £450,000 is to be purchased in February to cope with the planned expansion of demand. 20% of payment is to be made on 1 February and the remainder retained until the machine is operational (expected 1 July 2006).

An advertising campaign is also to be launched, involving payments of £20,000 in each of February and May.

Corporation tax of £56,000 is due on 30 June 2006.

The company is financed by share capital of 1 million £1 shares and a debenture of £0.5 million paying semi-annual interest of 3.5% on 30 June and 31 December.

The directors plan to pay a dividend of £0.10 per share in May.

An overdraft of £0.5 million has been agreed with Wilson Ltd's bankers.

The current overdraft interest rate is 7.2% per annum on the prior month closing balance.

Interest is received on cash balances at 6.0% per annum on the prior month closing balance.

On 1 January the firm expects to have £185,000 in the bank.

b) An alternative technique to the receipts and payments method used in a) for budgeting cash involves preparing a comparison of the present and forecast balance sheets (a cash flow forecast method).

Tasks

i)   Suggest TWO advantages for the receipts and payments cash budget method.
ii)   Suggest TWO advantages for the cash flow forecast technique.
iii)   Describe how each would be used together.

chapter 3:
FURTHER ASPECTS OF CASH BUDGETING

1 Given below are the daily takings in a shop that is open five days a week, Monday to Friday.

	Mon	Tues	Wed	Thurs	Fri
	£	£	£	£	£
Week 1	1,260	1,600	1,630	1,780	1,830
Week 2	1,340	1,750	1,640	1,850	1,980
Week 3	1,550	1,660	1,620	1,870	1,970

Calculate the five day moving average for the daily takings.

2 In time series analysis explain what is meant by the following:

i) trend
ii) cyclical variation
iii) seasonal variation
iv) random variation

3 Given below are the quarterly sales figures for a business for the last three years.

		£
2004	Q1	448,700
	Q2	449,900
	Q3	423,500
	Q4	436,700
2005	Q1	450,100
	Q2	451,600
	Q3	428,600
	Q4	439,800
2006	Q1	453,500
	Q2	455,100
	Q3	429,900
	Q4	441,500

Calculate the trend of these sales figures using a centred four quarter moving average.

4   Using the figures from activity 3 calculate the seasonal variations using the additive model.

5   Using the figures from activity 3 calculate the seasonal variations using the multiplicative model.

6   Using the figures from activity 3 and the seasonal variations from activities 4 and 5 estimate the following:

i)   sales for Q1 and Q2 of 2007 using the additive model
ii) sales for Q1 and Q2 of 2007 using the multiplicative model

7   What are the problems involved with using time series analysis for budgeting purposes?

8   Ben owns a small factory, and has become concerned about how output has varied according to the day of the week. He has analysed output over the last three weeks.

	Week 1 Units	Week 2 Units	Week 3 Units
Monday	560	574	588
Tuesday	840	875	910
Wednesday	728	770	812
Thursday	658	679	700
Friday	434	448	462

Ben has used regression analysis to calculate a trend line for output of: $y = 2.94x + 648.9$

Task

Find the seasonal variation for each of the fifteen days, and the average seasonal variation for the week using:

a)   the additive model
b)   the multiplicative model

Assume Monday of the first week is 0, Friday of the third week is 14. Therefore for Monday of the first week, output $y = (2.94 \times 0) + 648.9 = 648.9$

9   Trend values for sales of barbecues by Hothouse Ltd over the last three years have been as follows:

Year	1st quarter	2nd quarter	3rd quarter	4th quarter
1	7,494	7,665	7,890	8,123
2	8,295	8,493	8,701	8,887
3	9,090	9,296	9,501	9,705

Average seasonal variations for the four quarters have been:

Quarter 1 + 53
Quarter 2 + 997
Quarter 3 + 1,203
Quarter 4 – 2,253

Task

Use the trend line and estimates of seasonal variations to forecast sales in each quarter of next year.

10   Your company wants to construct a price index for three commodities Rag, Tag and Bobtail. The prices in the base month of September were :

Rag £8
Tag £5
Bobtail £2

and the quantities sold were

Rag 2,500 units
Tag 5,000 units
Bobtail 27,500 units

The prices of the items in October and November were as follows:

	October £	November £
Rag	8.24	8.40
Tag	5.25	5.50
Bobtail	2.00	2.12

Task

Using the sales revenues in September to weight the items, construct a price index for October and November.

11 A business currently sells its product for £30 but it is anticipated that there will be a price increase of 4% from 1 February. The sales quantities are expected to be as follows:

January	21,000 units
February	22,000 units
March	22,800 units

All sales are on credit and 40% of cash is received in the month following the sale and the remainder two months after the sale.

What are the receipts from sales that are received in March?

12 A business has production overheads of £347,000 in December 2006 but it is anticipated that these will increase by 1.25% per month for the next few months. Overheads are paid the month after they are incurred.

What is the cash outflow for overheads that is paid during the month of March 2007?

13 A business makes purchases of a raw material which has a cost of £2.60 per kg in November 2006. The actual and estimated price index for this material is as follows:

	Price index
November (actual)	166.3
December (estimate)	169.0
January (estimate)	173.4
February (estimate)	177.2

What is the expected price per kg (to the nearest penny) of the raw material in each of the months of December, January and February?

14 A business currently pays its suppliers with the following pattern:

60% one month after the date of purchase

40% two months after the date of purchase

30% of purchases are offered a 3% discount for payment during the month of purchase but in the past the business has not taken advantage of this. If it did take advantage then 30% of purchases would be paid for in the month of purchase, 40% in the month following purchase and 30% two months after the date of purchase.

Purchases are estimated to be as follows:

	£
August	520,000
September	550,000
October	560,000
November	580,000
December	600,000

You are required to calculate the payments to suppliers for each of the three months of October, November and December on the following bases:

i) the current situation continues where no settlement discounts are taken

ii) the settlement discounts are taken as described above from suppliers who are paid in the month of purchase (assume that this policy begins in October).

15 At 31 March a business had debtors of £260,000. Planned sales for the following three months in units are:

April	140,000 units
May	150,000 units
June	155,000 units

On average 40% of debtors pay during the month after the sale and the remainder pay two months after the date of sale.

The debtors at 31 March can be assumed to pay as follows:

	£
In April	140,000
In May	120,000
	260,000

Sales are made at a price of £1.00 per unit.

i) Calculate the receipts from sales in each of the three months April to June and the debtors at 30 June.

ii) If the sales price is reduced to £0.90 per unit from 1 April calculate the impact on the cash balance at 30 June and the level of debtors at 30 June.

16 You have been asked to prepare a cash budget for the three months ending 30 June using a computer spreadsheet. You have been given the following information:

■ the balance in the bank account is anticipated to be £22,000 at 1 April

■ sales in February and March were £360,000 and £368,000 respectively. It is anticipated that there will be a growth rate in these sales of 2% per month. 20% of the sales are for cash and

50% of the sales will be paid for in the month after the sale and the remaining 30% will be paid for in the following month

■ purchases are all paid for in cash in the month of their sale and they are generally 60% of the sales value

■ overheads in March were £72,000 and these have generally increased at a rate of 0.5% per month

■ a dividend payment of £60,000 is due in June

You are required to set up the columns and rows of the spreadsheet and produce formulae for all of the figures that will appear in the spreadsheet. Enter the formulae that you have derived into the appropriate cells in the spreadsheet.

17   a)   Describe briefly the benefits for cash budgeting from the use of a particular type of software package.

   b)   Give three examples of forecasting models that take account of the uncertainties involved in forecasting.

18   You have received the following note from your manager who has unexpectedly been called away to a conference.

'I have left a copy of the cash flow forecast and actual cash flow for the final three months of last year for the Goring factory on my desk. Please compare the two and write me a memo listing any differences and suggesting corrective action.

The bank has asked me to comment on how we would be affected by an increase in inflation higher than the 4% assumed in our forecasting. Could you give me some brief comments on this, relating them to the forecast for the factory.

We base our forecasts on past forecasts and any new assumptions. I wonder if there are any disadvantages in working this way? Again the bank has asked me why we do this – could you suggest any problems we may experience with this approach.'

Tasks

In a memo to your manager:

a)   compare the cash flow forecast and actual cash flow for the Goring factory for the final three months of last year, listing any variance and suggesting why they may have occurred, together with any corrective action.

b)   explain one way in which cash flow could be affected by an increase in inflation higher than 4%.

c)   explain one disadvantage of the method used to project cash flow for the factory.

Cash flow forecast for the final three months of last year
Goring factory

	October £000	November £000	December £000
Cash received			
Sales: Cash	10	10	10
Credit	80	90	90
Sales of assets	0	0	10
	90	100	110
Cash paid			
Purchase of: Machinery	25	0	5
Vehicles	10	0	0
Rent	12	12	12
Wages	15	16	16
Purchases	40	43	44
Selling/administration	10	10	10
	112	81	87
Net cash flow	(22)	19	23
Cash balance b/f	5	(17)	2
Cash balance c/f	(17)	2	25

Cash flow actuals for the final three months of last year
Goring factory

	October £000	November £000	December £000
Cash received			
Sales: Cash	9	9	10
Credit	82	89	91
Sales of assets	0	0	10
	91	98	111
Cash paid			
Purchase of: Machinery	28	0	5
Vehicles	10	0	0
Rent	12	12	12
Wages	17	17	18
Purchases	45	45	46
Selling/administration	10	10	10
	122	84	91
Net cash flow	(31)	14	20
Cash balance b/f	5	(26)	(12)
Cash balance c/f	(26)	(12)	8

chapter 4:
MANAGING CASH BALANCES

1 Explain what is meant by primary banks and secondary banks.

2 What are the main benefits of financial intermediation?

3 Briefly explain the four main contractual relationships between a bank and its customer.

4 What are a bank's duties to its customer?

5 Pravina, an eighteen year old who lives next door to you, is about to open her first bank account. Explain to her the rights the bank has in its relationship with her.

6 Give three examples of ways in which a customer can maintain a good relationship with its bank in order to raise finance on the most favourable terms.

7 What are the most common reasons underlying a business's identification of a future cash deficit or the need to raise additional finance?

8 During the year ending 30 June a business made sales of £2,600,000 and its cost of sales totalled £1,800,000. At 30 June there were stocks of £250,000, debtors of £550,000 and creditors of £200,000.

What is the operating cycle of the business, in days?

9 Kitten Ltd buys raw materials on 3 months' credit, holds them in store for 4 months and then issues them to production. The production cycle is a couple of days, and then finished goods are held for 1 month before they are sold. Debtors are normally allowed 2 months' credit.

Task

Calculate Kitten's operating cycle.

10 What are the main features of overdraft finance?

11 What are the main terms and conditions that would be found in a typical short term loan agreement?

12 What are the main advantages of overdraft finance compared to loan finance?

13 Distinguish between a finance lease and an operating lease.

14 Briefly explain the three main general factors that should influence any decisions regarding investment of surplus funds.

15 i) Explain what is meant by gilt edged securities
ii) Explain what is meant by a flat yield and a redemption yield on gilts
iii) Explain any risks associated with investing in gilts

16 A business has £100,000 to invest for a period of approximately 6 months. Investment in either a bank deposit account or gilt edged securities is being considered.

What would be the effect of a change in base rates on both of these potential investments?

17 A business makes a proportion of its sales for cash through a factory outlet. What security procedures should be adopted for the safe custody of this cash?

18 One of the roles of a central bank is to provide advice to the government on strategies to control inflation. Briefly outline FOUR possible consequences of inflation on organisations engaged in business.

19 Describe the factors that a bank must take into account when considering the total amount of credit it is prepared to give to its customers.

20 A bank manager is considering two possibilities for security on a loan to a company.

a)   The company's factory
b)   The company's fleet of new motor cars

The current open market value of both is more than the amount to be advanced.

Task

Discuss the main factors that the bank will consider when deciding what security to take.

21 Describe the main advantages of overdraft and loan finance for small businesses, and indicate when each might be the most appropriate source of finance.

22 Explain the advantages of leasing assets from the viewpoint of managing an organisation's cash balances.

23 RT plc has forecast the following cash movements for the next six months.

Cash available now	£2,000,000
Inflow in two months	£4,000,000
Outflow in four months	£2,000,000
Outflow in six months	£4,000,000

Assume that all movements of cash take place on the *last day* of each two-month period.

The structure of short-term interest rates is as follows.

Current		Expected in 2 months		Expected in 4 months	
Maturity period	Annual yield %	Maturity period	Annual yield %	Maturity period	Annual yield %
2 months	7.3	2 months	8.0	2 months	8.3
4 months	7.4	4 months	8.1	4 months	8.4
6 months	7.5	6 months	8.2	6 months	8.3

The company invests surplus cash balances in marketable securities. Company policy is to hold such securities to maturity once they are purchased. Every purchase transaction of marketable securities costs £100.

Task

Calculate which securities should be purchased to maximise income.

24 Azrina Ltd manufactures cycles. The company's long-term cash flow forecast for the year ended 31 December 2008 suggests a cash surplus of £1 million will be generated in 2007 and £1.75 million in 2008.

The company is considering its future cash management strategy and is considering four business strategies. For each of the following four scenarios, suggest what action you would take to manage the cash surplus and the reason for your recommendation:

a) No further growth in Azrina Ltd's existing business and no plans for further capital investment

b) Plans for an acquisition of a cycle parts manufacturer (valued up to £5 million) when a suitable opportunity arises

c) Development in 2007 and 2008 of several new product lines requiring capital investment of £2.5 million

d) Phased development of two new product lines requiring capital investment of £1.25 million and the intention to acquire another cycle parts manufacturer (value up to £3 million) when a suitable opportunity arises

25 On 31 December last year your company placed cash of £150,000 on a four-month deposit account earning interest at the rate of 6% per annum. An extract from the Financial Times gilt prices shows that Treasury stock 9¾% 2009 may be purchased at a price of £112½. The flat yield is 8.66% and the redemption yield is 6.2%.

Task

Prepare notes for the directors of your company explaining what is meant by gilt-edged securities and the advantages and disadvantages of investing at the price shown in Treasury Stock 9³/₄% 2009.

26 a) What is the interest yield on 7% Treasury Stock 2008 if its market value is £109.5675?

b) You have been advised to purchase 9% Treasury Stock 2009 with a nominal value of £10,000. The transaction is carried out by a stockbroker who charges commission of 0.5%. The price of the Treasury Stock is £109.0485. Accrued interest is 45 days. What is the total cost you will have to pay?

chapter 5:
CREDIT CONTROL

1   What are the stages in the ordering cycle and the collection cycle for the sale of goods on credit?

2   The normal credit terms for a business are that payment should be made within 60 days of the invoice date but a settlement discount of 2% is offered for payment within 14 days of the invoice. How would this be expressed on the sales invoice to the customer?

3   Briefly describe the role of the credit control department.

4   You have recently taken over the position of credit manager in a building supplies company. The company sells building materials on credit to building contractors. Yours is a new position established on the advice of the company's auditors to deal with poor credit control and a high incidence of bad debts. The auditors have suggested that an early priority should be the development of a credit control manual which covers policy and procedures in respect of:

a)   New customer credit acceptance
b)   Setting credit levels
c)   Setting credit terms
d)   Ensuring prompt payment

Task

Write an introductory note, suitable for inclusion in the proposed credit control manual, for each of the four credit control procedures listed above.

5   i)   What is meant by a cheque crossing?
      ii)   What is the specific meaning of an account payee only cheque crossing?

6   What is the difference between a standing order and a direct debit?

7   What are the three fundamental elements of a contract?

8   In contract law distinguish between an offer and an invitation to treat.

9   In contract law how can an offer be brought to an end?

10   Explain the meaning of each of the following within a contract:

  i)   express terms
  ii)   conditions
  iii)   warranties
  iv)   implied terms

11   What are the eight guiding principles of good practice of the Data Protection Act?

chapter 6:
GRANTING CREDIT

1   Summarise the normal methods of establishing the creditworthiness of potential new customers.

2   Identify three external sources of information that may be available regarding a company that is requesting credit from your business.

3   What potential problems might there be with a trade reference received regarding a potential new customer?

4   A bank reference has been received regarding a potential new customer who is requesting a credit facility of £10,000. The bank reference reads "should prove good for your figures".

   As the credit controller what would be your reaction to such a bank reference?

5   A business has a gross profit of £125,000 and a net operating profit of £60,000. The annual turnover was £500,000 and the total net assets of the business were £600,000.

   Calculate the following ratios:

   i)   gross profit margin
   ii)   net profit margin
   iii) return on capital employed
   iv)   net asset turnover

6   The following analysis has been compiled from the sales ledger of Dandy Ltd at 30 September 2006.

	Sales a) £	Unpaid b) £
September	40,000	30,000
August	45,000	18,000
July	50,000	15,000
June	35,000	7,000
Total debtors		70,000

Credit sales for the year to 30 September 2006 were £400,000.

Tasks

Calculate how many days' sales are represented by debtors using:

a)   debtors' turnover
b)   count-back method
c)   partial month method

7   Given below is an extract from the balance sheet of a business:

	£000	£000
Fixed assets		1,200
Current assets:		
Stock	80	
Debtors	120	
Cash	10	
	210	
Current liabilities		
Trade creditors	100	
Tax	8	
	108	
Net current assets		102
		1,302
Long term loans		(500)
		802

The summarised profit and loss account for the year is also given:

	£000
Sales	750
Cost of sales	500
Gross profit	250
Operating expenses	180
Interest paid	40
Profit before tax	30
Tax	8
Retained profit	22

You are to calculate the following accounting ratios:

i) current ratio
ii) quick ratio
iii) stock turnover
iv) debtors turnover
v) creditors turnover
vi) return on capital employed
vii) gearing ratio
viii) interest cover

8   You are the credit controller for a business which has received a request for £20,000 of credit from a potential new customer, Faverly Ltd. Faverly Ltd have provided you with their latest set of financial statements which are summarised below:

Profit and loss account for the year ended 30 June

	2006	2005
	£000	£000
Turnover	2,400	2,250
Cost of sales	(1,870)	(1,770)
Gross profit	530	480
Operating expenses	(230)	(210)
Operating profit	300	270
Interest payable	(70)	(48)
Profit before tax	230	222
Taxation	(57)	(55)
Profit after tax	173	167
Dividends	(60)	(50)
Retained profit for the year	113	117

Balance sheets at 30 June

	2006 £000	2005 £000
Fixed assets	3,200	2,867
Current assets		
Stocks	264	216
Debtors	336	360
	600	576
Current liabilities		
Trade creditors	384	380
Bank overdraft	720	480
	1,104	860
Net assets	2,696	2,583
Share capital	1,500	1,500
Profit and loss reserve	1,196	1,083
	2,696	2,583

You have also received a bank reference from Faverly Ltd's bank which reads "should prove good for your figures". Finally you have received the following trade references:

We have received a request for credit from Faverly Ltd who have quoted yourselves as a referee. We would be grateful if you could answer the following questions and return in the stamped addressed envelope enclosed.

How long has the customer been trading with you?	3 years 6 months
Your credit terms with customer per month	£10,000
Period of credit granted	30 days
Payment record	Prompt/occasionally late/slow
Have you ever suspended credit to the customer?	Yes/No
If yes - when and for how long?	2004 for six months
Any other relevant information	

We have received a request for credit from Faverly Ltd who have quoted yourselves as a referee. We would be grateful if you could answer the following questions and return in the stamped addressed envelope enclosed.

How long has the customer been trading with you?   5 years 3 months

Your credit terms with customer per month   £10,000

Period of credit granted   30 days...............................

Payment record   Prompt/occasionally late/slow

Have you ever suspended credit to the customer?   Yes/No

....

Any other relevant information   ....

....

You are required to carry out an assessment of the information provided for Faverly Ltd and to record your results and recommendation as to whether credit of £20,000 should be extended to Faverly Ltd in a memo to the finance director of your business.

9   You are the credit controller for a business and you have received a request from Fisher Ltd for credit of £15,000 from your company on a 30 day basis. Two trade references have been provided but no bank reference. You have also received the last set of published financial statements which include the previous year's comparative figures.

The trade references appeared satisfactory although one is from Froggett & Sons and it has been noted that the managing director of Fisher Ltd is Mr N Froggett. Analysis of the financial statements has indicated a decrease in profitability during the last year, a high level of gearing and fairly low liquidity ratios.

Draft a letter to the finance director of Fisher Ltd on the basis that credit is to be currently refused but may be extended once the most recent financial statements have been examined.

10   What information is required in order to set up an account in the sales ledger for a new customer with whom your business is to trade on credit?

11   Identify four possible reasons for the refusal of credit to a new customer.

12 When refusing credit to a new customer how should this be communicated and what matters should be discussed?

13 A business has normal credit terms of payment within 60 days of the invoice date. It is considering offering a settlement discount of 1% for payment within 10 days of the invoice date.

What is the approximate annual cost of this discount?

14 Widmerpool Ltd makes sales to certain customers of £100,000 with an average collection period of two months. Kenneth, its managing director, is considering whether to introduce a discount of 3% on sales to these customers in return for immediate cash settlement. Widmerpool normally requires a 15% return on its investments.

Task

Advise Kenneth whether to introduce the discount.

15 Brickwood grants credit terms of 60 days net to its major customers, but offers an early settlement discount of 2.5% for payment within seven days.

Tasks

a)   Calculate the cost of this discount.

b)   Identify two reasons why Brickwood might choose to offer its major customers such a generous discount.

16 Herbage Ltd is proposing to increase the credit period it gives to customers from one calendar month to two calendar months in order to raise turnover from the present annual figure of £18 million. The price of the product is £10 and it costs £6.40 to make. The increase in the credit period is likely to generate an extra 60,000 unit sales per year.

Task

Calculate whether the extra sales are enough to justify the extra costs given that the company's required rate of return is 15%. Assume no changes to stock levels, as the company is increasing its operating efficiency. Assume that existing debtors will take advantage of the new terms.

17 To improve your organisation's credit control procedures, the Credit Manager has asked you to assist in drafting formal procedures for the acceptance of new customers. As a start, he has asked you to summarise the factors to be considered when assessing the creditworthiness of new customers.

Task

Prepare the summary.

18 You are employed as an assistant accountant in Fastover Ltd. Your company's Financial Controller wants you to assess the creditworthiness of Whittle Ltd. Whittle has placed a large order with your company and any problems paying would have an impact on your company's cash flow.

You have received references from two of Whittle's suppliers and also extracts from Whittle's accounts over the last two years. You also have a copy of Fastover's credit control procedures manual which sets guidelines on when credit should be granted.

Task

Using the information given below and bearing in mind the guidelines in the quality control procedures manual, recommend in a memo to the Financial Controller whether Whittle Ltd should have credit terms extended to it.

Your ratio analysis should include the following ratios.

- current ratio (current assets: current liabilities)
- acid test ratio (current assets less stock: current liabilities)
- debt ratio (long-term liabilities: total assets less current liabilities)

Extract from procedures manual

Extending credit to new customers

The supply of goods/services on credit necessarily involves risk. To minimise that risk the following steps should be taken before extending credit to a new customer.

1. Two references from independent referees should be obtained. Any problems raised by the references should be followed up and further references should be taken if appropriate.

2. The latest set of accounts of a company should be obtained and ratio analysis undertaken. Any problems raised by the analysis should be followed up.

3. Assuming point 1 and 2 are satisfactory, a credit limit should be set by the Credit Control Manager. This should initially be a very conservative limit which is closely monitored. The limit may be reviewed after six months.

FASTINFO LTD
11 Beal Street
Wallington
WL1 9PO

Tel: 0331 8676767

5 January 2006

PRIVATE AND CONFIDENTIAL

Credit Manager
Greatlygrow Ltd
Long Street
Wallington
WL7 9ZW

Dear Sir or Madam

We have recently received a request from a customer of ours, Whittle Ltd, giving yourselves as a reference. We would be grateful if you would answer the following questions and return them in the enclosed stamped addressed envelope.

1.   For how long has Whittle Ltd been trading with you?

1 year

2.   Did you take up references for Whittle Ltd when you began trading with them?

2 references

3.   How long a credit period do you normally extend to Whittle Ltd?

6 weeks

4.   Does Whittle Ltd make payments in accordance with credit terms?

Yes

5.   Have you ever suspended credit being extended to Whittle Ltd?

No

      If YES please give date and period of suspension.

6.   Please supply any information which you consider relevant.

Thank you for your help.

Yours faithfully

Brian Herbert

Brian Herbert – Credit Control Manager

FASTINFO LTD
11 Beal Street
Wallington
WL1 9PO

Tel: 0331 8676767

5 January 2006

PRIVATE AND CONFIDENTIAL

Credit Manager
Weston Ltd
Weston Court
Wallington, WL5 8PP

Dear Sir or Madam

We have recently received a request from a customer of ours, Whittle Ltd, giving yourselves as a reference. We would be grateful if you would answer the following questions and return them in the enclosed stamped addressed envelope.

1. For how long has Whittle Ltd been trading with you?

    5 years

2. Did you take up references for Whittle Ltd when you began trading with them?

    2 references

3. How long a credit period do you normally extend to Whittle Ltd?

    Two months

4. Does Whittle Ltd make payments in accordance with credit terms?

    Usually

5. Have you ever suspended credit being extended to Whittle Ltd?

    Yes

    If YES please give date and period of suspension.

    Once two years ago for 6 months

6. Please supply any information which you consider relevant.

Thank you for your help.

Yours faithfully

Brian Herbert

Brian Herbert – Credit Control Manager

Extracts from the accounts of Whittle Ltd
Balance sheet

	This year £	Last year £
Fixed assets		
Intangible fixed assets	200	180
Tangible fixed assets	790	670
Investments	900	600
	1,890	1,450
Current assets		
Stocks	200	170
Debtors	800	750
Cash	90	105
	1,090	1,025
Current liabilities		
Trade creditors	900	890
Other	70	68
	970	958
Total assets less		
current liabilities	2,010	1,517
Less: Long term liabilities	500	400
	1,510	1,117
Financed by:		
Called up share capital	1,000	1,000
Profit and loss:		
b/f	117	7
retained	393	110
	1,510	1,117
Profit and loss account		
Profit after interest and taxation	500	190

19 You work as an Accounting Technician for Sleepy Ltd. You have recently received a request for credit facilities from the Finance Director of Dreams Ltd. The company has supplied its profit and loss account for the year ended 30 June 2006. In addition, in accordance with the credit policy of Sleepy, trade references have been obtained from two of Dreams Ltd's suppliers, Carpets Ltd and Wardrobes Ltd. The request for credit, profit and loss account and references are set out below.

Tasks

a) Prepare a memo setting out any concerns you have in connection with the request. You should include an analysis of the profit and loss account of Dreams Ltd and refer to the trade references.

b) Draft a letter to Mr D Jones at Dreams Ltd in reply to the original request for credit facilities.

DREAMS LTD

17 High Street
Newport
South Wales

Mr S Wilks
Financial Controller
Sleepy Ltd
Tregarn Trading Estate
Cardiff
CF1 3EW   21 December 2006

Dear Mr Wilks

We are a long-established company and trade as a retailer of furniture. We are keen to do business with your company. In order to facilitate this we would be grateful if you could confirm that you will be able to provide us with £20,000 of credit on 60 days terms.

I enclose a copy of our latest audited profit and loss account. You may also wish to contact two of our existing suppliers for trade references. I would suggest the following two:

Carpets Ltd
Monnow Way
Bristol
BS7 6TY

Wardrobes Ltd
Pansy Park
Liverpool
L4 1HQ

I look forward to hearing from you shortly.

Yours sincerely

D Jones

David Jones – Finance Director

CARPETS LTD
MONNOW WAY
BRISTOL
BS7 6TY

Pat King
Accounting Technician
Sleepy Ltd
Tregarn Trading Estate
Cardiff
CF1 3EW   28 December 2006

Dear Sir/Madam

In response to your request for credit information on Dreams Ltd our response is as follows:

·   We have traded with the company for four years.
·   We allow the company £10,000 of credit on 30-day terms.
·   We find that on average the company takes 60 days to settle their account with us.
·   We are not aware of any other information which you should consider.

Yours faithfully

A Evans

Anne Evans – Credit Controller

WARDROBES LTD
Pansy Park
Liverpool
L4 1HQ

Pat King
Accounting Technician
Sleepy Ltd
Tregarn Trading Estate
Cardiff
CF1 3EW   28 December 2006

Dear Sir/Madam

In response to your request for credit information on Dreams Ltd our response is as follows:

-     We have traded with the company for 3 months.
-     We allow the company £2,500 of credit on 30 days terms.
-     The company settles its account with us in accordance with our credit terms.
-     We are not aware of any other information which you should consider.

Yours faithfully

J Corkhill

J Corkhill – Credit Controller

Dreams Ltd
Profit and loss account for the year ended 30 June

	2006	2005
	£'000	£'000
Turnover	1,800	1,750
Cost of sales	(1,250)	(1,190)
Gross profit	550	560
Net operating expenses	(500)	(550)
Operating profit	50	10
Interest payable and similar charges	(30)	(20)
Profit(loss) before taxation	20	(10)
Taxation	–	3
Profit/(loss) after taxation	20	(7)
Dividends	(10)	–
Retained profit/(loss) for the year	10	(7)

chapter 7:
MANAGEMENT OF DEBTORS

1 What is a credit customer's credit limit and why is it important that it should not be exceeded?

2 A customer of your business has an outstanding balance on its sales ledger account of £24,519 at 31 July. This balance is made up as follows:

		£
10 May	Inv 042644	1,473
25 May	Inv 042712	3,265
6 June	Inv 042785	4,273
25 June	Inv 042846	4,175
6 July	Credit note 02764	(400)
10 July	Inv 042913	4,463
16 July	Inv 042962	3,143
25 July	Inv 042987	4,127
		24,519

The customer's name is Knightly Ltd and the company has a credit limit of £30,000.

Complete the aged debtor analysis given below for this customer as at 31 July.

Total £	Credit limit £	Current <30 days £	31–60 days £	61–90 days £	> 90 days £

3 Given below is an extract from an aged debtor analysis for your business at 31 August.

	Total £	Credit limit £	Current <30 days £	31–60 days £	61–90 days £	> 90 days £
Jeremy Ltd	8,236	10,000	3,757	3,589		890
Lenter Ltd	5,378	8,000	1,873	1,967	1,538	
Friday Partners	400	4,000			400	
Diamond & Co	6,256	5,000	4,227	2,029		

What does the aged debtor analysis indicate for each of these debtors and what action if any should be taken?

4   Given below are the totals of the aged debtor analysis for your business at 31 August.

	Total £000	Credit limit £000	Current <30 days £000	31–60 days £000	61–90 days £000	> 90 days £000
	1,442	1,800	782	468	160	32

The sales for the year ending 31 August totalled £13,150,000 and were made up as follows:

	£000
Before June	9,812
June	1,234
July	1,004
August	1,100
	13,150

The business policy is that debts should be paid within 30 days of the invoice date.

Calculate the following figures:

i)   the ratio of overdue debt to the total outstanding debt
ii)   the average period of credit taken using the debtors turnover method
iii)   the average period of credit taken using the count back method
iv)   the average period credit taken using the partial month method

5   Pretty Office Furniture has been in business for 18 months. The firm was offered a £5,000 credit limit by Sitting Duck Ltd in May 2005, increased, after being slightly exceeded, to £10,000 in January 2006. The account is due for review shortly.

2006 Month	Average balance £	Limit £
January	(5,032)	(10,000)
February	(4,103)	(10,000)
March	(10,214)	(10,000)
April	(6,745)	(10,000)
May	(11,744)	(10,000)
June	(11,570)	(10,000)
July	(9,218)	(10,000)
August	(11,538)	(10,000)
September	(12,010)	(10,000)

As Sitting Duck's credit controller, describe the interpretation that you place on the working of the account and the future action that you might consider taking. (Hint: is Pretty using working capital for operational reasons only?)

6 You are working in Paddington Ltd's credit control section. The Sales Manager has asked for your views on the credit status of four organisations to whom Paddington Ltd supplies goods.

Task

Using the extracts from the aged analysis of debtors given below, analyse these four accounts and write a memorandum to the Sales Manager.

Your memorandum should:

a)   provide an opinion of the creditworthiness of the customer and the status of the account
b)   suggest how the account should be managed in the future

Extract from: Aged analysis of debtors

Customer name and address	Total due £	Up to 30 days £	Up to 60 day £	Up to 90 days £	Over 90 days £
Megacorp PLC, Oakham, Rutland	72,540	21,250	12,250	15,500	23,540
Credit limit £85,000.					
Terms of sale: 60 days net.					
Goodfellows Cycles Ltd, Manchester	24,000	19,000			5,000
Credit limit £50,000.					
Terms of sale: 30 days net.					
Hooper-bikes Ltd, Sheffield	26,750	6,250	9,875	5,275	5,350
Credit limit £25,000.					
Terms of sale: 60 days net.					
Dynamo Cycles Ltd, Nottingham	2,750	2,750			
Credit limit £7,500.					
Terms of sale: 30 days net.					

7 What evidence might be found for potential bad or doubtful debts?

8 During the year ending 30 June 2005 a business had total credit sales of £1,300,000 and bad debts of £65,000. During the year ending 30 June 2006 sales increased to £2,000,000 and bad debts in the year were £130,000.

i)   What is the bad debt ratio for each of the two years?
ii)   What might an increase in the bad debt ratio indicate for a business?

9 Given below is the credit control policy for a business and an extract from its aged debtor analysis at 30 September.

Credit control policy

1   Invoices must be issued on the same day as goods are despatched

2   An aged analysis of trade debtors is to be produced monthly

3   Credit terms are strictly 30 days from the date of invoice

4   Statements are despatched on the first working day of each month

5   A reminder letter must be sent when a debt is 14 days overdue

6   A telephone call to chase payment must be made when a debt is 21 days overdue

7   The customer will be placed on the stop list when the debt is 30 days overdue and a meeting arranged with the customer to discuss the operation of the account

8   A letter threatening legal action will be sent when the debt is 45 days overdue

9   Legal proceedings are to be commenced when a debt is 60 days overdue subject to the agreement of the Finance Director.

Aged debtor analysis at 30 September: extract

	Total	Credit limit	Current <30 days	31–60 days	61–90 days	> 90 days
	£	£	£	£	£	£
Carnford Ltd	12,430	15,000				12,430
Luxford Ltd	3,400	4,000	2,500	720		180
KLP Ltd	1,560	2,000		600	960	
Flanders Ltd	18,450	20,000	10,240	6,225	1,985	

For each debtor:

- set out the action to be taken with regard to each of the four customer accounts
- state how discussion should be conducted with the overdue accounts
- recommend whether any provisions for doubtful debts are required.

10 Your company holds regular credit meetings each month, reviewing each item on the latest receivables report.

The meeting includes representatives from the sales and finance departments (including yourself) to facilitate discussions on the general background of customers and their current levels of trade. Normally only overdue items will be reviewed and follow up actions will be agreed between the members.

At this meeting you have to take action regarding a number of customers who are overdue.

An efficient system for collection of overdue receivables is essential in the credit collection process. Routine letters from an anonymous credit control section to the accountant of the debtor company concerned are frequently ignored and not given any priority.

Task

Consider each of the contact levels listed below and suggest how and when each might be usefully employed in the collection process.

a) Telephone the accounting technician processing payments in the debtor company.
b) Send a fax to the accounting technician.
c) Send collection letters to the finance director.
d) Hold meetings with the debtor.
e) Take legal action.
f) Stop supplies.

11 The new Finance Director of your company has made an initial review of the credit collection process and has decided that, as part of it, a proper system of sending out collection (or reminder) letters to credit customers should be put in place.

You have been asked to design a reminder letter system.

Tasks

a) Write a memorandum to the Finance Director, outlining how your proposed system will operate and the type of letters to be despatched. Your answer should describe the whole of the reminder system and explain the rationale for the operations.

b) Design three different suitable reminder letters to be used for three different situations. Highlight the circumstances in which they would be used.

12 Draft a first reminder letter to a customer whose debt of £1,350.46 is 14 days overdue. The customer's name is Harvey Ltd and its account number is 204764.

13 Draft a letter to a customer whose debt of £976.80 is 30 days overdue and who is to be placed on your business's stop list. The customer's name is Bart & Sons and their account number is B245.

chapter 8:
COLLECTION OF DEBTS

1   Briefly explain the three main services of a debt factor.

2   Give TWO advantages and TWO disadvantages of debt factoring.

3   You have recently received a memo from your company's new sales director stating that he does not understand the difference between with recourse and without recourse.

   Task

   Explain the difference between 'with recourse' and 'without recourse' in relation to factoring debts.

4   Explain what is meant by invoice discounting and how it differs from debt factoring.

5   Briefly explain three types of debt insurance.

6   Give ONE advantage and ONE disadvantage of debt insurance.

7   Your company is reconsidering its methods of managing debtors. These include:

   a)   credit insurance through a whole turnover policy
   b)   factoring

   Task

   Write a memorandum to the managing director outlining your understanding of how each of these two methods may improve credit control. Your note should describe briefly the principles involved in each method, who will be involved in its operation, the effect on customer relationships, the impact on cash flow and the effect on the company's financial statements.

8   What are the possible remedies for a breach of contract? Which of these remedies is most appropriate for a seller of goods where the buyer has not paid?

9   What is the procedure for bringing an action to court against a debtor for non-payment? Which court should the action be brought in?

10   Your business has obtained a County Court judgement against a debtor who owes the business £5,500. Give a description of two methods which may be used to enforce this judgement.

11   i)   How is a petition for bankruptcy brought against an individual?
       ii)   What are the consequences of a petition for bankruptcy?
       iii) What are the consequences of a bankruptcy order?

12   If a customer is declared bankrupt what is the order in which their assets are used to make payments due? As an unsecured creditor how would your business claim payment from a bankrupt debtor?

13   Explain what is meant by a liquidation. What is the order of distribution of assets once a company is being liquidated?

14   Your managing director feels that there is a lack of information in your company's credit control manual about signs of possible future insolvency of your company's business customers.

Task

Prepare a section for your company's credit control manual that sets out possible signs of insolvency.

15 a)   Describe the characteristics and advantages of collection agencies.

  b)   Explain the considerations that would influence a firm when choosing whether to employ a solicitor to help collect debts.

16 a)   A company is insolvent when it cannot pay its debts as they fall due. Identify TWO routes for a creditor to recover bad debts and briefly describe what is involved.

  b)   Using the courts to recover bad debts is costly and time consuming. Describe THREE methods of enforcing a judgement in the county courts.

PRACTICE SIMULATION 1

UNIT 15

FH PANELS LTD

DATA AND TASKS

This simulation is designed to test your ability to operate a cash management and credit control system.

The situation is set out on page 325.

The tasks for you to perform are detailed on pages 325 to 337.

You are allowed **four hours** to complete your work.

Correcting fluid may be used but it should be used in moderation. Any errors should be crossed out neatly and clearly. The use of pencils for your written answers is not acceptable.

You should read the whole simulation before commencing work so as to gain an overall picture of what is required.

Coverage of performance criteria and range statements

It should be recognised that it is not always possible to cover all performance criteria and range statements in a simulation; some may be more appropriate and entirely natural in the workplace and others may not be practicable within the scope of a particular simulation. Where performance criteria and range statements are not covered they must be assessed by other means by the assessor before a candidate can be deemed competent.

Pages 343 and 344 of this book give an indication of the performance criteria coverage for this simulation and also flag up the need to ensure all areas of the range statement are covered.

The situation

Your name is Peter Long and you work as an Accounting Technician at FH Panels Ltd, a company that manufactures and sells fencing panels. The company was established ten years ago and has consistently increased its turnover and profitability over that period.

Fencing panels are made out of separate wood strips purchased from a number of suppliers. The company operates from leasehold factory premises and supplies building contractors and Do It Yourself retailers throughout the United Kingdom.

Personnel

Accounting technicians	Yourself (Peter Long) and your assistant Steve Rudd
Financial Controller	Jenny Spiers
Production Director	Graham Baker
Sales Director	Angus Clarke

Today's date is 1 July 2006.

Tasks to be completed

Task 1

Refer to the e-mail from Steve Rudd, and the cash budget for the three months ended 30 June 2006, set out at the end of these tasks.

Prepare a memo to Jenny Spiers in which you should:

- reconcile the actual cash balance at 30 June 2006 with the budgeted cash balance at that date;

- identify three significant deviations from the cash budget and suggest what action could have been taken to avoid each of these variances.

Write your answers in the blank memo on the following page.

MEMO

To:

From:

Date:

Subject:

_____
_____
_____
_____
_____
_____
_____
_____
_____
_____
_____
_____
_____
_____
_____
_____
_____
_____
_____
_____
_____
_____
_____
_____
_____
_____
_____
_____
_____
_____
_____
_____
_____
_____
_____
_____
_____

Task 2

The latest balance sheet of FH Panels Ltd is set out at the end of these tasks. Refer to this and the information provided in the memos from Graham Baker, Angus Clarke and Jenny Spiers also to be found at the end of these tasks.

a) Jenny Spiers has asked you to prepare a cash flow forecast for each of the three months ending 30 September 2006 based upon the information provided and using the proforma below. There is also space for any workings you may have.

b) The company is considering introducing a settlement discount of 2% for payments made in the month following sale. This policy is expected to result in 60% of debtors paying in the month following sale, 30% paying two months following the sale and 10% paying three months following sale. In a memo to Jenny Spiers calculate the effect on forecast receipts from trade customers for each of the three months to 30 September 2006 if this policy is introduced. Use the blank memo on the following page.

Cash flow forecast for three months ending 30 September 2006

	July £	August £	September £
Receipts from debtors			
Payments to suppliers			
Wages			
Production overheads			
Selling overheads			
Repairs and maintenance			
Capital expenditure			
Dividend	____	____	____
Cash flow for the month			
Opening cash balance	____	____	____
Closing cash balance	____	____	____

Workings

MEMO

To:

From:

Date:

Subject:

Task 3

In the past the company has invested surplus funds in a variety of Treasury stocks and also in fixed term deposits with the bank.

Jenny Spiers has asked you to prepare notes to brief the directors on:

■   what is meant by gilt edged securities

■   the effects of possible changes in base rates on the company's short term investment strategy

Use the space below.

Task 4

The directors of FH Panels Ltd have identified an opportunity to acquire a freehold factory which would allow them to expand production. The price of the factory is £300,000.

Explain in a memo to the Board of Directors:

- the advantages and disadvantages of funding the purchase with:

  i) a bank overdraft
  ii) a bank loan

- which is the preferred method of financing

Use the blank memo on the following page.

MEMO

To:

From:

Date:

Subject:

_____
_____
_____
_____
_____
_____
_____
_____
_____
_____
_____
_____
_____
_____
_____
_____
_____
_____
_____
_____
_____
_____
_____
_____
_____
_____
_____
_____
_____
_____
_____
_____
_____
_____
_____
_____

Task 5

Carmen Contractors Ltd have applied to FH Panels for credit facilities. The company has provided its profit and loss accounts for each of the two years ended 31 March 2005 and 2006 and balance sheets as at those dates (to be found at the end of these tasks) but has included no further information. Jenny Spiers has asked you to do the following.

- Prepare a memo for Jenny Spiers in which you compute three key accounting ratios for both years which will assist in making a recommendation on whether to extend credit or not. You should comment on the trend in each ratio given your objective of making a decision on extending credit. Use the memo on the following page.

- Draft a letter to the Purchasing Manager of Carmen Contractors Ltd declining the request for credit facilities. You should also state in your letter four additional items of information you require before you would be able to agree to offer credit terms to the company. Use the letterhead provided at the end of this task.

MEMO

To:

From:

Date:

Subject:

FH Panels Ltd
Hellingford Industrial Estate
Newtown
NT6 4XL

Task 6

Your assistant, Steve Rudd, is to be trained to open new credit accounts for customers.

As part of this training, you should prepare notes to cover:

- TWO factors to be considered when agreeing credit terms with a customer

- TWO sources of internal information and TWO sources of external information for evaluating the credit status of customers

- THREE items of data required when setting up a new customer's account

Use the space below.

Task 7

The credit control policy and an extract from the aged debtor analysis are set out after these tasks. You should continue to assume that today's date is 1 July 2006. On the basis of this information write a memo to Jenny Spiers which should include the following:

- any credit control action required for each account
- any suggestions for any provisions for doubtful debts

Use the blank memo on the following page.

MEMO

To:

From:

Date:

Subject:

Task 1

```
                                    E-mail

To:        Peter Long
From:      Steve Rudd
Subject:   Actual cash flows
Date:      1 July 2006
```

The information you requested is as follows

Actual cash flows

The actual cash flows for each of the three months ended 30 June 2006 were as follows:

	April £	May £	June £
Receipts from debtors	86,500	91,200	84,400
Payments to suppliers	(33,200)	(33,200)	(32,700)
Wages	(16,250)	(16,500)	(16,750)
Production overheads	(10,000)	(10,000)	(10,000)
Selling overheads	(3,100)	(3,400)	(3,500)
Repairs and maintenance	(4,100)	(3,900)	(2,700)
Capital expenditure		(50,000)	
Dividend			(30,000)
Cash flow for the month	19,850	(25,800)	(11,250)
Opening cash balance	41,100	60,950	35,150
Closing cash balance	60,950	35,150	23,900

Task 1

Cash budget for the three months ended 30 June 2006

	April £	May £	June £
Receipts from debtors	91,500	96,700	92,400
Payments to suppliers	(31,400)	(28,800)	(30,100)
Wages	(16,250)	(16,500)	(16,750)
Production overheads	(10,000)	(10,000)	(10,000)
Selling overheads	(3,300)	(3,000)	(3,000)
Repairs and maintenance	(1,100)	(1,500)	(1,100)
Capital expenditure			
Dividend			(30,000)
Cash flow for the month	29,450	36,900	1,450
Opening cash balance	41,100	70,550	107,450
Closing cash balance	70,550	107,450	108,900

Task 2

FH Panels Ltd Balance sheet as at 30 June 2006

	£	£
Fixed assets:		
Leasehold buildings		400,000
Plant and machinery	450,000	
Less: depreciation	172,800	
		277,200
		677,200
Current assets:		
Stock – wood	32,000	
Stock – finished goods	30,000	
Debtors	166,710	
Cash	23,900	
	252,610	
Current liabilities:		
Trade creditors	(33,500)	
Net current assets		219,110
		896,310
Represented by:		
Share capital		500,000
Retained profits		396,310
		896,310

Task 2

Memo

To: Peter Long, Accounting Technician
From: Graham Baker, Production Director
Date: 30 June 2006
Subject: Budgetary information

I have set out below the information that you have requested:

1   The cost of a strip of wood is expected to remain at £0.20 per strip for the next six months.

2   Each fence panel requires 25 strips of wood.

3   Each panel takes 20 minutes of labour time to manufacture and we currently pay our production staff £7.50 per hour. I expect to pay our production staff £7.80 per hour from 1 September 2006.

4   Fixed production overheads are expected to remain at £14,000 for July 2006 which includes £4,000 of depreciation. The overheads other than depreciation are expected to increase by 5% from 1 August 2006.

5   Wood stocks at 30 June 2006 are 160,000 strips valued at £32,000 and finished stocks of fence panels amount to 4,000 at 30 June 2006 valued at £30,000.

6   I plan to increase fence panel stocks by 300 each month but I shall reduce stocks of wood to 150,000 at the end of August and 120,000 at the end of September.

7   Repairs and maintenance costs should be budgeted at an average of £2,500 per month.

Memo

To: Peter Long, Accounting Technician
From: Angus Clarke, Sales Director
Date: 30 June 2006
Subject: Budgetary information

The sales information you requested is as follows:

1   Sales are expected to be 6,800 panels in July, 7,000 panels in August and 7,300 panels in September.

2   The current price of a fence panel is £13.20 per panel but there is to be a 5% price increase from 1 August 2006.

3   Sales department costs are expected to be £4,000 per month including depreciation of £800 per month.

Task 2

Memo

To: Peter Long, Accounting Technician
From: Jenny Spiers, Financial Controller
Date: 30 June 2006
Subject: Budgetary information

In preparing the cash flow forecast to 30 September please incorporate the following:

1   Although our policy is for all trade customers to pay within 30 days, for budgetary purposes you should assume that 20% of customers pay one month after the date of sale, 70% pay two months after the date of sale and 10% pay three months after the date of sale.

2   You should assume that our debtors at 30 June will pay as follows:

In July	£87,248
In August	£70,618
In September	£8,844
	£166,710

3   All purchases of wood will continue to be paid for one month in arrears as at present. All other costs will be paid for in the month in which they are incurred.

4   Capital expenditure of £20,000 should be budgeted for in August 2006.

Task 5

Carmen Contractors Ltd
Profit and loss accounts for the years ending 31 March

	2006	2005
	£000	£000
Turnover	560	500
Cost of sales	440	400
Gross profit	120	100
Operating expenses	85	80
Operating profit	35	20
Interest payable	10	10
Profit before tax	25	10
Taxation	8	2
Profit after tax	17	8

341

Task 5

Carmen Contractors Ltd
Balance sheets for the 12 months ended:

	2006 £000	2005 £000
Fixed assets	215	194
Current assets		
Stock	42	40
Debtors	22	14
	64	54
Current liabilities		
Trade creditors	56	52
Overdraft	105	95
	161	147
Net assets	118	101
Share capital	80	80
Profit and loss reserve	38	21
	118	101

Task 7

FH Panels Ltd
CREDIT CONTROL POLICY

1   Invoices must be issued on the same day as goods are despatched

2   An aged analysis of trade debtors is to be produced monthly

3   Credit terms are strictly 30 days from the date of invoice

4   Statements are despatched on the first working day of each month

5   A reminder letter must be sent when a debt is 14 days overdue

6   A telephone call to chase payment must be made when a debt is 21 days overdue

7   The customer will be placed on the stop list when the debt is 30 days overdue and a meeting arranged with the customer to discuss the operation of the account

8   A letter threatening legal action will be sent when the debt is 45 days overdue

9   Legal proceedings are to be commenced when a debt is 60 days overdue subject to the agreement of the Financial Controller.

AGED DEBTOR ANALYSIS – EXTRACT AT 30 JUNE 2006

	Total £	Credit limit £	Current <30 days £	31–60 days £	61–90 days £	> 90 days £
Castle Builders	10,800	12,000				10,800
DD DIY Ltd	6,800	10,000	5,200	1,200		400
AP Partners	3,250	4,000	1,000	1,000	1,250	
Gatfield Ltd	17,640	25,000	8,200	8,600	840	

COVERAGE OF PERFORMANCE CRITERIA

All performance criteria for this Unit are covered in this simulation.

Element	PC Coverage	Task(s)
15.1	**Monitor and control cash receipts and payments**	
	a) Cash receipts and payments are monitored and controlled against budgeted cash flow	1
	b) Appropriate staff are consulted to determine the likely pattern of cash flows over the accounting period and to anticipate any exceptional receipts or payments	2
	c) Forecasts of future cash payments and receipts are in accord with known income and expenditure trends	2
	d) Cash budgets are prepared in the approved format and clearly indicate net cash requirements	2
	e) Significant deviations from the cash budget are identified and corrective action is taken within defined organisational policies	2
15.2	**Manage cash balances**	
	a) Overdraft and loan facilities are arranged in anticipation of requirements and on the most favourable terms available	4
	b) Surplus funds are invested in marketable securities within defined financial authorisation limits	3
	c) The organisation's financial regulations and security procedures are observed	3
	d) Account is taken of trends in the economic and financial environment in managing cash balances	3
	e) An adequate level of liquidity is maintained in line with cash forecasts	1
15.3	**Grant credit**	
	a) Credit terms are agreed with customers in accordance with the organisation's policies	5
	b) Internal and external sources of information are identified and used to evaluate the current credit status of customers and potential customers	5
	c) New accounts are opened for those customers with an established credit status	6
	d) The reasons for refusing credit are discussed with customers in a tactful manner	5

Element	PC Coverage	Task(s)
15.4	**Monitor and control the collection of debts**	
	a) Information relating to the current state of debtors' accounts is regularly monitored and appropriate action taken	7
	b) Information regarding significant outstanding accounts and potential bad debts is promptly sent to relevant individuals within the organisation	7
	c) Discussions and negotiations with debtors are conducted courteously and achieve the desired outcome	7
	d) Debt recovery methods used are appropriate to the circumstances of individual cases and are in accordance with the organisation's procedures	7
	e) Recommendations to write off bad and doubtful debts are based on a realistic analysis of all known factors	7
	Any missing range statements will need to be assessed by other means.	

PRACTICE SIMULATION 2

UNIT 15

HAPPY CHIEF LTD

DATA AND TASKS

Instructions

This Simulation is designed to let you show your ability to operate a cash management and credit control system.

You should read the whole Simulation before you start work, so that you are fully aware of what you will have to do.

You are allowed **four hours** to complete your work. You should spend two hours on Tasks 1 and 2, and two hours on the remaining tasks.

Write your answers in the Answer Booklet provided.

The situation

Your name is George Benson and you work as an Accounting Technician for Happy Chefs Ltd. Happy Chefs Ltd is a catering company which provides catering and meals for corporate and private clients for functions and events.

Today's date is 4 January 2006.

Personnel

Accounting Technicians	Yourself, Clare Kavanagh and your assistant Kevin Timms
Finance Director	Gary Taylor
Financial Controller	Fiona Lim
Managing Director	Paula James

Tasks to be completed

Task 1

Refer to the memo from Kevin Timms on page 349. Prepare a memo to Fiona Lim in which you should:

- identify **three** significant differences between the actual cash flow for December 2005 and the budgeted cash flow for that month;

- suggest **three** actions which the company could have taken to avoid using its overdraft

Use the blank memo on page 353 in the Answer Booklet.

Task 2

Refer to the memos from Paula James and Fiona Lim given on pages 350 and 351.

a) Gary Taylor has asked you to prepare a cash budget for each of the three months ending 31 March 2006, based on the information provided and using the proforma on page 354 in the Answer Booklet. There is also space in the Answer Booklet for any workings you may have.

b) The company is considering offering a 2% settlement discount for payment within the same month as the invoice date. This is expected to mean that 70% of debtors will pay within this period and the 20% will pay in the month after invoice and 10% will pay two months after the invoice date. In a memo to Gary Taylor recommend whether the company should pursue this policy. Use page 355 in the Answer Booklet.

Task 3

At the current time the company has an overdraft. The Board of Directors is also considering the purchase of substantial new premises at a cost of about £300,000.

Explain in a memo to the Board:

- the advantages and disadvantages of funding the new premises with a bank overdraft or a bank loan
- which is the preferred method of financing

Use the blank memo page on page 356 of the Answer Booklet.

Task 4

The company is due to open a cash sales outlet for prepacked gourmet meals from its current factory.

Fiona Lim has asked you to draft a note setting out **three** procedures which should be adopted for the safe custody of cash.

Use the blank note page on page 357 of the Answer Booklet.

Task 5

Your assistant Kevin Timms has recently been required to draft letters to potential credit customers refusing them credit terms. He has asked for your advice and you are to write him a note setting out the main factors that should be considered and communicated when refusing credit terms to a customer.

Use the blank note page on page 358 of the Answer Booklet.

Task 6

Paula James has recently been reading an article on debt factoring and invoice discounting.

She is interested in these areas and asks you to set out in a memo **two** advantages and **two** disadvantages of debt factoring and **one** advantage and **one** disadvantage of invoice discounting.

Use the blank memo on page 359 of the Answer Booklet.

Task 7

The debt collection policy, and extract from the aged debtor analysis and supporting customer notes, are set out on pages 351 and 352.

On the basis of this information you are to write a memo to Fiona Lim stating any credit control action that is required for these customers.

Use the blank memo on page 360 of the Answer Booklet.

Task 8

Refer to the memo from Paula James on page 352 regarding Trevor Lightman. Paula would like clarification of Happy Chefs' legal position.

Write a note to Paula concerning the legal position of this debt. Your note should cover:

- the fundamental elements of a contract
- the action which Happy Chefs has for breach of contract
- how that action can be pursued.

Use the blank note on page 361 of the Answer Booklet.

Task 1

MEMO

To: George Benson
From: Kevin Timms
Date: 2 January 2006
Subject: December cash flow

As requested I now set out the actual and budgeted cash flows for the month of December 2005.

	Actual £	Budget £
Sales receipts	154,000	175,000
Food costs	(72,500)	(64,000)
Salaries	(43,000)	(43,000)
Administration costs	(25,400)	(27,600)
Capital expenditure	(64,000)	(18,000)
Dividend	(20,000)	–
Deposit account interest	100	100
Net cash flow for month	(70,800)	22,500
Opening cash balance	31,400	30,000
Closing cash balance	(39,400)	52,500

Task 2a

```
                            MEMO

To:          George Benson
From:        Paula James
Date:        2 January 2006
Subject:     Budgetary information
```

Please incorporate the following assumptions into your cash budget for the three months to 31 March 2006.

1 January is always a quiet month and I anticipate that we will only be invoicing £104,000 that month. However February invoicing should be £140,000 and March £155,000.

2 From 1 February we are opening a factory sales outlet for sales to the public of some of our pre-packaged foods. In the early months I expect sales to be for cash and to total £800 a month.

3 Salaries are due to increase by 5% from 1 March.

4 Administration costs should be £27,000 in January but due to a rent increase will go up by £3,000 from 1 February onwards.

5 We are investing in new refrigeration equipment and there is to be a down payment of £20,000 on 1 February and a monthly payment thereafter of £6,000.

6 There will be no movement in the deposit account and the monthly interest will remain as in previous months.

Task 2a

```
                                MEMO

To:          George Benson
From:        Fiona Lim
Date:        2 January 2006
Subject:     Budgetary information

Please use the following assumptions when preparing the cash budgets for the three months
to 31 March 2006.

1    Debtors at 31 December 2005 were £210,000 and of these it is anticipated that
     £175,000 will be received in January and the remainder in February.

2    Cash inflows from sales invoices will be as follows:

     40% in the month the invoice is issued
     50% in the month after the invoice is issued
     10% two months are the invoice is issued

3    Our gross profit margin (after deduction of food purchases) will remain at 60% with
     constant stock levels. Our food purchases will continue to be paid for one month after
     purchase.

4    Creditors for food purchases at 31 December 2005 were £70,000 and these will all be
     paid for in January.

5    All salaries and administration costs are paid for in the month they are incurred.
```

Task 7

DEBT COLLECTION POLICY

Invoices must be sent out the day after the goods/service is provided.

All customers are required to pay within 30 days of the invoice date.

An aged debt analysis is produced monthly.

Statements are sent to all debtors in the first week of each month.

When a debt is 7 days overdue a telephone call is made to the customer.

When a debt is 14 days overdue a reminder letter is sent to the customer.

If a debt becomes 30 days overdue the customer is put on the stop list and a meeting with the customer is arranged.

When a debt is 60 days overdue it is put into the hands of a debt collector.

When a debt is 90 days overdue legal proceedings are commenced subject to the agreement of the Managing Director.

Aged debtor analysis at 31 December 2005 – extract

Customer	Amount due £	Current £	31 to 60 days £	61 to 90 days £	> 90 days £
Havanna Ltd	1,250.00		1,250.00		
Jones Partners	800.00			800.00	
Norman Bros	1,1,00.00	700.00	400.00		

Notes

- the outstanding invoice for Havanna Ltd is dated 20 November 2005

- the outstanding invoice for Jones Partners is dated 14 October 2005

- the invoices for Norman Bros were dated as follows:

  - £700 12 December 2005

  - £400 17 November 2005 - a telephone call was made on 28 December to chase this debt but there has been no response

Task 8

MEMO

To: George Benson
From: Paula James
Date: 2 January 2006
Subject: Trevor Lightman

We provided this customer with catering services on 28 August 2005 after receiving a signed order from the customers and invoiced him on the following day for £1,500.00. We have still received no payment and the debt collectors were also unsuccessful in obtaining payment from the customer.

Answer Booklet

Task 1

```
                              MEMO

To:
From:
Date:
Subject:
_____

_____

_____

_____

_____

_____

_____

_____

_____

_____

_____

_____

_____

_____

_____

_____

_____

_____
```

Task 2

a) **Cash budget for three months ending 31 March 2006**

	Jan £	Feb £	Mar £	Total £
Cash inflows				
From opening debtors				
January invoices				
February invoices				
March invoices				
Shop sales				
Deposit account interest				
Total receipts				
Cash outflows				
Food supplies				
Salaries				
Administration costs				
Capital expenditure				
Total payments				
Movement for the month				
Opening cash balance				
Closing cash balance				

Workings

Task 2

b)

MEMO

To:

From:

Date:

Subject:

_____

_____

_____

_____

_____

_____

_____

_____

_____

_____

_____

_____

_____

_____

_____

_____

_____

_____

_____

Task 3

MEMO

To:
From:
Date:
Subject:

_____

_____

_____

_____

_____

_____

_____

_____

_____

_____

_____

_____

_____

_____

_____

_____

_____

_____

_____

_____

_____

Task 4

NOTE

Task 5

NOTE

Task 6

MEMO

To:
From:
Date:
Subject:

_____

_____

_____

_____

_____

_____

_____

_____

_____

_____

_____

_____

_____

_____

_____

_____

_____

_____

_____

_____

_____

_____

_____

Task 7

MEMO

To:
From:
Date:
Subject:

_____

_____

_____

_____

_____

_____

_____

_____

_____

_____

_____

_____

_____

_____

_____

_____

_____

_____

_____

_____

_____

_____

Task 8

NOTE

COVERAGE OF PERFORMANCE CRITERIA

All performance criteria for this Unit are covered in this simulation.

Element	PC Coverage		Task(s)
15.1	**Monitor and control cash receipts and payments**		
	a)	Cash receipts and payments are monitored and controlled against budgeted cash flow	1
	b)	Appropriate staff are consulted to determine the likely pattern of cash flows over the accounting period and to anticipate any exceptional receipts or payments	2
	c)	Forecasts of future cash payments and receipts are in accord with known income and expenditure trends	2
	d)	Cash budgets are prepared in the approved format and clearly indicate net cash requirements	2
	e)	Significant deviations from the cash budget are identified and corrective action is taken within defined organisational policies	1
15.2	**Manage cash balances**		
	a)	Overdraft and loan facilities are arranged in anticipation of requirements and on the most favourable terms available	2
	b)	Surplus funds are invested in marketable securities within defined financial authorisation limits	N/A
	c)	The organisation's financial regulations and security procedures are observed	4
	d)	Account is taken of trends in the economic and financial environment in managing cash balances	N/A
	e)	An adequate level of liquidity is maintained in line with cash forecasts	1
15.3	**Grant credit**		
	a)	Credit terms are agreed with customers in accordance with the organisation's policies	5
	b)	Internal and external sources of information are identified and used to evaluate the current credit status of customers and potential customers	7
	c)	New accounts are opened for those customers with an established credit status	5
	d)	The reasons for refusing credit are discussed with customers in a tactful manner	5

Element	PC Coverage	Task(s)
15.4	**Monitor and control the collection of debts**	
	a) Information relating to the current state of debtors' accounts is regularly monitored and appropriate action taken	7
	b) Information regarding significant outstanding accounts and potential bad debts is promptly sent to relevant individuals within the organisation	7
	c) Discussions and negotiations with debtors are conducted courteously and achieve the desired outcome	5
	d) Debt recovery methods used are appropriate to the circumstances of individual cases and are in accordance with the organisation's procedures	6
	e) Recommendations to write off bad and doubtful debts are based on a realistic analysis of all known factors	7

Any missing range statements will need to be assessed by other means.

AAT SAMPLE SIMULATION

UNIT 15
LUCENT LTD

DATA AND TASKS

This simulation is designed to test your ability to operate a cash management and credit control system.

The situation is set out on page 367.

The tasks for you to perform are detailed on pages 367 and 368.

You are allowed **four hours** to complete your work.

Correcting fluid may be used but it should be used in moderation. Any errors should be crossed out neatly and clearly. The use of pencils for your written answers is not acceptable.

You should read the whole simulation before commencing work so as to gain an overall picture of what is required.

Write your answers in the separate Answer Booklet provided starting on page 375. Paper for rough work is provided on pages 376 and 377 of the Answer Booklet.

Coverage of performance criteria and range statements

It should be recognised that it is not always possible to cover all performance criteria and range statements in a simulation; some may be more appropriate and entirely natural in the workplace and others may not be practicable within the scope of a particular simulation. Where performance criteria and range statements are not covered they must be assessed by other means by the assessor before a candidate can be deemed competent.

Pages 373 and 374 of this book give an indication of the performance criteria coverage for this simulation and also flag up the need to ensure all areas of the range statement are covered.

THE SITUATION

Your name is Pat Smith and you work as an accounting technician at Lucent Ltd, a company which manufactures and sells candles. The company was established ten years ago.

The company sells candles from its own shop, and to other retailers throughout the UK.

Personnel

Assistant Accountant	Yourself, Pat Smith
Financial Controller	Amy Williams
Production Director	Ross Morris
Sales Director	Ben Mohammed

TASKS TO BE COMPLETED

Task 1

The latest balance sheet of Lucent Ltd is set out on page 369. Refer to this and the information provided in the memo from Ross Morris on page 369, the memo from Ben Mohammed on page 370 and the memo from Amy Williams on page 370.

- Amy Williams asks you to prepare a cash budget for each of the three months ending 30 June 2006 based on the information provided and using the proforma on page 378 of the Answer Booklet. You should use pages 376 and 377 in the Answer Booklet to set out your workings for the number of candles to be produced, the raw materials to be purchased and the receipts from trade sales for each of the three months.

- Amy Williams asks you to calculate the impact on the forecast levels of cash and trade debtors at 30 June 2006 if sales to credit customers are made at a price of £1.50 and not £1.65 for each of the three months. Suggest two actions the company could take to reduce any adverse impact on cash flow that such a policy may create. Use page 378 of the Answer Booklet.

Task 2

The company has an overdraft facility of £225,000 with its bank is due for renewal in April 2006. Amy Williams has asked you to draft a memo to the Board setting out the size of facility required and whether an overdraft facility or term loan is more appropriate for the company's needs. You should date your memo 10 April 2006.

Use page 379 of the Answer Booklet

Task 3

An offer has been received to purchase the company's freehold retail site for £400,000. The company has accepted the offer and completion of the sale is expected to take place in July 2006. The Board of Directors has asked Amy Williams to consider how this money might be invested. In preparation for her meeting she has now asked you to prepare notes on the following matters.

- Gilt edged securities and bank deposits as investment opportunities appropriate for any surplus funds from the sale of the property.

- The security procedures which should be arranged for each type of investment.

- The effect of any increase in base rate on both types of investment.

Use page 380 of the Answer Booklet.

Task 4

A copy of a request for credit facilities from a director of Fancy Goods Ltd, a retailer of candles and other decorative products, is set out on page 371.

You should draft a letter to Mr S Redmond in reply to the original request for credit facilities. Your letter should set out the information you require from the company in order to progress the granting of credit facilities. You should use page 381 of the Answer Booklet for this task. Date your letter 10 April 2006.

Task 5

You have recently employed a trainee credit controller. Draft a memo to him setting out:

- six reasons why trade credit facilities might be refused
- how such a decision should be communicated to the applicant

You should use page 382 of the Answer Booklet for this task. Date your memo 10 April 2006.

Task 6

An extract of the aged debtor analysis and the company's credit control policy is set out on page 372. In a memo to Amy Williams, you should:

- set out the action to be taken with regard to each of the four customer accounts
- state how discussion should be conducted with overdue accounts
- recommend whether any provisions for doubtful debts are required

You should use page 383 of the Answer Booklet for this task.

LUCENT LTD – BALANCE SHEET AT 31 MARCH 2006

	£	£
Fixed assets		
Land and buildings		150,000
Plant and machinery	280,000	
Less: depreciation	120,000	
		160,000
		310,000
Current assets		
Stock		
Raw materials	60,000	
Finished goods	55,000	
Debtors	380,000	
Cash in hand at retail shop	1,000	
	496,000	
Current liabilities		
Bank overdraft	220,000	
Trade creditors for raw materials	120,000	
	340,000	
Net current assets		156,000
Total assets less current liabilities		466,000
Capital and reserves		
Share capital		100,000
Retained profits		366,000
		466,000

MEMO

To: Pat Smith, Assistant Accountant
From: Ross Morris, Production Director
Re: Budgetary information
Date: 2 April 2006

I set out below the information you recently requested.

1   The cost of raw materials for each candle is 60 pence. No price increase is expected in the budgetary period.

2   Each candle takes six minutes of labour time to manufacture and we currently pay our production staff £5 per hour.

3   Our fixed production overheads are £25,000 per month. This includes depreciation of £5,000.

4   At 31 March 2006 our raw materials stocks were sufficient to manufacture 100,000 candles and we also hold 50,000 candles in stock.

5   I plan to increase candle stocks by 5,000 each month but I shall maintain raw material stocks at their current level.

MEMO

To: Pat Smith, Assistant Accountant
From: Ben Mohammed, Sales Director
Re: Budgetary information
Date: 29 March 2006

The sales information you requested is as follows.

1   Sales to the retail trade are expected to be 120,000 candles in April, 125,000 in May and 130,000 in June. In addition, we expect to sell 5,000 candles from our own shop in each of the next three months.

2   Candles will be sold to the retail trade at £1.65. Sales made from our own shop will be made at £3 each.

3   Sales department costs are expected to be fixed at £12,000 per month including depreciation of £500 per month.

4   The costs for the shop are fixed and are £7,000 per month including depreciation of £800.

MEMO

To: Pat Smith, Assistant Accountant
From: Amy Williams, Financial Controller
Re: Budgetary information
Date: 30 March 2006

In preparing the budgeted cash flow to June please incorporate the following assumptions.

1   Although it is our policy for all trade customers to pay within 30 days, for budgetary purposes you should assume that 30% of retail trade customers pay one month after the date of sale and 70% pay two months after the date of sale.

2   You should assume that the debtors at 31 March will pay as follows.

	£
In April	200,000
In May	180,000
	380,000

3   All purchases of raw materials will be paid for one month in arrears as at present. All other costs will be paid in the month in which they are incurred.

4   Sales from our own shop will be made for cash.

5   Administration overheads should be budgeted to be £25,000 each month.

6   Overdraft interest is charged by the bank each month and should be budgeted at the rate of 1% per month on the overdrawn balance at the end of the previous month.

Fancy Goods Ltd

20 High Street

Bristol BS1 2FG

Pat Smith
Assistant Accountant
Lucent Ltd
Tylers Trading Estate
Gloucester GL15 3EW

21 March 2006

Dear Mr Smith

Request for credit facilities

I am seeking credit facilities for my chain of 10 decorative product shops. Although we have never purchased products from you I am keen to establish a trading relationship with you. To facilitate this I would be grateful if you could arrange for a credit facility of £10,000 on thirty days terms.

I look forward to receiving confirmation of this facility.

Yours sincerely

Stephen Redmond

Stephen Redmond
Director

AGED DEBTOR ANALYSIS

Customer	Amount due £	Current £	31–60 days £	61–90 days £	91 + days £
Candles Ltd	12,500.65				12,500.65
Lux Ltd	3,250.00	2,250.00	850.00		150.00
Lights Ltd	1,475.00		475.00	1,000.00	
Flames Ltd	16,815.75	9,275.50	6,120.25	1,420.00	

CREDIT CONTROL POLICY

1   Invoices must be issued on the same day as goods are despatched.

2   An aged analysis of trade debtors is to be produced monthly.

3   Statements are to be despatched on the first working day of each month.

4   A reminder letter must be sent when a debt is 14 days overdue.

5   A telephone call to chase payment must be made when a debt is 21 days overdue.

6   The customer will be placed on the stop list when the debt is 30 days overdue and a meeting arranged with the customer to discuss the operation of the account.

7   A letter threatening legal action will be sent when the debt is 45 days overdue.

8   Legal proceedings to be commenced when a debt is 60 days overdue, subject to agreement with the Financial Controller.

COVERAGE OF PERFORMANCE CRITERIA

All performance criteria for this unit are covered in this simulation.

Element	PC Coverage	Task(s)
15.1	**Monitor and control cash receipts and payments**	
	a) Cash receipts and payments are monitored and controlled against budgeted cash flow	1
	b) Appropriate staff are consulted to determine the likely pattern of cash flows over the accounting period and to anticipate any exceptional receipts or payments	1
	c) Forecasts of future cash payments and receipts are in accord with known income and expenditure trends	1
	d) Cash budgets are prepared in the approved format and clearly indicate net cash requirements	1
	e) Significant deviations from the cash budget are identified and corrective action is taken within defined organisational policies	1
15.2	**Manage cash balances**	
	a) Overdraft and loan facilities are arranged in anticipation of requirements and on the most favourable terms available	2
	b) Surplus funds are invested in marketable securities within defined financial authorisation limits	3
	c) The organisation's financial regulations and security procedures are observed	3
	d) Account is taken of trends in the economic and financial environment in managing cash balances	3
	e) An adequate level of liquidity is maintained in line with cash forecasts	2
15.3	**Grant credit**	
	a) Credit terms are agreed with customers in accordance with the organisation's policies	4
	b) Internal and external sources of information are identified and used to evaluate the current credit status of customers and potential customers	4
	c) New accounts are opened for those customers with an established credit status	5
	d) The reasons for refusing credit are discussed with customers in a tactful manner	5

Element	PC Coverage	Task(s)
15.4	**Monitor and control the collection of debts**	
	a) Information relating to the current state of debtors' accounts is regularly monitored and appropriate action taken	6
	b) Information regarding significant outstanding accounts and potential bad debts is promptly sent to relevant individuals within the organisation	6
	c) Discussions and negotiations with debtors are conducted courteously and achieve the desired outcome	6
	d) Debt recovery methods used are appropriate to the circumstances of individual cases and are in accordance with the organisation's procedures	6
	e) Recommendations to write off bad and doubtful debts are based on a realistic analysis of all known factors	6
	Any missing range statements will need to be assessed by other means.	

AAT SAMPLE SIMULATION

ANSWER BOOKLET

UNIT 15

ROUGH WORK

ROUGH WORK

ANSWERS (Task 1)

LUCENT LTD

Cash flow forecast for the three months ending 30 June 2006

	April £	May £	June £
Receipts			
Trade sales			
Own retail sales			
Total receipts			
Payments			
Trade suppliers			
Production wages			
Production overheads			
Sales department costs			
Retail shop costs			
Administration costs			
Overdraft interest			
Total payments			
Movement for month			
Bank balance b/f			
Bank balance c/f			

Impact of reduction in sales price

_____

_____

_____

_____

_____

_____

_____

_____

_____

_____

_____

_____

ANSWERS (Task 2)

MEMO

To:

From:

Re:

Date:

ANSWERS (Task 3)

Briefing notes on gilt edged securities and bank deposits

ANSWERS (Task 4)

LUCENT LIMITED
Tylers Trading Estate, Gloucester GL15 3EW

ANSWERS (Task 5)

MEMO

To:

From:

Re:

Date:

_____

_____

_____

_____

_____

_____

_____

_____

_____

_____

_____

_____

_____

_____

_____

_____

_____

_____

_____

_____

_____

_____

_____

ANSWERS (Task 6)

MEMO

To:
From:
Re:
Date:

_____

_____

_____

_____

_____

_____

_____

_____

_____

_____

_____

_____

_____

_____

_____

_____

_____

_____

_____

_____

_____

_____

_____

_____

_____

REVISION COMPANION UNIT 15

answers

answers to chapter 1: MONITORING CASH RECEIPTS AND PAYMENTS

1   Profit is where a business charges more for its sales in a period than the costs that it incurs. The costs will be the cost of the goods sold and all other expenses of the business but if the amount charged for the goods that are sold exceeds these costs then a profit has been made.

Cash flow however is the net amount of cash coming into the business from sales and other sources and going out of the business in the form of payments for goods, wages and other expenses. If all transactions are for cash and all expenses are cash expenses then cash flow and operating profit should be equal. However this will rarely be the case in practice and therefore cash flow and profit will not equate to the same figures.

2   **Tutorial note**. In your simulation, you will be asked to write memos to other staff, some of whom may lack accounting knowledge. You therefore need to be able to explain key concepts in a way that is understandable to non-accountants.

To:	Mr Blaze
From:	Carla Lark, Accounts
Date:	17 July
Subject:	Cash cycles etc

Introduction

The principles underlying the bank manager's request are basically simple, but the language can seem a little obscure.

Profitability and liquidity

These are two different ideas. Both of them can be used to assess the performance of a business.

a)   If a business is **profitable**, this means that there is a **surplus of income** over expenditure, and so there is a positive return on money invested.

b)   **Liquidity** means the ability of a business to **pay its debts** as they fall due. In practice this means that cash receipts and payments must at least balance, or that facilities for borrowing can be obtained.

Profitability and liquidity differ for many reasons.

a)   A customer who takes credit will **hand over payment some time** (for example a month) **after** the **transaction** took place. The timings of cash receipts and reported sales will therefore differ.

b)   The same is true of payments. Goods bought in one period may only **actually be paid for after the end of the period**. Also, some stocks will not be used until the next period.

c) **Cash** may **arise** from a **transaction** which **does not reflect profit**, such as the receipt of a loan.

d) Some assets in a business are **depreciated**. In other words, their cost is spread over their useful life, even though the expenditure was incurred on one occasion.

Cash cycle

The cash cycle relates to liquidity. The cash cycle refers to the amount of time between:

a) **Paying for goods** and
b) **Receiving the money** from the customer for the sale of the goods

This is relevant to a bank manager, as the cash cycle means that the delay results in the business having to borrow money from the bank. If the cash cycle were shorter, in other words if you took longer to pay your suppliers and if you collected your debts sooner, you would have to borrow less.

Operating cash flows

The bank manager is trying to find out how easy or difficult it will be for you to make the **loan repayments**. He wants to know whether you will have sufficient cash surplus each period to pay off both the interest on the loan and the principal (the sum initially advanced).

Operating cash flows are the result of **trading**, and relate to sales and debtors, purchases and creditors, and stocks. If there is a surplus, the bank will be confident that the principal and interest can be paid: hopefully the new investment will enhance the business's ability to generate cash surpluses.

3   There are a number of reasons for the difference between the profit that a business makes and the cash balance. These include the following:

Accruals accounting

Under the accruals concept revenue from sales and the cost of goods and expenses are accounted for in the period in which they are earned or incurred rather than in the period in which the cash is received or paid. Therefore even though a business may appear to have made a profit in a period it may not yet have the cash to show for it.

Non-cash expenses

Generally expenses of a business will reduce the amount of cash that the business has as these expenses will have to be paid for. However there are some expenses which have no effect on cash at all. The most familiar of these is the annual depreciation charge on fixed assets. Although this is an expense of the business it is not an amount of cash leaving the business.

Receipts/payments not affecting profit

Many businesses will find that on occasions they have receipts of cash into the business which do not affect profit. For example if a sole trader pays more capital into his business or a company issues additional shares for cash there are receipts of cash into the business but the profit of the business is not affected.

Purchase of fixed assets

When fixed assets are purchased by a business this will often mean a large payment of cash in order to acquire the asset however this does not affect the profit and loss account as only the annual depreciation charge on the asset is an expense rather than the full cash cost.

Sale of fixed assets

When a fixed asset is sold then this will mean cash coming into the business, being the selling price of the asset. However the profit of the business is only increased or decreased by any amount of profit or loss on the sale of this asset rather than the cash received.

4   Regular cash receipts might include:

- receipts from cash sales
- receipts from credit sales
- interest on bank deposit accounts

Irregular cash receipts might include:

- proceeds from sales of fixed assets
- dividends from investments held

5   Regular cash payments might include:

- payments to suppliers for purchases on credit
- payment of wages
- payment of expenses

Irregular cash payments might include:

- purchase of fixed assets
- payment of drawings to a sole trader/dividends to shareholders

6   a)   Payments to employees for wages are a **revenue expense**. They must be paid **regularly** (or else the employees will leave), but are **predictable**. They are likely to be a **significant expense** (how great depends on the nature of the company and industry), but should be met out of **business revenues**, or **temporarily**, out of an **overdraft**.

b)   Payment for new plant and machinery is **capital expenditure** that will be needed once every few years. It may be postponed for a year or two if cash is short, but ultimately the business must pay for up-to-date, reliable machinery to remain operational. (In addition if investment is postponed, another type of expenditure, **repairs**, will probably increase because of the unreliability of ageing machinery.)

Because expenditure on plant and machinery may be for very large amounts, a business may not be able to meet it out of cash-in-hand. Extra finance may be needed, either **loans** or **proceeds from the issue** of shares. If the business obtains funds in these ways, it will be following the principle of **matching**, obtaining long-term finance to meet expenditure that will give it long-term benefits.

7   A cash flow forecast can be prepared using an opening and closing budgeted balance sheet and a budgeted profit and loss account by firstly reconciling the budgeted operating profit to the budgeted net cash flow from operating activities. This is done by adjusting the budgeted operating

profit for non-cash expenses, such as depreciation, and then for changes in working capital. This will give the budgeted cash flow from operating activities as follows:

	£
Budgeted net operating profit	X
Adjustments for:	
Depreciation	X
Profit on sale of fixed assets	(X)
Working capital adjustments:	
Increase in stocks	(X)
Decrease in debtors	X
Increase in creditors	X
Budgeted net cash flow from operations	X

Other cash flows which are not part of the operating profit cash flows are then included by considering interest and tax payments and other changes in the balance sheet balances. This would lead to the final part of the cash flow forecast:

	£
Budgeted net cash flow from operations	X
Non-operating cash flows	
Interest payments	(X)
Purchase of fixed assets	(X)
Proceeds from sale of fixed assets	X
Issue of shares	X
Payment of dividend	(X)
Budgeted net cash flow	X
Opening cash balance	X
Closing cash balance	X

8 i) Cash budget June

	Budget £	Actual £	Variance £	
Receipts:				
Cash sales receipts	101,000	94,000	7,000	Adv
Credit sales receipts	487,000	475,000	12,000	Adv
Total receipts	588,000	569,000	19,000	Adv
Payments:				
Credit suppliers	(303,000)	(294,000)	9,000	Fav
Wages	(155,000)	(162,000)	7,000	Adv
Variable expenses	(98,600)	(99,400)	800	Adv
Fixed expenses	(40,000)	(40,000)	–	
Capital expenditure	–	(45,000)	45,000	Adv
Total payments	(596,600)	(640,400)	43,800	Adv
Net cash flow for the month	(8,600)	(71,400)	62,800	Adv
Bank b/f	20,300	20,300		
Bank c/f	11,700	(51,100)	62,800	Adv

ii)   Possible actions to reduce or eliminate the overdraft at the end of June might have been:

- to collect receipts due from credit sales earlier
- to delay payments to credit suppliers
- to delay the capital expenditure
- to find an alternative method of buying the fixed asset such as leasing or hire purchase

9   i)   Reconciliation of budgeted cash balance at 31 July to actual cash balance

	£
Budgeted cash balance	61,900
Additional cash sales	13,000
Shortfall in receipts from credit sales	(25,000)
Additional receipt from sale of fixed asset	22,000
Additional payments to suppliers	(35,000)
Additional variable overheads	(7,400)
Additional fixed overheads	(2,000)
Purchase of fixed assets	(46,000)
Actual cash balance	(18,500)

ii)   Possible actions to prevent the use of overdraft finance at the end of the month might be:

- to collect receipts from credit customers earlier

- to delay payment to credit suppliers

- to delay payment of any overheads paid for on credit

- to delay payment for the fixed assets

- to find an alternative method of purchasing the fixed assets such as leasing or   hire purchase

- to delay payment of the dividend

10   Possible actions include:

- improving credit control procedures to ensure money is received from credit   customers sooner

- increasing the proportion of cash sales in comparison to credit sales

- selling surplus fixed assets

- increasing the period of credit taken from suppliers therefore paying suppliers later

- negotiating credit terms for expenses that are currently paid in cash

- delaying payments for fixed assets

- changing the method of financing the purchase of fixed assets

- waiving or delaying dividend payments

answers to chapter 2:
PREPARING CASH BUDGETS

1

		October £	November £	December £
Cash sales	280,000 x 30%	84,000		
	250,000 x 30%		75,000	
	220,000 x 30%			66,000
Credit sales				
August	240,000 x 30%	72,000		
September	265,000 x 40%	106,000		
	265,000 x 30%		79,500	
October	280,000 x 40%		112,000	
	280,000 x 30%			84,000
November	250,000 x 40%			100,000
Total cash receipts		262,000	266,500	250,000

2

		October £	November £	December £
August	180,000 x 35%	63,000		
September	165,000 x 45%	74,250		
	165,000 x 35%		57,750	
October	190,000 x 20% x 98%	37,240		
	190,000 x 45%		85,500	
	190,000 x 35%			66,500
November	200,000 x 20% x 98%		39,200	
	200,000 x 45%			90,000
December	220,000 x 20% x 98%			43,120
Total cash payments		174,490	182,450	199,620

3

	August £	September £	October £
July purchases 5,000 x £50 x 60%	150,000		
August purchases 5,200 x £50 x 60%		156,000	
September purchases 5,500 x £50 x 60%			165,000

4 **Tutorial note**. In this question you are told that there are no opening and closing stocks, therefore purchases = cost of sales

a) Remember **mark up** is on **purchases**.

If purchases 100%, mark up $33\frac{1}{3}$,

Sales = $100 + 33\frac{1}{3} = 133\frac{1}{3}\%$

Purchases $= \dfrac{100}{133\frac{1}{3}} \times 6,000$

$= £4,500$

b) Remember **margin** is on **sales**.

If sales 100% margin 20%

Purchases = $100 - 20 = 80\%$

Sales $= \dfrac{100}{80} \times 12,000$

$= £15,000$

c) i) Mark up $= \dfrac{\text{Profits}}{\text{Purchases}}$

$= \dfrac{6,000}{16,000 - 6,000}$

$= 60\%$

ii) Margin $= \dfrac{\text{Profits}}{\text{Sales}}$

$= \dfrac{6,000}{16,000}$

$= 37\frac{1}{2}\%$

5

		April £	May £	June £
March sales	650,000 x 70%	455,000		
April sales	600,000 x 25% x 97%	145,500		
	600,000 x 70%		420,000	
May sales	580,000 x 25% x 97%		140,650	
	580,000 x 70%			406,000
June sales	550,000 x 25% x 97%			133,375
Total cash receipts		600,500	560,650	539,375

6

	Profit £	Operational cash flow £
Sales	300,000	300,000
Opening debtors (\ received in year)		20,000
Closing debtors (outstanding at year end)		(25,000)
Cash in		295,000
Cost of sales	200,000	200,000
Closing stock (bought, but not used, in year)		19,000
Opening stock (used, but not bought, in year)		(15,000)
Purchases in year		204,000
Opening creditors (\ paid in year)		12,000
Closing creditors (outstanding at year end)		(14,000)
Cash out		202,000
Profit/operational cash flow	100,000	93,000

7   i)   Production budget

	April Units	May Units	June Units	July Units	Aug Units
Sales	1,000	1,200	1,300	1,500	1,600
Less: opening stock	(180)	(200)	(220)	(240)	(260)
Add: closing stock	200	220	240	260	280
Production	1,020	1,220	1,320	1,520	1,620

ii) **Purchases budget**

	April Kg	May Kg	June Kg	July Kg
Materials required for production				
1,220 x 2kg	2,440			
1,320 x 2kg		2,640		
1,520 x 2kg			3,040	
1,620 x 2kg				3,240
Less: opening stock	(550)	(500)	(450)	(400)
Add: closing stock	500	450	400	350
Purchases in kg	2,390	2,590	2,990	3,190

	£	£	£	£
2,390 x £40	95,600			
2,590 x £40		103,600		
2,990 x £40			119,600	
3,190 x £40				127,600

iii) **Cash payments to suppliers**

	May £	June £	July £
Cash payments	95,600	103,600	119,600

8 Production budget

	March Units	April Units	May Units	June Units
Sales next month	7,200	7,050	6,550	6,150
Less: opening stock	(1,000)	(1,000)	(1,000)	(900)
Add: closing stock	1,000	1,000	900	750
Production in units	7,200	7,050	6,450	6,000

Labour budget – hours

	April Hours	May Hours	June Hours
7,050/3	2,350		
6,450/3		2,150	
6,000/3			2,000

Labour budget – £

	April £	May £	June £
Hours x £8.40	19,740	18,060	16,800

9   Cash budget – July to September

	July £	August £	September £
Cash receipts:			
Receipts from credit sales (W1)	438,400	467,840	488,520
Proceeds from sale of equipment		7,500	
Total receipts	438,400	475,340	488,520
Cash payments:			
Payments to suppliers (W2)	246,000	256,000	288,000
Wages	60,000	60,000	60,000
Overheads (W3)	44,000	47,750	49,000
Selling expenses	48,000	50,000	52,000
Equipment		42,000	
Overdraft interest	820	424	233
Total payments	398,820	456,174	449,233
Net cash flow	39,580	19,166	39,287
Opening balance	(82,000)	(42,420)	(23,254)
Closing balance	(42,420)	(23,254)	16,033

WORKINGS

1)   Receipts from credit sales

		July £	August £	September £
April sales	420,000 x 12%	50,400		
May sales	400,000 x 25%	100,000		
	400,000 x 12%		48,000	
June sales	480,000 x 40%	192,000		
	480,000 x 25%		120,000	
	480,000 x 12%			57,600
July sales	500,000 x 20% x 96%	96,000		
	500,000 x 40%		200,000	
	500,000 x 25%			125,000
August sales	520,000 x 20% x 96%		99,840	
	520,000 x 40%			208,000
September sales	510,000 x 20% x 96%			97,920
		438,400	467,840	488,520

2) **Payments to suppliers**

		July £	August £	September £
May purchases	250,000 x 60%	150,000		
June purchases	240,000 x 40%	96,000		
	240,000 x 60%		144,000	
July purchases	280,000 x 40%		112,000	
	280,000 x 60%			168,000
August purchases	300,000 x 40%			120,000
		246,000	256,000	288,000

3) **Overheads**

	July £	August £	September £
June overheads (50,000 – 6,000) x 25%	11,000		
July overheads (50,000 – 6,000) x 75%	33,000		
(50,000 – 6,000) x 25%		11,000	
August overheads			
(55,000 – 6,000) x 75%		36,750	
(55,000 – 6,000) x 25%			12,250
September overheads			
(55,000 – 6,000) x 75%			36,750
	44,000	47,750	49,000

10   Cash budget – October to December

	October £	November £	December £
Cash receipts:			
Receipts from credit sales (W1)	378,000	391,500	417,000
Cash payments:			
Purchases of raw materials (W2)	144,180	156,060	164,880
Wages (W3)	118,800	127,440	131,760
Production overheads	50,000	50,000	50,000
General overheads	60,000	60,000	68,000
Total payments	372,980	393,500	414,640
Net cash flow	5,020	(2,000)	2,360
Opening balance	40,000	45,020	43,020
Closing balance	45,020	43,020	45,380

WORKINGS

1) **Receipts from credit sales**

	October £	November £	December £
August sales			
5,000 x £75 x 60%	225,000		
September sales			
5,100 x £75 x 40%	153,000		
5,100 x £75 x 60%		229,500	
October sales			
5,400 x £75 x 40%		162,000	
5,400 x £75 x 60%			243,000
November sales			
5,800 x £75 x 40%			174,000
	378,000	391,500	417,000

2) **Purchases of raw materials**

Production budget

	Aug Units	Sept Units	Oct Units	Nov Units	Dec Units
Sales	5,000	5,100	5,400	5,800	6,000
Less: opening stock	(500)	(500)	(500)	(600)	(700)
Add: closing stock	500	500	600	700	800
Production	5,000	5,100	5,500	5,900	6,100

Purchases budget

	Aug Kg	Sept Kg	Oct Kg	Nov Kg
Required for production x 3kg	15,300	16,500	17,700	18,300
Less: opening stock	(3,000)	(3,000)	(3,000)	(3,200)
Add: closing stock	3,000	3,000	3,200	3,500
Purchases in kg	15,300	16,500	17,900	18,600
	£	£	£	£
Kg x £9	137,700	148,500	161,100	167,400

Payments to suppliers

	October £	November £	December £
August purchases			
137,700 x 40%	55,080		
September purchases			
148,500 x 60%	89,100		
148,500 x 40%		59,400	
October purchases			
161,100 x 60%		96,660	
161,100 x 40%			64,440
November purchases			
167,400 x 60%			100,440
Total payments to suppliers	144,180	156,060	164,880

3) **Wages**

Production budget

	Aug Units	Sept Units	Oct Units	Nov Units	Dec Units
Sales	5,000	5,100	5,400	5,800	6,000
Less: opening stock	(500)	(500)	(500)	(600)	(700)
Add: closing stock	500	500	600	700	800
Production	5,000	5,100	5,500	5,900	6,100

Labour budget – hours

	Oct Hours	Nov Hours	Dec Hours
Production x 3 hours	16,500	17,700	18,300
	£	£	£
Wages – production x £7.20	118,800	127,440	131,760

11   **Cash flow forecast for the three months ending 31 December**

	£000
Operating profit	140
Add: depreciation	20
	160
Increase in stocks	(20)
Increase in debtors	(30)
Increase in creditors	25
Net cash flow from operating activities	135
Interest paid	(10)
Tax paid	(40)
	85
Payments for fixed assets (W1)	(310)
Long term loan	200
Net cash outflow	(25)

WORKING

Payment for fixed assets

<table>
<tr><td colspan="4" style="text-align:center">Fixed assets at NBV</td></tr>
<tr><td></td><td>£000</td><td></td><td>£000</td></tr>
<tr><td>Opening balance</td><td>760</td><td>Depreciation</td><td>20</td></tr>
<tr><td>Additions (bal fig)</td><td>310</td><td>Closing balance</td><td>1,050</td></tr>
<tr><td></td><td>1,070</td><td></td><td>1,070</td></tr>
</table>

12   **Tutorial note**. Don't get caught out by putting all the rent in the budget. Task b) discusses measures to alter the operating cycle.

a)   **Marquis Marketing Ltd**
     Cash budget: July to September 2006

	July £000	August £000	September £000	Total £000
Inflows				
Receipts from sales	160	320	80	560
Outflows				
Payments for purchases	60	40	120	220
Salaries	36	36	36	108
Rent (£48,000 ÷ 4)	12	–	–	12
	108	76	156	340
Net movement in month	52	244	(76)	220
Opening balance	(112)	(60)	184	(112)
Closing balance	(60)	184	108	108

b)   The trading information given in the question denotes an erratic, highly seasonal trend. It would be more informative to have the **information** for **at least one year**, if not longer, to give a full picture of the trading cycle.

    It would help to reduce the fluctuations in the monthly cash balance of the receipts from sales and the payments for **purchases** if the receipts and payments could be **'matched'**. A way of doing this would be to reduce the length of credit terms allowed to customers to one month.

    Another option is to **negotiate the rent** so that it is paid monthly, which would help to spread the payment out more evenly over the year.

    It would be even more beneficial if the company could **pay the suppliers after a longer period**. By negotiating the company might be able to pay in two months' time rather than one, and therefore could keep the credit terms for customers at two months.

    If the credit terms given to customers were reduced to one month and if rent was paid monthly, then the cash budget would appear as follows.

	July £000	August £000	September £000	Total £000
Inflows				
Receipts from sales	320	80	80	480
Outflows				
Payments for purchases	60	40	120	220
Salaries	36	36	36	108
Rent	4	4	4	12
	100	80	160	340
Net movement in month	220	–	(80)	140
Opening balance	(112)	108	108	(112)
Closing balance	108	108	28	28

This shows a slightly more even cash flow although obviously the same months are still better or worse than others.

13 a) **Wilson Ltd – cash budget 2006**

Month ending (£)

	January	February	March	April	May	June
Inflows						
Receipts from cash sales	32,800	41,000	49,200	53,300	57,400	68,800
Receipts from debtors	114,800	131,200	131,200	164,000	196,800	213,200
Interest received	925	1,059	646	822	1,064	829
Total inflows	148,525	173,259	181,046	218,122	255,264	282,829
Outflows						
Payments to creditors	40,000	48,000	48,000	56,000	60,000	60,000
Variable costs	80,000	96,000	96,000	112,000	120,000	120,000
Fixed costs	1,800	1,800	1,800	1,800	2,200	2,200
Advertising		20,000			20,000	
Capital expenditure		90,000				
Corporation tax						56,000
Dividend					100,000	
Interest on overdraft						
Interest on long-term loan						17,500
Total outflows	121,800	255,800	145,800	169,800	302,200	255,700
Net cash flow	26,725	(82,541)	35,246	48,322	(46,936)	27,129
Opening cash balance	185,000	211,725	129,184	164,430	212,752	165,816
Closing cash balance	211,725	129,184	164,430	212,752	165,816	192,945

b)   i)   The receipts and payments cash budget method is:

- relatively **easy to use** and to understand
- suitable for time periods of up to about **three months**

     ii)   The cash flow forecast method is:

- more **easily reconciled** to financial accounting statements
- able to prevent items such as **negative stocks** appearing in forecasts

     iii)   To use both methods together, differences which arise between the two should be reconciled regularly in order to create a more accurate forecast.

answers to chapter 3: FURTHER ASPECTS OF CASH BUDGETING

1

			Takings £	Five day moving average £
Week 1	Mon		1,260	
	Tues		1,600	
	Wed		1,630	1,620
	Thurs		1,780	1,636
	Fri		1,830	1,666
Week 2	Mon		1,340	1,668
	Tues		1,750	1,682
	Wed		1,640	1,712
	Thurs		1,850	1,754
	Fri		1,980	1,736
Week 3	Mon		1,550	1,732
	Tues		1,660	1,736
	Wed		1,620	1,734
	Thurs		1,870	
	Fri		1,970	

2 i) The trend is the general movement in the time series figures over a period of time.

ii) Cyclical variations are the long term variations caused by general economic factors which often extend over a period of many years.

iii) Seasonal variations are variations in the time series figures due to the seasonality of the business.

iv) Random variations are other variations that are not due to the trend, cyclical or seasonal variations.

3

		Time series £	Four quarter moving average £	Trend £
2004	Q1	448,700		
	Q2	449,900		
			439,700	
	Q3	423,500		439,875
			440,050	
	Q4	436,700		440,263
			440,475	
2005	Q1	450,100		441,113
			441,750	
	Q2	451,600		442,138
			442,525	
	Q3	428,600		442,950
			443,375	
	Q4	439,800		443,813
			444,250	
2006	Q1	453,500		444,413
			444,575	
	Q2	455,100		444,788
			445,000	
	Q3	429,900		
	Q4	441,500		

4

		Time series £	Trend £	Seasonal variation £
2004	Q1	448,700		
	Q2	449,900		
	Q3	423,500	439,875	− 16,375
	Q4	436,700	440,263	− 3,563
2005	Q1	450,100	441,113	+ 8,987
	Q2	451,600	442,138	+ 9,462
	Q3	428,600	442,950	− 14,350
	Q4	439,800	443,813	− 4,013
2006	Q1	453,500	444,413	+ 9,087
	Q2	455,100	444,788	+ 10,312
	Q3	429,900		
	Q4	441,500		

	Q1	Q2	Q3	Q4
2004			− 16,375	− 3,563
2005	+ 8,987	+ 9,462	− 14,350	− 4,013
2006	+ 9,087	+10,312		
Total	+18,074	+19,774	− 30,725	− 7,576
Average	+ 9,037	+ 9,887	− 15,363	− 3,788
Adjustment	+ 57	+ 57	+ 57	+ 56
Seasonal variation	+ 9,094	+ 9,944	− 15,306	− 3,732

5

		Time series £	Trend £	Seasonal variation %
2004	Q1	448,700		
	Q2	449,900		
	Q3	423,500	439,875	96.3
	Q4	436,700	440,263	99.2
2005	Q1	450,100	441,113	102.0
	Q2	451,600	442,138	102.1
	Q3	428,600	442,950	96.8
	Q4	439,800	443,813	99.1
2006	Q1	453,500	444,413	102.0
	Q2	455,100	444,788	102.3
	Q3	429,900		
	Q4	441,500		

	Q1	Q2	Q3	Q4
2004			96.3	99.2
2005	102.0	102.1	96.8	99.1
2006	102.0	102.3		
Total	204.0	204.4	193.1	198.3
Seasonal variation	102.0	102.2	96.6	99.2

6 The increase in the trend is from £439,875 to £444,788 over a period of 7 increases. Therefore the average increase is £702 per quarter ((£444,788- 439,875)/7). To these average increases the seasonal variation must then be applied.

i) Q1 2007 = £444,788 + (3 x 702) + 9,094
           = £455,988

   Q2 2007 = £444,788 + (4 x 702) + 9,944
           = £457,540

ii) Q1 2007 = (£444,788 + (3 x 702)) x 102.0%
           = £455,832

   Q2 2007 = (£444,788 + (4 x 702)) x 102.2%
           = £457,443

7 The problems involved with using time series analysis for budgeting purposes include the following:

■   the less historic data available the less reliable will be the results

■   the further into the future we forecast the less reliable will be the results

■   there is an assumption that the trend and seasonal variations from the past will continue into the future

■   cyclical and random variations have been ignored.

8   **Tutorial note**. It would be acceptable to add an extra column to the first table for the seasonal percentage if you had room; it would save you repeating the actual and trend figures.

a)   The seasonal variation for the 15 days using the **additive** model are as follows:

		Actual	Trend	Seasonal variation
Week 1	Monday	560	648.90	−88.90
	Tuesday	840	651.84	+188.16
	Wednesday	728	654.78	+73.22
	Thursday	658	657.72	+0.28
	Friday	434	660.66	−226.66
Week 2	Monday	574	663.60	−89.60
	Tuesday	875	666.54	+208.46
	Wednesday	770	669.48	+100.52
	Thursday	679	672.42	+6.58
	Friday	448	675.36	−227.36
Week 3	Monday	588	678.30	−90.30
	Tuesday	910	681.24	+228.76
	Wednesday	812	684.18	+127.82
	Thursday	700	687.12	+12.88
	Friday	462	690.06	−228.06

Average variations

	Monday	Tuesday	Wednesday	Thursday	Friday	
Week 1	−88.90	+188.16	+73.22	+0.28	−226.66	
Week 2	−89.60	+208.46	+100.52	+6.58	−227.36	
Week 3	−90.30	+228.76	+127.82	+12.88	−228.06	
Total	−268.80	+625.38	+301.56	+19.74	−682.06	
Average	−89.60	+208.46	+100.52	+6.58	−227.36	−1.40
Adjustment to reduce variation to 0	+0.28	+0.28	+0.28	+0.28	+0.28	+1.40
Adjusted average	−89.32	+208.74	+100.80	+6.86	−227.08	0

b) The seasonal variation for the 15 days using the multiplicative model are as follows:

		Actual	Trend	Seasonal percentage
Week 1	Monday	560	648.90	86.3
	Tuesday	840	651.84	128.9
	Wednesday	728	654.78	111.2
	Thursday	658	657.72	100.0
	Friday	434	660.66	65.7
Week 2	Monday	574	663.60	86.5
	Tuesday	875	666.54	131.3
	Wednesday	770	669.48	115.0
	Thursday	679	672.42	101.0
	Friday	448	675.36	66.3
Week 3	Monday	588	678.30	86.7
	Tuesday	910	681.24	133.6
	Wednesday	812	684.18	118.7
	Thursday	700	687.12	101.9
	Friday	462	690.06	67.0

Average variations

	Monday	Tuesday	Wednesday	Thursday	Friday	
Week 1	86.3	128.9	111.2	100.0	65.7	
Week 2	86.5	131.3	115.0	101.0	66.3	
Week 3	86.7	133.6	118.7	101.9	67.0	
Total	259.5	393.8	344.9	302.9	199.0	
Average	86.5	131.3	115.0	101.0	66.3	500.1
Adjustment to reduce variation to 500		−0.1				−0.1
Adjusted average	86.5	131.2	115.0	101.0	66.3	500

9 Average increase in trend line value $= \dfrac{9{,}705 - 7{,}494}{11}$

$= 201$ units

Future trend values

Quarter 1   9,906 units
Quarter 2 10,107 units
Quarter 3 10,308 units
Quarter 4 10,509 units

Quarter	Trend forecast	Average seasonal variation	Forecast of actual sales
1	9,906	+53	9,959
2	10,107	+997	11,104
3	10,308	+1,203	11,511
4	10,509	−2,253	8,256

10 Relative price for each item

	October	November
Rag	103 (8.24/8 × 100%)	105 (8.40/8 × 100%)
Tag	105 (5.25/5 × 100%)	110 (5.50/5 × 100%)
Bobtail	100 (2/2 × 100%)	106 (2.12/2 × 100%)

Weightings for each item

	Price/Quantity sold in September	Weighting
Rag	8 × 2,500 = 20,000	20
Tag	5 × 5,000 = 25,000	25
Bobtail	2 × 27,500 = 55,000	55

Price indices

Relative price × Weighting

Period	Rag	Tag	Bobtail	Total
September (Rag: 100 × 20)	2,000	2,500	5,500	10,000
October (Rag: 103 x 20)	2,060	2,625	5,500	10,185
November (Rag: 105 × 20)	2,100	2,750	5,830	10,680

$$\text{Price index for October} = \frac{10,185}{10,000} \times 100$$

$$= 101.9$$

$$\text{Price index for November} = \frac{10,680}{10,000} \times 100$$

$$= 106.8$$

11

	£
January sales 21,000 x £30 x 60%	378,000
February sales 22,000 x £30 x 1.04 x 40%	274,560
March receipts	652,560

12   March cash outflow for overheads   = £347,000 x 1.0125 x 1.0125
                                             = £355,729

13   December = £2.60 x 169.0/166.3 = £2.64
         January   = £2.60 x 173.4/166.3 = £2.71
         February = £2.60 x 177.2/166.3 = £2.77

14   i)

		October £	November £	December £
August purchases	520,000 x 40%	208,000		
September purchases	550,000 x 60%	330,000		
	550,000 x 40%		220,000	
October purchases	560,000 x 60%		336,000	
	560,000 x 40%			224,000
November purchases	580,000 x 60%			348,000
		538,000	556,000	572,000

   ii)

		October £	November £	December £
August purchases	520,000 x 40%	208,000		
September purchases	550,000 x 60%	330,000		
	550,000 x 40%		220,000	
October purchases	560,000 x 30% x 97%	162,960		
	560,000 x 40%		224,000	
	560,000 x 30%			168,000
November purchases	580,000 x 30% x 97%		168,780	
	580,000 x 40%			232,000
December purchases	600,000 x 30% x 97%			174,600
		700,960	612,780	574,600

15   i)

		April £	May £	June £
March debtors		140,000	120,000	
April sales	140,000 x 40%		56,000	
	140,000 x 60%			84,000
May sales	150,000 x 40%			60,000
Cash receipts		140,000	176,000	144,000

		£
Debtors at 30 June		
May sales	150,000 x 60%	90,000
June sales		155,000
		245,000

ii) Cash receipts at £0.90

		April £	May £	June £
March debtors		140,000	120,000	
April sales	140,000 x 0.90 x 40%		50,400	
	140,000 x 0.90 x 60%			75,600
May sales	150,000 x 0.90 x 40%			54,000
		140,000	170,400	129,600

Total cash receipts at a price of £1 (from part (i)) = 140 + 176 + 144 = £460,000

Total cash receipts at a price of £0.90 = £440,000

This is £20,000 less than under the current price of £1.00.

Debtors at 30 June	£
May sales 150,000 x 0.90 x 60%	81,000
June sales 155,000 x 0.90	139,500
	220,500

Debtors are £24,500 less than under the current price of £1.00.c

16

	A	B	C	D
		April	May	June
		£000	£000	£000
1	Sales	375.36	=+B1*B18	=+C1*B18
2	**Cash receipts**			
3	Cash sales	=+B1*B21	=+C1*B21	=+D1*B21
4	One month after sale	184.0	=+B1*B22	=+C1*B22
5	Two months after sale	108.0	110.4	=+B1*B23
6	Total receipts	=+B3+B4+ B5	=+C3+C4+C5	=+D3+D4+D5
7	**Cash payments**			
8	Purchases	=+B1*B20	=+C1*B20	=+D1*B20
9	Overheads	72.36	=+B9*B19	=+C9*B19
10	Fixed assets			
11	Tax			
12	Dividends			60.0
13	Total payments	=+B8+B9+ B10+B11+ B12	=+C8+C9+ C10+C11+ C12	=+D8+D9+ D10+D11+ D12
14	Net cash flow	=+B6-B13	=+C6-C13	=+D6-D13
15	Opening balance	22.0	+B16	+C16
16	Closing balance	=+B14+B15	=+C14+C15	=+D14+D15
17				
18	Sales growth rate	1.02		
19	Overheads growth rate	1.005		
20	Cost of sales	0.6		
21	Cash sales	0.2		
22	Debtors within one month	0.5		
23	Debtors within two months	0.3		

17 **Tutorial note**. In b) you were only asked for three examples.

a)   The use of a spreadsheet package simplifies cash budgeting considerably.

A budget can be set up using the accustomed format. It can then be **altered** at will, so that the preparer can see the effects, for instance, of increased sales, different debt collection periods and so on.

Time is saved, accuracy is improved, and amendments can be made very speedily and easily.

b)   **Sensitivity analysis**

Sensitivity analysis is the measurement of the effect of a given change in a key assumption in a forecast. The change can be a change in **income** or in **quantities** purchased or sold. Alternatively the effects of a change in the timing of activities can be investigated in this way, or the consequences of a particular event, for example the introduction of a competing product.

Different forecasts

If a business faces a **variety** of **possible scenarios**, different forecasts can be prepared using appropriate assumptions for each possible scenario.

Different outcomes

Alternatively forecasts can be based on a **range** of **possible outcomes**. Outcomes which will particularly concern the business are the worst and best possible outcomes, and the most likely outcome.

Probability analysis

Probability analysis assigns probabilities to **uncertain values**, **quantities** or **outcomes** in order to assess expected values of the uncertain outcomes.

18 a)

To: Accountant
From: Accounting Technician
Date: 9 January
Subject: Differences between forecast and actual cash flows for Goring factory

	Forecast £000	Actual £000	Difference £000	Comment
Cash sales	30	28	−2	Reason should be ascertained. Possible action includes giving cash purchasers an incentive.
Credit sales	260	262	+2	No action required.
Machine	30	33	−3	Investigation is needed of why the difference arose as terms should have been agreed in advance. If increase is due to problems with supplier, a different supplier should be used in the future.
Wages	47	52	−5	Possible reasons for a difference include labour problems and higher than expected overtime. Any labour problems should be sorted out, and close control kept over overtime levels.
Purchases	127	136	−9	Possible reasons include use of different suppliers, a need for emergency deliveries or tighter terms (for example loss of discounts). Action may include taking steps to ensure emergency deliveries are not needed in future, and seeking new suppliers offering more favourable terms.
Cash balance	25	8	−17	

b) **Effect of inflation**

   i)   An increase in inflation higher than expected could increase the **cost of purchases and operating costs**. If sales price rises did not match cost rises, **profits** could **decrease**.

   ii)   The Bank of England might respond to an increase in inflation by increasing interest rates. This would **increase borrowing costs** and could **lower profits**.

c) **Problems with method used**

   i)   Basing forecasts on past cash flows could mean that **past inefficiencies are repeated**, and **possible improvements ignored**.

   ii)   The **assumptions** made about future sales may not be accurate. For example labour hours may be more than expected, hence overtime payments greater than planned.

   iii) The forecasts do not appear to take into account **complications** such as seasonal variations.

answers to chapter 4:
MANAGING CASH BALANCES

1   Primary banks are those which operate the money transmission service in the economy. This means that they are the banks which operate cheque accounts and deal with cheque clearing. They are sometimes also known as the commercial banks, retail banks or clearing banks.

The secondary banks are made up of a wide range of merchant banks, other British banks and foreign banks in the UK. They do not tend to take part in the cheque clearing system.

2   The main benefits of financial intermediation are:

-   small amounts deposited by savers can be combined to provide larger loan packages to businesses

-   short term savings can be transferred into long term borrowings

-   search costs are reduced as companies seeking loan finance can approach a bank directly rather than finding individuals to lend to them

-   risk is reduced as an individual's savings are not tied up with one individual borrower directly

3   The four main contractual relationships between a bank and its customers are as follows:

Debtor/creditor relationship

When the customer deposits his money with the bank then the bank becomes the debtor and the customer is of course a creditor of the bank. If the customer's account is overdrawn however the bank becomes the creditor and the customer the debtor.

Bailor/bailee relationship

This element of the relationship concerns the bank accepting the customer's property for storage in its safe deposit. The bank will undertake to take reasonable care to safeguard the property against loss or damage and also to re-deliver it only to the customer or someone authorised by the customer.

Principal/agent relationship

An agent is someone who acts on behalf of another party, the principal. Within banking the principal/agent relationship exists where for example the customer pays a crossed cheque into the bank. The bank then acts as an agent when presenting the cheque for payment and paying the proceeds into the customer's account.

Mortgagor/mortgagee relationship

If the bank asks the customer to secure a loan with a charge over its assets then the relationship between the two is that of mortgagor and mortgagee. If the customer does not repay the loan then the bank has the right to sell the asset and use the proceeds to pay off the loan.

4   A bank's main duties to its customer are:

- it must honour a customer's cheques provided that they are correctly made out, there is no legal reason for not honouring it and the customer has enough funds or overdraft limit to cover the amount of the cheque

- the bank must credit cash/cheques that are paid in to the customer's account

- if the customer makes a written request for repayment of funds in its account, for example by writing a cheque, the bank must repay the amount on demand

- the bank must comply with the customer's instructions given by direct debit mandate or standing order

- the bank must provide a statement showing the transactions on the account within a reasonable period and provide details of the balance on the customer's account

- the bank must respect the confidentiality of the customer's affairs unless the bank is required by law, public duty or its own interest to disclose details or where the customer gives his consent for such disclosure

- the bank must tell the customer if there has been an attempt to forge the customer's signature on a cheque

- the bank should use care and skill in its actions

- the bank must provide reasonable notice if it is to close a customer's account.

5   **Use of money**

You cannot restrict the ways in which the bank uses your money; the money can be used in any ways that are **legally and morally acceptable**. However the bank must make the money available to you according to the terms of your deposit; if you are opening a current account it must be **available on demand**.

Overdrawn balances

If your account shows a negative or debit balance (an **overdraft**), the bank has the right to be repaid this balance on demand. The only exception is if the bank has granted you an **overdraft facility**, which requires the bank to give you a period of notice if it wishes you to pay back what you owe it.

Charges and commissions

The bank can charge you **interest** on overdrawn balances, and can also levy **other charges and commissions** for use of its services. Depending on the terms of your account, this could even include charges for drawing cheques from your account, and withdrawing money from cashpoint machines.

Duty of care

You owe the bank a duty of care, particularly when **drawing cheques**. You should not issue cheques that are signed but lack other details such as payee or amount, nor should you write cheques out in pencil as they can easily be altered.

You should also **take care of cards** that the bank issues to you (credit, debit and cashpoint cards) and keep your **PIN number** (the number that you need to enter to use the bank's cashpoint machines) secure.

6   **Tutorial note**. Other examples that you might have thought of include informing the bank promptly if there are any queries on the bank statements, or if any cheques have been mislaid.

   a)   **Maintaining** the **value of any security** which is pledged to secure a loan

   b)   **Informing the bank** as to the **progress of the business**, especially its demands for cash (Forecasts of expected future cash flow are often required for credit to be advanced.)

   c)   **Only using the overdraft** for **appropriate financial needs** and within authorised limits

7   The most common reasons for a business identifying a future cash deficit or the need to raise additional finance are:

   ■   to fund day-to-day working capital
   ■   to increase working capital
   ■   to reduce creditors
   ■   to purchase fixed assets
   ■   to acquire another business

8   Operating cycle:

	Days
Stock turnover 250/1,800 x 365	51
Debtors turnover 550/2,600 x 365	77
	128
Less: creditors turnover 200/1,800 x 365	(41)
Operating cycle	87

9

	Months
Raw material stock turnover period	4.0
Less: Credit taken from suppliers	(3.0)
Finished goods stock turnover period	1.0
Debtors' payment period	2.0
Operating cycle	4.0

10   The main features of overdraft finance are:

   ■   overdraft facility and actual overdraft – there is a distinction between the overdraft facility offered by the bank, the maximum amount of overdraft finance available, and the actual overdraft that the business makes use of

- interest – the interest charged on an overdraft is usually at quite a high margin over and above the bank's base rate. However interest is only charged on the amount of the actual overdraft, calculated on a daily basis, rather than on the total overdraft facility

- commitment fee – in some cases an initial fee will be charged for the granting of the overdraft facility

- repayment – technically an overdraft is repayable on demand to the bank. However in practice it would be rare for a bank to enforce this.

11   The main terms and conditions that would be found in a typical short term loan agreement would cover the following matters:

- the term of the loan
- the interest rate
- the way in which the interest is charged
- the repayment date/dates
- any security required for the loan
- any covenants attached to the loan.

12   The main advantages of overdraft finance compared to loan finance are as follows:

- flexibility – the full overdraft facility does not need to be used and therefore the precise amount of funding required does not need to be estimated provided that the facility granted is greater than the amount of overdraft anticipated to be required. If necessary an application can be made to the bank to increase an overdraft facility at some point in the future.

- cost – although the interest rate on an overdraft may be higher than the interest rate negotiated for a loan the overdraft interest paid is calculated daily on the amount of the actual overdraft rather than on a fixed amount for a loan.

- short term – technically an overdraft is repayable on demand and therefore should normally only be used to fund short term working capital requirements. The benefit of this is that when the short term funding requirement is over the overdraft facility is simply not required. There is no necessity to negotiate paying off a loan early or incurring a penalty for early repayment.

- security – for a loan the bank will normally require some form of security, either a fixed or a floating charge, however this is often not the case for an overdraft

- covenants – for a loan the bank may impose certain restrictions or covenants which will limit the freedom of action of the management of the business whereas this will not normally be the case for an overdraft

13   Under a finance lease the lessee has the use of the asset for most, if not all of its useful life. The lessee may even be able to sell the asset at the end of its life with only a proportion of the sale proceeds being returned to the lessor. However the lessee although having use of the asset never actually gains legal title to the asset.

The lessee will normally be responsible for the upkeep and maintenance of the asset and to all intents and purposes owns the asset. The regular finance lease charges will reflect the repayment of the value of the asset and the finance charge to the lessor.

An operating lease is more like short term hire of an asset. This is where the lessor hires out the asset to the lessee for a short period which is normally substantially less than the asset's total life.

Once the lease period is over then the lessor will lease the same asset to another lessee. The lessor will tend to be responsible for maintaining the asset and the lessee simply gets the use of the asset for the lease period in return for the lease payments.

14 The three main general factors that should influence any decisions regarding investment of surplus funds are:

- risk
- return
- liquidity

When cash is invested there are two main risks. There is the risk that the value of the investment will fall and there is also the risk that the return from the investment will be lower than expected due to changes in market interest rates. When a business is investing surplus funds it will generally wish to invest in investments where the risk of loss is fairly minimal.

The return on an investment has two potential aspects, the income return and the capital return. Most investments will pay some form of interest or dividend which is the income return. However most investments will also tend to fluctuate in value over time and this is the capital return (or capital loss). In general the higher the risk of an investment the higher will be the expected rate of return and vice versa.

Liquidity is the term used for the ease and speed with which an investment can be converted into cash. Any investments which are widely traded on a market, such as the money markets, will be very liquid but investments such as a bank deposit account which requires 3 months notice to withdraw the funds would not be a liquid investment. The more liquid an investment is the lower the return is likely to be as less liquid investments will pay higher returns to attract investors.

15 i) Gilt edged securities or gilts are marketable British Government securities which form the major part of the fixed interest market. The securities pay a fixed amount of interest twice a year and have a variety of redemption dates. They are highly marketable securities on the fixed interest market.

ii) The flat yield on a gilt is the coupon rate of interest as a percentage of the current price of the gilt. The redemption yield is the total interest to the date of redemption and the redemption value compared to the current price of the gilt.

iii) Gilts are low risk securities as they are underwritten by the UK government. However there is a risk regarding the value of gilts as this will fluctuate with changes in interest base rates. If interest rates in general rise then the value of gilts will tend to fall.

16 If the money is invested in a bank deposit account then whatever happens to base interest rates the amount invested will be repaid together with the interest earned. If base rates increase then the interest rate paid on the deposit will also normally tend to increase.

If the money is invested in gilt edged securities the amount of interest paid will remain constant at the coupon rate whatever happens to interest base rates. However if base rates increase then the market value of the gilts will tend to decrease in order to provide a high enough return to attract investors.

17 Security procedures for the safe custody of cash include the following:

Physical procedures – any cash or cheques received must be kept safe at all times and must only be accessible to authorised individuals within the organisation. Therefore cash should be kept under lock and key either in a cash box, lockable till or safe. Only authorised individuals should have access to the keys.

Checks for valid payment – payments received in cash will of course be valid provided that any notes are not forged. However if cheques are accepted as payment then they must be supported by a valid cheque guarantee card and be correctly drawn up, dated and signed. If debit or credit cards are accepted then basic checks should be made on the card and signature and authorisation must be sought for payments which exceed the floor limit.

Reconciliation of cash received – when payments are received in the form of cash, cheques or debit and credit cards then a list of all cash, cheque and card receipts taken during the day must be kept. This list must then be reconciled at the end of each day to the amount of cash in the till, cash box or safe. The list may be manual as each sale is made or may be automatically recorded on the till roll as each sale is rung in.

This reconciliation should not be carried out by the person responsible for making the sales but by some other responsible official. Any discrepancies between the amount of cash recorded as taken during the day and the amount physically left at the end of the day must be investigated.

Banking procedures – any cash, cheques and card vouchers should be banked as soon as possible and intact each day. This not only ensures the physical safety of the cash but also that it cannot be used by employees for unauthorised purposes. It also means that once the money is in the bank it is earning the business the maximum amount of interest. All cash should be banked as soon as possible but if it is not possible to bank it until the following day then either the cash must be left in a locked safe overnight or in the bank's overnight safe.

Recording procedures – for security purposes the paying-in slip for the bank should be made out by someone other than the person paying the money into the bank. The total on the paying in slip should be reconciled to the till records or cash list for the day.

18 **Tutorial note**. You were only asked for four consequences.

Some of the consequences of inflation are as follows:

a) the **costs** of materials, labour and energy will **rise**. If the market is competitive, it may not be possible to pass these increases on to the customer, thereby leading to a reduction in profits.

b) the Bank of England is likely to **increase interest rates** in an attempt to control inflation. Higher interest rates mean that the cost of investment will increase, and this may lead to the company's investment plans being cut back.

c) long-term inflation will lead to the **devaluation of the currency**. This will benefit exporters, but lead to an increase in the cost of imported raw materials.

d) the government may seek to control inflation by **imposing price and wage controls**. This will impact on the operating flexibility of businesses.

e) high inflation results in an **increased level of economic uncertainty** since prices are continually changing. This leads to companies adopting more cautious investment policies than would otherwise be the case, or worse still seeking to cut labour costs by redundancies. **Unemployment** may therefore **rise**.

19 The total credit that a bank gives its customers will be limited by:

a) the **bank's own policy decisions** as to the amount of credit it is allowed to give

b)   the **cash ratio deposits** imposed by the Bank of England

c)   **governments** placing **restrictions** on the amount of credit banks can offer

d)   consumers choosing to keep cash-in-hand, or keep cash in the bank only for the very short-term, thus restricting the **cash** available to be **loaned** to other customers

e)   the bank's **own creditworthiness** (how cheaply it can borrow)

f)   the **general economic climate**

20   **Tutorial note**. Valuation is the key consideration here. Another possibility might be for the bank to have a floating charge over all of the company's business.

The bank will consider the following factors:

a)   **Title**

The bank will check that the company owns, not leases, the fleet of motor cars, but if it does so, there should be no difficulty in **passing title**.

Title over property may be more problematic, and the bank should seek **legal advice** if there appear to be any complications in the title deeds.

b)   **Realisation**

Sale of a large fleet of motor vehicles will be more complicated than selling one or two; the fleet may have to be split up and sold to different dealers but the **extra administration involved** should not be excessive.

Realising the property may present more problems. There may only be a limited demand for the factory on an **existing use basis**. Selling the land to a buyer for another use might limit the proceeds available, and might be difficult if there are **legal complications**.

c)   **Valuation**

This is likely to be the decisive factor in the bank's decision. Security should be stable or increasing in value, but the value of a fleet of motor cars will **decline rapidly**. Unless the loan is on a short-term basis, and the value of the fleet is significantly in excess of the amount loaned, the bank is unlikely to want the fleet to be its sole security.

If the considerations outlined in (b) are of limited importance, there is a good possibility that the value of the factory will be **stable or increase** over the long-term. The bank will take into account the current or future state of the property market, but may well opt for taking the factory as sole security.

21   **Tutorial note**. This exercise summarises the key considerations you will need to consider when deciding the most appropriate means of obtaining short and medium-term finance.

Advantages of an overdraft

a)   The customer **only pays interest when he is overdrawn**.

b)   The bank has the flexibility to **review** the customer's overdraft facility periodically, and perhaps agree to additional facilities, or insist on a reduction in the facility.

c) An overdraft can do the same job as a **medium-term loan**: a facility can simply be renewed every time it comes up for review.

d) Being short-term debt, an overdraft will not affect the calculation of a company's **gearing**.

Bear in mind, however, that overdrafts are normally **repayable on demand**.

Advantages of a loan

a) Both the customer and the bank **know exactly** what the repayments of the loan will be and how much interest is payable, and when. This makes planning (budgeting) simpler.

b) The customer does not have to worry about the bank deciding to reduce or **withdraw** an overdraft facility before he is in a position to repay what is owed. There is an element of 'security' or 'peace of mind' in being able to arrange a loan for an agreed term.

c) Medium-term loans normally carry a **facility letter** setting out the precise terms of the agreement.

Appropriateness of each means of finance

a) In most cases, when a customer wants finance to help with **'day to day' trading** and cash flow needs, an overdraft would be the appropriate method of financing. The customer should not be short of cash all the time, and should expect to be in credit on some days, but in need of an overdraft on others.

b) When a customer wants to borrow from a bank for **only a short period of time**, even for the purchase of a major fixed asset such as an item of plant or machinery, an overdraft facility might be **more suitable** than a loan. This is because the customer will stop paying interest as soon as his account goes into credit.

c) When a customer wants to borrow from a bank, but cannot see his way to repaying the bank except over the course of a few years, the **medium-term nature** of the financing is best catered for by the provision of a loan rather than an overdraft facility.

22 The **advantages of leasing** are as follows.

a) Leasing **reduces the amount of capital** needed to operate the company, as compared with purchasing the asset which requires a capital outlay.

b) When the asset is being used to generate additional business, the use of a lease allows **costs and revenues** to be **matched** as the income from the use of the asset can be applied to pay the lease premiums.

c) Lease finance can be arranged relatively **cheaply, quickly and easily**.

d) Cash budgeting is **made easier** since the timing and amount of the premiums are known at the outset.

23 **Tutorial note**. One source of evidence for this part of the unit is a report containing investment recommendations which may include calculations. Note all the cash is put on deposit for the minimum maturity period, and this means selling the original investments at the end of two months, and purchasing new two month investments with a higher interest rate.

Since interest rates are forecast to rise, the best solution is likely to be one in which only short-term deposits are made, thus allowing **advantage** to be taken of the rise in rates. Options structured in this way include the following.

If you are unsure how to proceed, think of the combinations of decisions that the company can make. For example if the company invests the £2 million it has at time 0 for two months, it will have to invest the amount again at the end of two months, but if it invests the £2 million at time 0 for four months, then it won't be available for further investment after two months. Remember also that the maximum it can invest between months 4 and 6 is £4 million (it cannot commit more than £4 million of the £6 million it has at the end of month 2 for more than two months).

In order to check whether you have taken account of all the money available in your calculations, remember that £2 million is available for the first two months, £6 million (the original 2 million + the £4 million available after 2 months) is available for the next two months, £4 million (the original £2 million + the £4 million available after two months – the £2 million outflow after 4 months) is available for the last two months.

The sum of amounts available x period available = ((2 x 2) + (6 x 2) + (4 x 2)) = 24. Therefore in your answer the sum of (amounts invested x periods invested) should also equal 24.

It can be seen that option 1 yields the best return.

	Amount £'000	Month invested	Period (in months)	Rate %	Value £
1	2,000	0	2	7.3	24,333
	6,000	2	2	8.0	80,000
	4,000	4	2	8.3	55,334
	Transaction costs				(300)
					159,367
2	2,000	0	4	7.4	49,333
	4,000	2	4	8.1	108,000
	Transaction costs				(200)
					157,133
3	2,000	0	4	7.4	49,333
	4,000	2	2	8.0	53,333
	4,000	4	2	8.3	55,334
	Transaction costs				(300)
					157,700
4	2,000	0	2	7.3	24,333
	2,000	2	2	8.0	26,667
	4,000	2	4	8.1	108,000
	Transaction costs				(300)
					158,700
5	2,000	0	6	7.5	75,000
	2,000	2	4	8.1	54,000
	2,000	2	2	8.0	26,667
	Transaction costs				(300)
					155,367
6	2,000	0	6	7.5	75,000
	4,000	2	2	8.0	53,333
	2,000	4	2	8.3	27,667
	Transaction costs				(300)
					155,700

24 a) **No further growth**

Action. An increased or **special dividend** should be paid to shareholders; the company could also consider a **share buyback**, by means of which shares would be repurchased from the shareholders and cancelled.

Reason. If no further investments are planned, cash surplus to the needs of the business should be **returned to shareholders** so that they can use it for other investment opportunities. A small cash surplus should however be maintained.

b) **Acquisition of manufacturer**

Action. Invest the cash surplus in **marketable securities** (eg Certificates of Deposit, commercial paper) or bank deposits.

Reason. Such investments ensure that the company will make a **return on its money** while retaining sufficient liquidity for when it makes an acquisition.

c) **Development of new product lines**

Action. **Spend** the **cash surplus** on the proposed capital investments.

Reason. Unless there is some other possible use for the funds, eg to fund an acquisition, it will be better to use the cash surplus rather than borrowing to **fund the capital investment**, since the cost of debt finance is likely to exceed the return achievable on cash investments.

d) **Acquisition of manufacturer and development of product lines**

Action. **Retain the cash** until required for the acquisition. Fund the new product lines by borrowing or raising additional equity finance.

Reason. The cash will be **needed at short notice** for the acquisition. It should be easy to raise finance for the new product lines from external sources.

25 **Gilts or gilt-edged securities** are marketable British government securities that can be traded on the Stock Exchange. Gilts are a low-risk investment in that the government is unlikely to default on them, but gilts can suffer falls in market values.

Gilts can be classified according to the length of their lives as follows:

- Shorts – lives up to 5 years
- Mediums – lives from 5 to 15 years
- Longs – lives of more than 15 years
- Undated – indefinite lives
- Index-linked – interest and eventual redemption value linked to inflation

Gilts and deposit account

As an alternative to investing £150,000 in a 6% deposit account, the company could invest in £150,000/1.125 = £133,333 worth of 9¾% gilt-edged stock.

Advantages of gilts

- Gilts offer a higher interest yield than the deposit account, 8.66% compared with 6%, and a higher redemption yield, 6.2% compared with 6%.

- Gilts can be bought or sold at any time, and do not need to be held to redemption. A fixed-term deposit must be held for a set length of time.

Disadvantages of gilts

- The market value of the stock will fall if interest rates rise.
- The company will have to pay transaction costs every time it wishes to buy or sell gilts.

26 a) Interest yield $= \dfrac{\text{Coupon rate}}{\text{Market price}} \times 100\% = \dfrac{7}{109.5675} \times 100\% = 6.39\%$

b)

	£
Purchase consideration (£10,000 @ £109.0485 per £100)	10,904.85
Accrued interest: 45 days at 9% (£10,000 ´ 0.09 ´ 45/365)	1,110.96
Broker's commission on consideration (0.5% on £10,904)	54.52
Total purchase cost	12,070.33

answers to chapter 5:
CREDIT CONTROL

1   The ordering cycle is made up of the following stages:

- customer places order
- customer credit status established
- customer offered credit
- goods despatched
- invoice despatched

The collection cycle is made up of the following stages:

- customer receives invoice
- statement sent to customer
- reminder letters sent
- telephone calls to customer
- cash received

2   Net 60 days 2% discount for payment within 14 days

3   **Tutorial note**. The credit control department's role has three main stages.

a)   The initial decision whether to grant credit

b)   Ongoing checks on credit limits when orders are made, and other routine tasks including dealing with queries, giving references and maintaining the sales ledger

c)   The pursuit of payment

Role of the credit control department

The roles of the credit control department can include the following.

a)   Maintaining the sales ledger
b)   Dealing with customer queries
c)   Reporting to sales staff about new enquiries
d)   Giving references about customers to third parties (eg credit reference agencies)
e)   In addition to checking out customers' creditworthiness, advising on payment terms
f)   Setting credit limits
g)   Visiting clients
h)   Monitoring customer payments

In fact the credit control function's jobs occupy a number of stages of the order cycle (from customer order to invoice despatch) and the collection cycle (from invoice despatch to the receipt of cash).

Order and collection cycles

The role of the credit control department in the order and collection cycles is as follows.

a)   Establish **credit status** for new customers or customers who request a credit extension.

b)   **Check credit limit**. If the order is fairly routine, and there is no problem with credit status, then credit control staff examine their records or at least the sales ledger records to see if the new order will cause the customer to exceed the credit limit.

c)   Issuing the delivery note, invoicing etc is not the job of the credit control department, but the credit control department will need to have **access to information**, such as invoice details, to do its job. Indeed the credit control department might well help in the design of the invoice, to ensure issues relating to payment are given their due prominence.

d)   The credit control department takes over the **collection cycle**, although the final payment is ultimately received by the accounts department. This includes:

- Issuing statements
- Sending demands
- Employing debt collectors
- Initiating legal action

4   The introductory notes below cover aspects of the company's procedures for granting credit and collecting debts. In the building supplies industry, we are exposed to **credit risk** for a number of reasons, as follows.

a)   We deal with a **large number of customers**, many of which are small in turnover terms.
b)   Many of our customers suffer from **cash flow problems** from time to time.
c)   There are **high levels of business failure** in our industry.

The **credit control manual** of which these notes form a part is designed to give guidance in the light of these general circumstances.

New customer credit acceptance

In this section, we detail the checks which are carried out when a trader applies to us to become a credit customer. This set of checks, which aims to assess the trading record of the business, its capacity to pay its debts and any special risk factors, is designed to **balance the risk of debts turning out** to be **bad** with the **commercial objective of maximising turnover**. In some cases, acceptance may be granted for a 'probationary' period and reviewed at the end of that specified period. New customers, or customers on which information is limited or is adverse, may be restricted to cash sales.

Setting credit levels

A **credit limit** is set for each prospective credit customer at the stage when they are accepted. This limit, which must be **authorised** as appropriate and will be reviewed regularly, is set with reference to **information** obtained about the customer together with the past trading record as a cash customer, if any. Procedures exist, as set out below, to ensure that sales which breach customers' credit limits are not made.

Setting credit terms

All credit control staff need to be fully familiar with our **standard terms and conditions** of sale, which are set out below and are also shown on the reverse side of invoice forms. Note that these cover various matters including retention of title, our reservation of a right to charge interest on overdue payments and the option to offset debts against any reciprocal trading account we may hold with the customer. Note that **specific credit terms** for particular customers must be in **writing and must be authorised** by the Credit Manager.

Ensuring prompt payment

Prompt payment is a key objective of all credit controllers. If **payment is late**, there is a **loss in interest**, or an **increase in overdraft interest**, for us, and a **risk of cash flow problems** in our business. We are not in the business of providing interest-free loans for our customers! There is also the risk that slow payers will turn into **non-payers**, and therefore into a greater loss to our business. Here, we outline the steps which can be taken to ensure **prompt payment**. These range from the use of initial reminder letters and telephone calls, through personal visits to customers and the eventual sanction of resorting to legal action, by which stage the Credit Manager will be involved. The steps must be followed consistently for all accounts.

5   i)   A cheque crossing is two parallel lines drawn vertically across the face of the cheque which means that the cheque must be paid into a bank account rather than being exchanged for cash.

      ii)   An account payee only crossing means that the cheque can only be paid into the bank account of the person or business named on the cheque as the payee.

6   A standing order is an instruction to a bank to pay a fixed amount on fixed dates to another party. The dates and amount are set by the payer.

      In contrast a direct debit is where the payer's bank is authorised to make periodic payments of varying amounts at the request of the payee.

7   The three fundamental elements of a contract are:

      ■   agreement (offer and acceptance)
      ■   value (consideration)
      ■   intention to create legal relations

8   An offer is an offer by one party to the other to enter into a contract. For example if you pick up some goods in a shop and try to pay for them you are making an offer to buy those goods from the shopkeeper.

      An invitation to treat however is an invitation from one party to the other to make an offer. For example the price tag on goods in the shop is an invitation to treat rather than an offer. The offer is made when the customer tries to pay for the goods.

9   An offer can be brought to an end in a variety of different ways:

      ■   if there is a set time period for an offer then the offer will lapse at the end of that time period. If there is no express time period set then the offer will lapse after a reasonable period of time

      ■   an offer can be revoked by the offeror at any point in time before it has been accepted - this means that the offer is cancelled

- an offer comes to an end if it is rejected. Rejection is not only by the offeree specifically saying no to the offer, as an offer can also be rejected by a counter-offer

- an offer also comes to an end when a valid acceptance is made.

10 i) Express terms are terms that are specifically stated in the contract and are binding on both parties.

ii) Conditions are terms that are fundamental to the contract and if they are broken then the party breaking them will be in breach of contract and can be sued for damages and the injured party can terminate the contract if they wish.

iii) Warranties are less important terms in a contract. If any of these are not fulfilled then there is still a breach of contract but the contract remains in force. However the injured party can still claim damages from the court for any loss suffered.

iv) Implied terms are terms of a contract which are not specifically stated but are implied in such a contract either by trade custom or by the law.

11 The eight guiding principles of good practice in the Data Protection Act are that personal information must be:

- fairly and lawfully processed

- processed for limited purposes

- adequate, relevant and not excessive

- accurate and up to date

- not kept for longer than necessary

- processed in line with the data subject's rights

- kept securely

- not transferred to countries outside the EU unless such data is adequately protected in those countries.

answers to chapter 6:
GRANTING CREDIT

1 **Tutorial note**. The question refers to new credit customers, so do not cite items such as the aged debtors analysis.

The main methods available are as follows.

a) **Bank and trade references**. Before credit is allowed, the new customer should be asked to provide at least two trade references and a bank reference. These should be followed up to ascertain the current level of trading, the amount of credit allowed and the timeliness or otherwise of payments.

b) **Credit rating agencies**. These can provide summaries of the financial information publicly available about a company, together with a rating of their creditworthiness based on the experience of other suppliers.

c) **Evaluation of publicly available information**. This includes both the annual report and accounts, and any press comment (which may well be more up to date).

d) **Personal visit**. A member of staff should visit the company to pick up general impressions and to establish a relationship with the staff there who are responsible for payment.

2 Any three of the following:

- bank reference
- trade reference
- credit reference agency
- Companies House
- publications and media
- the Internet

3 The potential problems with even a good trade reference include the following:

- some firms deliberately pay two or three suppliers promptly in order to use them as trade referees whilst delaying payment to their other suppliers

- the trade referee may be connected or influenced in some way by the potential customer, for example it may be a business owned by one of the directors of the customer

- the trade referee given may not be particularly strict themselves regarding credit control therefore their replies might not be typical – the genuine nature of the trade referee should be checked

- even if the reference is genuine and good it may be that trade with this supplier is on a much smaller basis or different credit terms to that being sought by the customer

4   This is not as good a reference as could have been hoped for and therefore the credit controller would almost certainly carry out further investigations including trade references and ratio analysis.

5   i)   Gross profit margin = 125/500 x 100 = 25%
         ii)   Net profit margin = 60/500 x 100 = 12%
         iii)   Return on capital employed = 60/600 x 100 = 10%
         iv)   Net asset turnover = 500/600 = 0.83 times

6   a)   Debtors' turnover $= \dfrac{\text{Total debtors}}{\text{Credit sales}} \times 365$

$$= \frac{70,000}{400,000} \times 365 = 64 \text{ days}$$

         b)   **Count-back method**

		£
Total debtors at end of September		70,000
Less: September sales		(40,000)
		30,000
Less: August sales, unpaid portion		(30,000)
		–

Days outstanding

	Days
September: entire turnover	30
August: $\dfrac{30,000}{45,000} \times 31$ days	21
	51

         c)   **Partial month method**

	Sales	Unpaid	Days	$\dfrac{\text{Unpaid}}{\text{Sales}} \times \text{Days}$
September	40,000	30,000	30	23
August	45,000	18,000	31	12
July	50,000	15,000	31	9
June	35,000	7,000	30	6
				50

7   i)   Current ratio = 210/108 = 1.9 : 1
         ii)   Quick ratio = 130/108 = 1.2 : 1
         iii)   Stock turnover = (80/500) x 365 = 58 days
         iv)   Debtors turnover = (120/750) x 365 = 58 days
         v)   Creditors turnover = (100/500) x 365 = 73 days
         vi)   Return on capital employed = ((250 – 180)/1,302) x 100 = 5.4%
         vii)   Gearing ratio = (500/1,302) x 100 = 38%
         viii) Interest cover = (250 – 180)/40 = 1.75 times

8

MEMO

To: Finance Director
From: Credit Controller
Date: X-X-2006
Subject: Request for credit from Faverly Ltd

After the request from Faverly Ltd for £20,000 of credit I have examined the information that we have available about the company which includes a bank reference, two trade references and the financial statements for the last two years.

Bank reference

The bank reference is reasonable but not as positive as it might be.

Trade references

Both trade referees note that Faverly Ltd is an occasional late payer and one of the referees did in fact suspend credit with the company for six months in 2004. It is interesting to note that both referees only allow Faverly Ltd credit of £10,000 on 30 days credit terms.

Financial statements

The financial statements for Faverly Ltd for the last two years have been examined and the following key ratios calculated under the headings of profitability, liquidity and gearing.

	2006	2005
Profitability		
Gross profit margin	22%	21%
Net profit margin	12.5%	12%
Return on capital employed	11.1%	10.5%
Liquidity		
Current ratio	0.54 : 1	0.67: 1
Quick ratio	0.3 : 1	0.4 : 1
Stock turnover	51 days	45 days
Debtors turnover	51 days	58 days
Creditors turnover	75 days	78 days
Gearing		
Interest cover	4.3 times	5.6 times

Although the company appears to be profitable and indeed to be increasing its profitability levels there has to be considerable concern about the company's liquidity. Both the current and quick ratios are seemingly very low and are decreasing. While the company has no long term debt it has been financed for the last two years by a substantial overdraft although the interest cover is still quite healthy at over 4 times.

Concern should also be raised about the creditors turnover period which although slightly improved is still long at 75 days and considerably longer than the company's debtors turnover period of 51 days.

> **Conclusion**
>
> In the absence of any further information I suggest that we offer Faverly Ltd a trial period of credit for say £10,000 on strictly 30 day terms. If these terms are not adhered to strictly then we must return to trading on a cash basis only with the company.

9   Finance Director
    Fisher Ltd

    Date:

    Dear Sir

    Re: Request for credit facilities

    Thank you for your enquiry regarding the provision of credit facilities of £15,000 on 30 day terms. We have taken up your trade references and examined your latest set of financial statements.

    We are concerned about your levels of profitability, gearing and liquidity in the most recent year and also have some concerns about one of the trade references from Froggett & Sons.

    On balance we are not in a position to grant your request for trade credit at the current time although we would of course be delighted to trade with you on a cash basis. If you do not wish to trade on this basis and would like to enquire about credit terms in the future then we would be delighted to examine your current year's financial statements when they are available.

    Thank you for your interest shown in our business.

    Yours faithfully

    Credit Controller

10 The information required to set up an account in the sales ledger for a new credit customer includes:

    ■   the business name of the customer
    ■   the contact name and title within the customer's business
    ■   business address and telephone number
    ■   the credit limit agreed upon
    ■   the payment terms agreed
    ■   any other terms such as settlement discounts offered

11 Any four of the following:

    ■   a non-committal or poor bank reference
    ■   poor trade references
    ■   concerns about the validity of any trade references submitted
    ■   adverse press comment about the potential customer
    ■   poor credit agency report
    ■   indications of business weakness from analysis of the financial statements
    ■   lack of historical financial statements due to being a recently started company

12 When refusing credit to a customer it is important that this is done politely and tactfully and the reasons for the refusal are made quite clear. It is also important to state that trading on a cash basis would be more than welcome and to encourage the customer to re-apply for credit terms when any conditions required are satisfied.

13 Cost of discount $= \dfrac{d}{100-d} \times \dfrac{365}{N-D}$

where d = discount percentage given
N = normal payment term
D = discount payment term

Cost of discount $= \dfrac{1}{100-1} \times \dfrac{365}{60-10} = 7.4\%$

14 Cost of early settlement $= \dfrac{d}{(100-d)} \times \dfrac{365}{(N-D)}$

$= \dfrac{3}{(100-3)} \times \dfrac{365}{(60-0)}$

$= 18.8\%$

As 18.8% is greater than the 15% the company uses to appraise investments, the discount is not worthwhile.

15 a)   Cost of discount $= \left(\dfrac{d}{100-d} \times \dfrac{365}{(N-D)} \right)\%$

$= \left(\dfrac{2.5}{100-2.5} \times \dfrac{365}{60-7} \right)\%$

$= 17.7\%$

b)   Brickwood may offer the discount for the following reasons.

i)   If its cost of borrowing (eg on overdraft) exceeds 17.7%, Brickwood will **save more in interest** from reducing its debt than it will have to pay out in discount.

ii)   Offering a generous settlement discount will encourage many customers to **pay early**, which will improve cash flow and may help to keep debts within borrowing limits.

16 The existing value of debtors is: $\dfrac{£18m}{12\,months} = £1.5m$

If sales increased by 60,000 units, the value of debtors would be:

$2 \times \dfrac{£18m + (60,000 \times £10)}{12\,months} = £3.1\ \text{million}$

The debtors have to be financed somehow, and the additional £1.6 million will cost £1,600,000 × 15% = £240,000 in financing costs.

The profit on the extra sales is: 60,000 units × (£10 − £6.40) = £216,000

The new credit policy is not worthwhile, mainly because existing customers would also take advantage of it.

17 a) New customers should give at least two **good references**, including one from a bank, before being granted credit.

b) Credit ratings can be checked using a **credit rating agency**.

c) For large value customers, a file should be maintained of any **available financial information** about the customer, and its contents regularly reviewed.

d) The company could send a **member of staff to visit** the customer's premises, to get a first hand impression of the customer and its prospects. This is particularly important in the case of prospective major customers.

18 To: Financial Controller
    From: Assistant Accountant
    Date: 17 January 2006
    Subject: Request for credit by Whittle Ltd

I have reviewed Whittle's accounts and the references that we have received.

Ratio analysis

	This year	Last year
Current ratio	$\dfrac{1,090}{970} = 1.12$	$\dfrac{1,025}{958} = 1.07$
Acid test ratio	$\dfrac{890}{970} = 0.92$	$\dfrac{855}{958} = 0.89$
Debt ratio	$\dfrac{500}{2,010} = 25\%$	$\dfrac{400}{1,517} = 26\%$

Current ratio

The current ratio is above 1, which means that **current assets** more than **cover current liabilities**. The current ratio has also risen since last year. The one reservation is that the rise has been due to an increase in stocks and debtors and cash has slightly fallen, indicating that control over working capital may be less efficient than previous years.

Quick ratio

As with the current ratio, the quick ratio has risen slightly during the years. Excluding stock, **current assets nearly cover current liabilities** should these need to be paid.

Debt ratio

Equity has remained at about three times long-term loan capital indicating that Whittle Ltd is **reasonably geared**. The debt ratio has fallen slightly this year despite extra long-term liabilities of £100,000, indicating that Whittle Ltd should be able to afford the extra debt.

References

The reference from **Greatlygrow Ltd** does not indicate any problems. However Whittle has only been trading with Greatlygrow Ltd for one year, a reasonably successful one for Whittle.

Whittle has had a **much longer trading relationship**, five years, with **Weston Ltd**. However the reference indicates that credit was suspended two years ago for six months, and the answer to question 3 in the letter suggests that there may have been other occasions when Whittle failed to meet credit terms. Despite the problems Weston is giving Whittle two months credit.

Recommendations

Before a final decision is taken about whether to grant credit to Whittle, **clarification of the reasons for the suspension of credit should be obtained**, and also whether there have been any other **breaches of credit terms**. A further reference, either from another long-term supplier or Whittle's bank needs to be obtained.

If the explanations and further reference is satisfactory, I recommend credit should be extended to Whittle. The credit period should initially be one month, and the account should be **closely monitored**. A **financial limit** ought also be set; you will want to consider the **size of the limit** and what should happen if the **value of the order exceeds** the desirable limit.

19 a)   To: Financial Controller
                 From: Accounting Technician
                 Date:
                 Subject: Request for credit facilities

We have received an application from David Jones, Financial Controller of Dreams Ltd, for credit of £20,000 on 60 day terms. However I have the following reservations about this request.

- Dreams Ltd has **only supplied the profit and loss account**, not the balance sheet, restricting the financial analysis we can carry out.

- The accounts are now **over six months old.**

- **Gross profit** and **gross profit margin** have **fallen slightly** between 2005 and 2006.

- The company made a **loss after tax** in 2005 and only a small profit in 2006.

- The terms given by the two suppliers who have provided references are stricter than the terms that Dreams Ltd has requested, £10,000 for 30 days in one case, £2,500 for 30 days in the other.

- Dreams Ltd has **not kept** to the **terms** set by Carpet Ltd, and has been taking on average 60 days to settle its account with Carpet Ltd.

- Wardrobes Ltd has **only traded** with Dreams Ltd for **three months**, and thus the assurance given by its reference is limited.

Appendix – Ratios

	2006	2005

Gross profit margin $\dfrac{550}{1,800} \times 100\% = 30.6\%$ $\qquad$ $\dfrac{560}{1,750} \times 100\% = 32.0\%$

Operating profit margin $\dfrac{50}{1,800} \times 100\% = 2.8\%$ $\qquad$ $\dfrac{10}{1,750} \times 100\% = 0.6\%$

b)

Sleepy Ltd
Tregarn Trading Estate
Cardiff
CF1 3EW

Mr D. Jones
Finance Director
Dreams Ltd
17 High Street
Newport
South Wales

Date:

Dear Mr Jones

Request for credit facilities

Thank you for your application for opening credit facilities. We are pleased that you are interested in doing business with our company.

We have considered your application against our prescribed credit criteria. At present we do not feel able to offer you the facilities you request, but may be able to offer a facility of £10,000 credit on 30 days terms. In order to be able to decide whether to offer this facility, we shall need to see copies of your balance sheet from last year and your most recent management accounts.

We look forward to hearing from you, and hope that we shall soon be trading with you.

Yours sincerely

answers to chapter 7:
MANAGEMENT OF DEBTORS

1   A customer's credit limit is the maximum amount that is allowed to be outstanding by the customer at any point in time. A customer's credit limit will be set by the credit controller on the basis of a detailed assessment of the customer's financial position with consideration to the amount of credit that is safe to grant to that customer. Therefore it is important that the credit limit that has been set is not exceeded.

2

	Total £	Credit limit £	Current <30 days £	31–60 days £	61–90 days £	> 90 days £
Knightly Ltd	24,519	30,000	11,333	8,448	4,738	

3   **Jeremy Ltd** There is one long outstanding debt of £890 which would appear to be a problem. The customer's file should be checked to see if there is any correspondence about this amount and if not a telephone call should be made to the customer to determine the problem with the payment. Consideration might be given to providing for this amount as a doubtful debt.

     Lenter Ltd This debtor would appear to be a consistent slow payer as the debts are equally stretched over the current period up to 90 days. The customer should be consulted about their slow payment record and incentives for earlier payment such as settlement discounts offered.

     Friday Partners This debt is of great concern as not only has it been outstanding for more than 61 days but there is no current trading with the customer. The customer should be urgently contacted in order to determine any problem with the payment of the debt.

     Diamond & Co This customer appears to be a slightly slow payer but of more importance is that their credit limit has been exceeded by over £1,000. The reason for this exceeding of the credit limit should be investigated and if necessary no further sales to this customer should be made until the earlier invoices are paid.

4   i)   Overdue debt to total debt = 660/1,442 x 100 = 46%
     ii)   Debtors turnover = 1,442/13,150 x 365 = 40 days

iii) **Count back method**

	£000
Debtors	1,442
August sales	(1,100)
July sales not yet received	342

Average credit period

	Days
August	31
Proportion of July sales	
342/1,004 x 31	11
	42

iv) **Partial month method**

	Sales	Unpaid amount		
	(a)	(b)	(c)	b/a x c
	£000	£000	Days	
Before June	9,812	32	273	0.9
June	1,234	160	30	3.9
July	1,004	468	31	14.5
August	1,100	782	31	22.0
	13,150	1,442	365	41.3

5   The company appears to be using trade credit as a permanent source of finance. It is not reducing its balance at all. Given that Sitting Duck approved a substantial increase in the limit, there may be a good (temporary) reason for the worsening cash flow; however Pretty is not keeping within the terms of the credit limit. The trend is firmly upwards, and it would be reasonable to expect Pretty to request another increase shortly. As a matter of prudent foresight, Sitting Duck's credit controller might wish to consider the following points.

a)   The report is rather crude, and shows **no analysis** of **debtors' ageing**. Perhaps Pretty is purchasing a lot more; an assessment of days sales in debtors would be useful. When viewed in the context of Pretty's overall business with Sitting Duck, Pretty's payment record might be improving.

b)   On the other hand the **costs** of the credit need to be assessed. It may be worthwhile for Sitting Duck to offer **settlement discounts** for earlier payment.

6   **MEMORANDUM**

To: Sales Manager
From: Credit Controller
Date: 6 December
Subject: Aged analysis of debtors

Megacorp plc

32% of this major customer's debt is over 90 days old. Although clearly a key customer, Megacorp appears to be taking unfair advantage of its 60 days net credit terms.

For the future, we should consider:

a) **Offering a discount** for early payment

b) **Improving communication** with Megacorp's purchase ledger department and senior management to help ensure prompt payment

c) Sending **prompt reminder letters**, followed up by telephone calls

d) **Reviewing the credit limit** for the company

Goodfellows Cycles Ltd

Goodfellows appears generally to be a prompt payer within the 30 days terms set for the customer. However, a debt of £5,000 is currently outstanding for over 90 days.

I recommend that:

a) The £5,000 **debt outstanding** for over 90 days should be **investigated** to check whether there is some dispute. Perhaps a relatively minor query is holding up payment.

b) We should consider ways of **increasing sales** to the customer.

c) Procedures for **dealing** with **customer queries** should be reviewed.

Hooper-bikes Ltd

Hooper-bikes has a total amount outstanding in excess of its credit limit. 60 days' credit is allowed to this customer, but 40% of its debt is overdue. This is not a satisfactory situation, and urgent action should be taken.

For the future, I recommend that:

a) The **credit limit** for the customer should be **reviewed**.

b) We make sure that the **debt outstanding** is brought to **within** the current **credit limit** as soon as possible.

c) We consider how to **improve** this **customer's payment record**, perhaps by insisting on cash with order.

d) We **review order procedures** to avoid customers being supplied with goods which take their account beyond its credit limit.

Dynamo Cycles Ltd

There are no current problems regarding this smaller customer's account. Credit taken up is within the credit limit and no debt is overdue.

For the future we might:

a)   Try to increase sales to Dynamo
b)   Review this customer's credit limit

7   The evidence for potential bad or doubtful debts might include the following:

- evidence of long outstanding debts from the aged debt analysis
- a one off outstanding debt when more recent debts have been cleared
- correspondence with debtors
- outstanding older debts and no current business with the customer
- a sudden or unexpected change in payment patterns
- request for an extension of credit terms
- press comment
- information from the sales team

8   i)   Bad debt ratio 2005 = 65/1,300 x 100 = 5%
           Bad debt ratio 2006 = 130/2,000 x 100 = 6.5%

     ii)   An increase in the bad debt ratio might indicate the following:

- sales being made to high risk customers
- poor assessment of creditworthiness
- lack of useful information for checking on creditworthiness
- weak sales ledger accounting
- poor follow up procedures for outstanding debts

9   **Carnford Ltd** The amount is more than 60 days overdue and a visit to the customer might be in order to see if we can obtain payment without resort to legal proceedings. If a visit is not successful then legal proceedings should be considered subject to the agreement of the Finance Director. As the amount is large and over 60 days overdue, provision should be made for the entire amount.

Luxford Ltd A telephone call should be made to remind the company that there is a balance of £900 overdue and in particular to discover the reason for the amount of £180 that has been overdue for more than 60 days. No provision is necessary as yet.

KLP Ltd All of the amount outstanding is overdue and £960 is 30 days overdue. The customer should be considered being placed on the stop list and a meeting arranged to clarify the position.

Flanders Ltd This appears to be a consistent customer but of the total overdue amount of £8,210, £1,985 is more than 30 days overdue. A reminder letter and telephone call should be made to the customer and consideration should be given to putting the customer on the stop list however as this seems to be regular customer this should be considered very seriously if other negotiations will suffice.

10   Each level of personnel might be contacted as follows.

     a)   A phone call to the accounting technician in the debtor company will be **made to enquire** as to the causes of the **delay in payment** once it becomes overdue.

     b)   A **fax** gives an enhanced sense of urgency. Hopefully the technician in the debtor company will give the creditor company's affairs higher priority. The fax may be of one or more of the late invoices.

     c)   **Collection letters** to the finance director are more urgent still. They become more severe: the last in the sequence should be followed by court action. The finance director should only be contacted when payment has obviously become a problem.

d) Meetings will be held:

    i)   When the initial customer **credit arrangement** was **set up**
    ii)   When the customer wishes to **reschedule payments**
    iii) In cases of **dispute**

e) **Legal action** will be taken if the customer fails to carry out his side of the bargain, ie pay for goods received. This will be a matter for both companies' solicitors.

f) **Stop supplies**. The threat of stopping supplies might ensure that the purchasing manager of the debtor puts pressure on the accounts department to expedite payment. The actual cessation of supplies should only be contemplated after alternatives (such as cash on delivery) have failed to work.

11 a)   To: Finance Director
            From: Accounting Technician
            Date:
            Subject: Credit collection letters

It has been agreed that a revised reminder letter system should be set up. Below I outline how a revised system could operate.

Purpose of the system

The purpose of a reminder letter is to **initiate action**. The debtor is reminded that payment is outstanding. This sets in motion the process of collecting the debt, which may involve a debt collection agency or Court action.

Number of reminder letters to be sent

Only **two reminder letters** should be sent in respect of any debt, unless the circumstances are exceptional. Sending numerous reminder letters would tend to reduce the impact of the message being conveyed.

Timing of reminder letters

The first reminder letter should be sent **14 days** after the **due date**. This allows for a 'period of grace' for any minor delay in payment, for example because of postal delays.

The **second (final) reminder letter** is sent **14 days** after the first reminder letter.

Style and content of letters

The reminder letters will adopt a **standard form**, and the style will be courteous and concise.

The **first reminder** will be **addressed to the Accounts Payable Manager**, by name if known. It will be signed by me.

The **second reminder**, advising of the **possibility of serious action**, will be addressed to the Chief Accountant/Finance Director/Company Secretary. It will normally be signed by you.

Design of the letter

Standard letters will be produced by the company's **computerised accounting system**, on headed company notepaper.

b) **First Reminder**

Our ref: [   ]
Your ref: [   ]

[date]

Mr/Ms [name]
Accounts Payable Manager
[address]
[postcode]

Dear [name]

We have not received payment for your [month] account, totalling [£???.??] which was due at the end of [month].

Your prompt attention to this will be appreciated.

Yours sincerely

[Name]
Credit Controller

Circumstance in which it might be used:
As a first reminder

Final Reminder

Our ref: [   ]
Your ref: [   ]

[date]

Mr/Ms [name]
[Chief Accountant, etc]
[address]
[postcode]

Dear [name]

FINAL NOTICE – [£???.??]

We have not received a response to our previous reminder about this account.

We are not aware of any reason why it should not be paid and we must demand you settle the account WITHIN SEVEN DAYS.

Failure to pay will result in the account being placed in the hands of third parties for collection without further reference to you.

Yours sincerely

[Name]
Finance Director

Circumstance in which it might be used:
As a final reminder

Part payment letter

Our ref: [   ]
Your ref: [   ]

[date]

Mr/Ms [name]
Accounts Payable Manager
[address]
[postcode]

Dear [name]

Thank you for your payment of [£???.??]

This reduces the balance outstanding on your overdue account, leaving a balance of [£???.??].

Your attention to this will be appreciated and we look forward to receiving a further cheque from you promptly.

Yours sincerely

[Name]
Credit Controller

Circumstance in which it might be used:
As a part payment letter

12 Finance Controller
Harvey Ltd

Date:

Dear Sir

Account No: 204764

I do not appear to have received payment of the amount of £1,350.46 which is 14 days overdue. I trust that this is an oversight and that you will arrange for immediate payment to be made. If you are withholding payment for any reason, please contact me urgently and I will be pleased to assist you.

If you have already made payment please advise me and accept my apology for having troubled you.

Yours faithfully

Credit controller

13 Financial Controller
Bart & Sons

Date

Dear Sir

Account No: B245

I do not appear to have received payment of the amount of £976.80 which is now 30 days overdue. I trust that this is an oversight and that you will arrange for immediate payment to be made. If you are withholding payment for any reason, please contact me urgently and I will be pleased to assist you.

I regret that unless payment is received within the next seven days I will have no alternative but to stop any further sales on credit to you until the amount owing is cleared in full. If you have already made payment please advise me and accept my apology for having troubled you.

Yours faithfully

Credit controller

answers to chapter 8:
COLLECTION OF DEBTS

1   There are three main services that a debt factor can provide.

Advance of funds

One of the primary reasons for using a debt factor is the advancement of funds. This means that the factor will typically pay over about 80% of the face value of the debts immediately rather than the company having to wait until the monies are paid by the debtors themselves. The factor will then collect the debts and pay over the remaining amount less their charges and commission.

Administration of the sales ledger

In many cases the debt factor will also take over the entire administration of the business's sales ledger. This will tend to include the following:

- assessment of credit status
- sending out sales invoices
- recording sales invoices and receipts
- sending out statements
- sending out reminders
- collecting payments from debtors

Insurance against bad debts

In some cases the factor will provide a "without recourse" arrangement which effectively means that the factor, rather than the business, bears the risk of bad debts without any recourse to the business.

2   **Advantages** include any two of the following:

- advance of cash which may not be available from other sources
- specialist debt administration skills of the factor
- specialist debt collection skills of the factor
- saving in in-house sales ledger costs
- reduction in bad debts cost
- frees up management time

Disadvantages include any two of the following:

- cost – interest and commission
- potential loss of customer goodwill
- problems of eventually reverting back to running the sales ledger internally
- without recourse factoring can be an expensive method of debt insurance

3   Memorandum

To: Sales Director
From: Accountant
Date:
Subject: Factoring

I am writing in response to your enquiry about the difference between with and without recourse factoring

With recourse means that we will suffer the consequences of bad debts, and will have to repay the factor the advance that has been lent in relation to those debts. **Without recourse** means that if the client does not pay what they owe, the **factor will not ask for its money back.**

4   Invoice discounting is where a financial organisation advances money to a business based upon the book value of their debtors but at a discount to that face value. Unlike a factoring agreement the business continues to collect its debts themselves and pays the amounts due to the invoice discounter.

5   A whole turnover type of policy can operate in one of two ways:

- the entire sales ledger can be covered but the amount paid out for any bad debt claim would only be normally about 80% of the claim

- alternatively approximately 80% of the debtors can be insured for their entire amount and any claim on these debtors would be paid in full.

Either way under this type of policy only a proportion of bad debts will be covered for loss.

A further type of policy is an annual aggregate excess policy where bad debts are insured in total above an agreed limit or excess in a similar way to household or car insurance policies.

It is possible to purchase insurance for a specific debtor account rather than debtors in total.

6   The main advantage of debt insurance is that it provides protection against a debt going bad.

Disadvantages include the cost of the insurance premium and that it is rare for a policy to provide cover for 100% of the business debts.

7   To: Managing Director
From: Accounting Technician
Date:
Subject: Credit insurance and factoring

a)   **Credit insurance**

With a credit insurance arrangement, the company will pay a fee to an insurance company in case debts go bad.

A **'whole turnover' policy** does not signify exactly what it implies: there is normally a maximum percentage that will be allowed. For example, 80% of each debt might be insured. Another arrangement might be 100% cover of 80% of the debts.

Insurance can be provided by a variety of companies. Their involvement will be to review our systems of credit control, and see the extent to which we are exposed to credit risk.

Customers need not know of the insurance arrangement unless, in case of default on a debt and the company making a claim, the insurance company's loss adjuster decides to make enquiries.

The **effect on cash flow** is the amount of the premium, whenever paid.

The effect on the company's **financial statements** is restricted to an **increase** in **selling expenses** or **administration expenses** in the profit and loss account.

Any **income received** as a **result of a claim** might be accounted for as 'other income' if the debt has been written off: otherwise only the uninsured part of the claim will be written off.

The policy will be run largely by the credit control department.

b) **Factoring**

Factoring is not normally a way of avoiding bad debts: the factor **passes these** back to the customer, unless the company has an expensive **'without recourse' arrangement**. However, factoring can improve cash flows and credit control.

A factoring arrangement exists where a **third party**, often a bank, **advances a sum of money** to a company representing the company's debts (up to a maximum percentage) and then collects the debts of the company. This service **combining**, effectively, **borrowing and debtor administration**, is carried out for a fee.

The relationship with the customer will be affected, as there is a **third party involved** and, however irrational, some customers may prefer to deal with us directly.

The **effect on cash flow** is quite **significant**. Invoices are **turned more quickly into cash** than if we managed our own system. However we shall need to pay a fee to use the service.

Normal credit control and **sales ledger procedures** must still be implemented.

The effect on the financial statements at the end of the year might be to **increase cash**, but also **increase borrowing**, in the balance sheet. There will also be the factoring charge to the profit and loss account.

8   Possible remedies for a breach of contract are:

- action for the price – a court action to recover the agreed price of the goods/services
- monetary damages – compensation for loss
- termination – one party refusing to carry on with the contract
- specific performance – a court order that one of the parties must fulfil their obligations
- quantum meruit – payment ordered for the part of the contract performed
- injunction – one party to the contract being ordered by the court not to do something

For a seller of goods who has not been paid by the buyer the most appropriate remedy would normally be an action for the price.

9   When it is decided to bring an action against a debtor for non payment in order to recover money owed then the first step is to instruct a solicitor. The solicitor will require details of the goods or services provided, the date the liability arose, the exact name and trading status of the debtor, any background information such as disputes in the past and a copy of any invoices that are unpaid.

The court in which the action is brought will depend upon the size of the outstanding amount. If the claim is for less than £5,000 then the claim will be made in the Small Claims Court. Any claims for less than £25,000 will normally be dealt with the County Court and for claims higher than this the High Court.

10   Any two of the following:

- attachment of earnings order – the business will be paid the amount owing directly by the debtor's employer as a certain amount is deducted from their weekly/monthly pay. However this is only viable for a debtor who is an individual and is in stable, consistent work

- third party debtor order – this allows the business to be paid directly by a third party who owes the debtor money

- warrant of execution – a court bailiff seizes and sells the debtor's goods on behalf of the business

- administrative order – the debtor makes regular, agreed payments into court to pay off the debt

11   i)   Before a petition for bankruptcy against an individual is issued a creditor for a debt of at least £750 must issue a statutory demand for payment of the amount due. This may result in the debtor offering a settlement. If however there is no settlement offer from the debtor a petition for bankruptcy will be received from the court.

ii)   The consequences of a petition for bankruptcy against a debtor are:

- if the debtor pays money to any other creditors or disposes of any property then these transactions are void

- any other legal proceedings relating to the debtor's property or debts are suspended

- an interim receiver is appointed to protect the estate

iii)   The consequences of a bankruptcy order are:

- the official receiver takes control of the assets of the business

- a statement of the assets and liabilities is drawn up – this is known as a statement of affairs

- the receiver summons a meeting of creditors within 12 weeks of the bankruptcy order

- the creditors appoint a trustee in bankruptcy

- the assets of the business are realised and distribution is made to the various creditors

12   The assets of a bankrupt individual will be distributed in the following order:

- secured creditors
- bankruptcy costs
- preferential creditors such as employees, pension schemes, HM Revenue & Customs etc
- unsecured creditors such as trade creditors
- the bankrupt

As an unsecured trade creditor a business with debts due from a bankrupt should submit a written claim to the trustee detailing how the debt is made up. This may also need to be substantiated with documentary evidence.

13   In a liquidation the company is dissolved and the assets are realised with debts being paid out of the proceeds and any excess being returned to the shareholders. This process is carried out by a liquidator on behalf of the shareholders and/or creditors. The liquidator's job is simply to ensure that the creditors are paid and once this is done the company can be wound up.

The order of distribution of the assets of a liquidated company are:

- secured creditors with fixed charges
- costs of winding up the company
- preferential unsecured debts such as employees
- secured creditors with floating charges
- unsecured creditors such as trade creditors
- deferred debts such as unpaid dividends to shareholders

14   **Tutorial note**. The problem is that by the time unmistakable signs of financial problems appear, the debts owed by the customer may be considerable. The credit control department needs to be aware of the 'early warning' signs; although these may not always be reliable indicators of future insolvency, acting upon them can limit the risk of future loss.

a)   **Poor organisation**

A poorly governed company is often a high risk company. It is useful to find out details about the company's board of directors or senior management to assess if they have a wide enough **range of expertise** for the industry in which they are in, and in particular whether there appears to be **sufficient financial expertise** at high levels.

We should also note any problems or delays we face caused by the customer's **poor accounting systems**.

b)   **High-risk strategy**

We should be aware of our customers' current business strategy. Problems may arise if they are failing to **diversify**, or are committing resources to one or a few projects which have uncertain returns. We should also be alert for **new financial burdens**, such as extra loans, being taken on.

Conversely a **failure to change**, a lack of investment in new technology or products can be an indicator of poor prospects. Problems may arise quickly if the company is in an industry where significant change is taking place elsewhere.

c)   **Accounting signs**

We should obtain copies of our customers' statutory accounts. Obvious signs of performance problems are **declining sales or profit levels**.

We should also look at the accounts for indications of **liquidity problems**. These include a high level of current liabilities compared with current assets, large increases in sales and debtors but a lack of cash, and increases in fixed assets having to be financed by increases in current, not long-term liabilities.

Other possible signs are a **change in accounting policies** which has a significantly favourable effect upon figures, a **qualified audit report**, and **late filing** of accounts at Companies House.

We should also take into account what we know about the customer's **industry**, in particular whether there are a lot of companies in the industry in **financial difficulties**, or whether our customer appears to be **performing poorly** compared with the rest of the industry.

d) **Other signs**

Our own **credit control information** can provide important indications, for example **increased credit** being taken or requested, or a **lengthening payment period**.

We should also be alert for information that can be picked up on the industry **grapevine**, such as other suppliers reporting difficulties in collecting debts.

If staff visit the customer's premises, they should be **alert** for signs of problems such as old-fashioned machinery, a lack of computerisation or excessive levels of stock.

e) **Sudden problems**

These are events that might not be predictable, but will by their nature have a significant impact upon the customer's cash flow. Examples include fire, the loss of a major customer of its own, or the sudden withdrawal of loan or overdraft facilities.

15 **Tutorial note**. You need to think about the factors that will influence whether a collection agency or solicitor will be used (costs, likelihood of success, freeing up of firms' staff for more profitable work).

(a) **Debt collection agencies** are the most effective way of pursuing debts. Some debt collection agencies offer a variety of credit control services, including running the credit control department in its entirety. There are over 250 such agencies in the UK. The **Credit Services Association** is a professional body for debt collection.

Unlike other sources of third party assistance, most debt collection agencies are happy to be **paid by results**. In other words, most debt collectors offer a **'no collection, no fee'** basis. (There are some exceptions, such as the **trade protection societies**, which are associations set up by businesses in the same industry for their mutual benefit.)

Some agencies require an advance subscription to be paid for their services, or require clients to submit a 'coupon' for each case submitted. Most, however, receive a **straight percentage.**

Important features of using an agency include the following:

i) the debt collector's investigations can provide **information** which will help the client decide whether it is worth suing in the first place.

ii) **older debts** are inevitably harder to collect and so command a higher fee.

iii) it is in the collector's interest to collect the debts **sooner** rather than later: their commission depends on it.

iv) the client's staff are more **usefully employed** on **new business**.

v) sometimes, the mere fact that a **third party** is being **employed** is enough to persuade the debtor to pay up.

Some businesses use debt collection agencies as a matter of course, largely as an alternative to having an in-house credit control department. Others will only go to agencies as a last resort.

Any collection agency will employ suitable techniques, depending on the client.

i)   Some collect on a **letter** and **telephone** basis. This is often the case where the client has passed on a large number of **consumer** debts.

ii) Others, especially for more difficult cases, collect **'on the doorstep'**.

A debt collection agency is likely to have procedures in the following areas.

i)   All **telephone conversations** are meticulously **recorded**.
ii) Collectors may negotiate a **payment plan** with individual debtors.
iii) Clients are presented with a **report** every month.

b)   A business might choose to use a firm of **specialist solicitors**. Using non-specialist solicitors may not be as effective as an agency. To use a solicitor effectively, the following should be noted:

i)   the debt should be **undisputed**.

ii) the **approach** to any action in court will **depend** on whether the debtor is an individual (ie consumer), a sole trader or partnership (ie an unincorporated business) or a limited company (ie a firm with the letters Ltd, Limited, or plc after its name).

iii) the **individual's full name** should be supplied.

iv) for an unincorporated business, the **firm's trading name** and the name of the proprietor(s) should be supplied.

v)   for a limited company, the name of the **company** should be that **registered** at Companies House.

Many court cases fail because the respondents in the case have not been named correctly.

Debt collection agencies are considered to be normal business services, and the use of a collection agency is unlikely to result in the end of a commercial relationship. Rightly or wrongly, however, employing a solicitor is seen as being more serious.

16   a)   The following are possible routes for debt recovery. (Note that you need only give two.)

1)   **Receivership**

A secured creditor (ie those holding a charge on the assets of the business) calls in a receiver to run the business so that they can be paid.

2)   **Administrative receivership**

A secured creditor holding a floating charge may appoint an administrative receiver.

3)   **Administration**

The Court prevents creditors from taking further action against the company while an Insolvency Practitioner attempts to secure a satisfactory resolution.

4) **Voluntary arrangement with creditors**

Assisted by an Insolvency Practitioner, the company agrees with creditors a way of resolving its problems.

5) **Liquidation**

The company is wound up, its assets are sold off and it is closed down.

b) Note that you were asked for three methods.

1) **Warrant of execution**

The Court orders an enforcement officer or bailiff to seize goods belonging to the debtor and to sell them by public auction.

2) **Attachment of earnings**

The Court can order a specific weekly or monthly amount to be deducted from the debtor's wages or salary.

3) **Third party debt order**

A person (often, a bank or building society) holding money owed to the debtor is instructed to hold it for the benefit of the creditor instead.

4) **Petition for bankruptcy**

The debtor may be declared bankrupt, with the result that the debtor's assets will be administered by someone else.

5) **Administrative order**

A debtor with multiple debts not totalling more than £5,000 (at least one being a judgement debt they are unable to settle immediately) is enabled to discharge all obligations by making regular payments into Court.

6) **Charging order**

The creditor obtains a charge on the debtor's property, for example their house. If the debtor later sells the property, the creditor will receive some of the proceeds.

PRACTICE SIMULATION 1

UNIT 15
SUGGESTED ANSWERS

FH PANELS LTD

ANSWERS

Task 1

MEMO

To: Jenny Spiers, Financial Controller
From: Peter Long, Accounting Technician
Date: 1 July 2006
Subject: Cash flow to 30 June 2006

The reconciliation of the actual and budgeted cash flow for the three months ending 30 June 2006 is as follows:

	£
Budgeted cash balance at 30 June	108,900
Shortfall in receipts from debtors	(18,500)
Increase in payments to suppliers	(8,800)
Increase in selling overheads	(700)
Increase in repairs and maintenance costs	(7,000)
Capital expenditure not budgeted for	(50,000)
Actual cash balance at 30 June	23,900

The three significant deviations from the cash flow budget together with the suggested actions to avoid the variances are as follows (any three of the following):

Shortfall in receipts from debtors

Collection procedures within the credit control section could have been improved in order to collect amounts due from debtors earlier.

Increase in payments to suppliers

Payments to suppliers are higher than budgeted. Either stock levels of raw materials could be reduced or longer periods of credit could be taken from suppliers.

Increase in repairs and maintenance

These costs are significantly higher than budgeted and as they are fairly significant consideration should be given to obtaining credit terms for payment of these costs rather than payment in the month incurred.

Capital expenditure

As this was not budgeted for it may be a budgeting error. However to improve the cash flow for the period consideration could be given to either delaying this capital expenditure or finding an alternative method of funding the capital expenditure such as leasing or hire purchase.

Task 2

Cash flow forecast for three months ending 30 September 2006

	July £	August £	September £
Receipts from debtors (W1)	87,248	88,570	91,080
Payments to suppliers (W3)	(33,500)	(35,500)	(34,500)
Wages (W4)	(17,750)	(18,250)	(19,760)
Production overheads	(10,000)	(10,500)	(10,500)
Selling overheads	(3,200)	(3,200)	(3,200)
Repairs and maintenance	(2,500)	(2,500)	(2,500)
Capital expenditure		(20,000)	
Dividend			
Cash flow for the month	20,298	(1,380)	20,620
Opening cash balance	23,900	44,198	42,818
Closing cash balance	44,198	42,818	63,438

WORKINGS

1   Receipts from debtors

	July £	August £	September £
From debtors at 30 June	87,248	70,618	8,844
July sales			
6,800 x £13.20 x 20%		17,952	
6,800 x £13.20 x 70%			62,832
August sales			
7,000 x £13.20 x 1.05 x 20%			19,404
	87,248	88,570	91,080

2   Production and purchases budgets

Production budget

	July Units	August Units	September Units
Sales	6,800	7,000	7,300
Less: opening stock finished goods	(4,000)	(4,300)	(4,600)
Add: closing stock finished goods	4,300	4,600	4,900
Production	7,100	7,300	7,600

Purchases budget

	July *Strips of wood*	August *Strips of wood*	September *Strips of wood*
Production requirements			
(7,100 x 25)	177,500		
(7,300 x 25)		182,500	
(7,600 x 25)			190,000
Less: opening stock – wood	(160,000)	(160,000)	(150,000)
Add: closing stock – wood	160,000	150,000	120,000
Purchases	177,500	172,500	160,000

3   Payments to suppliers

	July £	August £	September £
Opening creditor	33,500		
July purchases 177,500 x £0.20		35,500	
August purchases 172,500 x £0.20			34,500

4   Wages

Production budget

	July Units	August Units	September Units
Sales	6,800	7,000	7,300
Less: opening stock finished goods	(4,000)	(4,300)	(4,600)
Add: closing stock finished goods	4,300	4,600	4,900
Production	7,100	7,300	7,600

Wage payments

	July £	August £	September £
July 7,100/3 x £7.50	17,750		
August 7,300/3 x £7.50		18,250	
September 7,600/3 x £7.80			19,760

MEMO

To: Jenny Spiers, Financial Controller
From: Peter Long, Accounting Technician
Date: 1 July 2006
Subject: Proposed discount policy

The effect of the proposed discount policy for the next three months' receipts from debtors would be as follows:

	July £	August £	September £
From debtors at 30 June	87,248	70,618	8,844
July sales			
6,800 x £13.20 x 60% x 98%		52,779	
6,800 x £13.20 x 30%			26,928
August			
7,000 x £13.20 x 1.05 x 60% x 98%			57,048
	87,248	123,397	92,820

Task 3

Gilt edged securities or gilts are marketable British Government securities. They pay a fixed amount of interest and are available with varying maturity dates from very short term, days or weeks, through to twenty years or more. There are also undated gilts with no redemption date. Gilts do not have to be held to maturity as there is a very large and active market in them making them an ideal short term investment.

Both a bank deposit account and gilts carry a stated rate of interest. However they will be affected differently by changes in base interest rates.

With the bank deposit account if base rates change then the interest payable on the deposit will also normally change. However the amount deposited will not be affected and when the deposit matures the initial deposit will be the amount returned plus any accumulated interest.

However gilts are marketable securities and as such their market value will fluctuate with changes in base rates. If the base rate of interest increases then the market value of any amount invested in gilts will fall. Whereas if market interest rates decrease the value of gilts will increase.

Therefore when any short term investment decisions are to be made by the company account should be taken of expected changes in the economic and financial environment and in particular expected changes in base rates of interest.

Task 4

MEMO

To: Board of Directors
From: Peter Long, Accounting Technician
Date: 3 July 2006
Subject: Bank loans and overdrafts

The company has identified an opportunity to purchase a freehold property at a cost of £300,000. However this purchase must be funded and here consideration is given to the use of either a bank overdraft or a bank loan for such funding.

a) **Bank overdraft**

A bank overdraft is technically repayable on demand and as such is traditionally used for short term financing requirements rather than long term investment. The main advantage of overdraft finance over a bank loan is that if a facility of say £300,000 is granted the company does not need to use all of this amount if there are other funds available and we will only be charged interest on the amount of the overdraft facility used each day rather than on £300,000. The main disadvantages of overdraft finance are that the interest rate will tend to be higher than that for a loan and if the company does not achieve satisfactory cash flows then the bank might force the overdraft to be repaid on demand.

b) **Bank loan**

A bank loan can be negotiated for a particular term (or time period), interest rate, repayment terms and possibly with security in the form of the freehold to be purchased. Term loans are generally most appropriate for the finance of long term assets since the repayment can be matched to the income expected from the assets.

The main advantages of a loan are that it can be tailored to the precise requirements of the business in terms of time scale and repayment and the interest rate will tend to be lower than that for a bank overdraft. The main disadvantages of a term loan are that there will often be financial penalties if the company wishes to repay the loan early and the bank may also include restrictive covenants in the terms of the loan.

Preferred method of financing

As the finance is required for the purchase of a freehold factory which will presumably be held for the long term and which will provide additional income for the company then the most appropriate form of finance would be that of a term loan rather than a bank overdraft.

Task 5

MEMO

To: Jenny Spiers, Financial Controller
From: Peter Long, Accounting Technician
Date: 1 July 2006
Subject: Carmen Contractors Ltd – request for credit

As requested I am setting out three key accounting ratios for Carmen Contractors Ltd which should help our credit assessment process. These ratios have been calculated from the financial statements provided by Carmen Contractors Ltd for the years ending 31 March 2005 and 2006.

	2006	2005
Gross profit margin	21.4%	20.0%
Interest cover	3.5 times	2.0 times
Trade creditors days	46 days	47 days

Gross profit margin

The gross profit margin has increased between 2005 and 2006 and if this increase continues this should also lead to an increase in net profitability. Such a profit profile should make the company an attractive customer to us.

Interest cover

The business is heavily financed by a bank overdraft with the related interest charges. Interest cover was low in 2005 but has improved in 2006 which is an encouraging sign even though the overdraft itself has increased.

Trade creditor days

The average time the company takes to pay its creditors has improved marginally from 47 days in 2005 to 46 days in 2006. Although this is not an excessively long period we would normally offer credit terms of 30 days and would therefore prefer the creditor days to be somewhat shorter.

The analysis of the financial statements is fairly positive but as this is the only information that we have from the company at the present time we should be seeking more information before extending credit to this company.

Note:

Other ratios that could have been usefully calculated are:

	2006	2005
Net profit margin	6.25%	4.0%
Return on capital employed	29.7%	19.8%
Current ratio	0.4 : 1	0.4 : 1

FH PANELS LTD
Hellingford Industrial Estate
Newtown
NT6 4XL

Purchasing Manager
Carmen Contractors Ltd

Date:

Dear Sir/Madam

Re: request for credit facilities

Thank you for your recent request for trade credit facilities from us and for having provided us with your most recent set of financial statements. I have examined those financial statements and despite obvious healthy signs I regret that at this time I am unable to offer credit facilities to you. I must stress that this decision is based solely on the information that you have currently provided us with which is insufficient for our purposes of assessing credit terms.

In order to establish credit facilities for you I would need the following additional information:

- your bank name, address, sort code and account numbers for a bank reference
- two current suppliers of yours from whom we may obtain trade references
- the amount of credit that you are seeking
- details of your registered office and trading name

I look forward to receiving this information shortly and hope that our two companies will be able to trade on credit together. In the meantime we would be happy to trade with you on a cash basis. Thank you for your interest in our company.

Yours faithfully

Peter Long
Accounting Technician

Task 6

Notes for opening accounts for new customers

Factors to consider when agreeing credit terms with a customer

- the status of the customer – is this a long established business? How large is the business?

- the credit risk of the business – the risk that the customer may not pay within the credit terms or not pay at all, ie a bad debt

Sources of information about potential customers

Internal information

Any two of:

- customer visits
- employee knowledge of customer
- analysis of financial statements

External information

Any two of:

- bank reference
- trade references
- Companies House information
- trade or general publications
- Internet

Data required when setting up a new account

Any three of:

- the business name of the customer
- the contact name and title within the customer's business
- business address and telephone number
- the credit limit agreed upon
- the payment terms agreed
- any other terms such as settlement discounts offered

Task 7

MEMO

To: Jenny Spiers, Financial Controller
From: Peter Long, Accounting Technician
Date: 1 July 2006
Subject: Aged debtor analysis

I have analysed the aged debtor analysis as at 30 June 2006 and recommend the following control actions:

Castle Builders The amount is more than 60 days overdue and a visit to the customer might be in order to see if we can obtain payment without resort to legal proceedings. If a visit is not successful then legal proceedings should be considered subject to your agreement. As the amount is over 60 days overdue, provision should be made for the entire amount.

DD DIY Ltd A telephone call should be made to remind the company that there is a balance of £1,600 overdue and in particular to discover the reason for the amount of £400 that has been overdue for more than 60 days. Provision might well be necessary for the amount of £400.

AP Partners £2,250 of the amount outstanding is overdue and £1,250 is over 30 days overdue. The customer should be considered being placed on the stop list and a meeting arranged to clarify the position.

Gatfield Ltd This appears to be a regular customer but of the total overdue amount of £9,440, £840 is 30 days overdue. A reminder letter and telephone call should be made to the customer and consideration should be given to putting the customer on the stop list however as this seems to be a significant customer this should be considered very seriously if other negotiations will suffice.

PRACTICE SIMULATION 2

UNIT 15
SUGGESTED ANSWERS

HAPPY CHEF LTD

Task 1

MEMO

To: Fiona Lim
From: George Benson
Date: 4 January 2006
Subject: Actual and budgeted cash flow

I have reviewed the comparison between the actual cash flows for December 2005 and the budgeted cash flows. The most significant differences between actual and budget are:

- sales receipts are £21,000 below budget
- food costs are £8,500 higher than budget
- capital expenditure is £46,000 higher than budget
- there has been a dividend of £20,000 paid which was not in the budget

(Note that only three differences were required.)

The differences in actual cash flows compared to budget have meant that the company has a significant overdraft at 31 December 2005 rather than a cash balance. Actions which the company could have taken to avoid using this overdraft include the following:

- collected money due from credit customers more quickly

- delayed payments to credit suppliers

- delayed capital expenditure

- changed method of financing capital expenditure, for example by leasing rather than outright purchase

- delayed or reduced payment of dividend

(Note that only three actions were required.)

Task 2

a) **Cash budget for three months ending 31 March 2006**

	Jan £	Feb £	Mar £	Total £
Cash inflows				
From opening debtors	175,000	35,000		210,000
January invoices (W1)	41,600	52,000	10,400	104,000
February invoices (W1)		56,000	70,000	126,000
March invoices (W1)			62,000	62,000
Shop sales		800	800	1,600
Deposit account interest	100	100	100	300
Total receipts	216,700	143,900	143,300	503,900
Cash outflows				
Food supplies (W2)	70,000	41,600	56,000	167,600
Salaries	43,000	43,000	45,150	131,150
Administration costs	27,000	30,000	30,000	87,000
Capital expenditure		20,000	6,000	26,000
Total payments	140,000	134,600	137,150	411,750
Movement for the month	76,700	9,300	6,150	92,150
Opening cash balance	(39,400)	37,300	46,600	(39,400)
Closing cash balance	37,300	46,600	52,750	52,750

Workings

1 Cash from invoiced sales

		Jan £	Feb £	Mar £
January invoices	104,000 x 40%	41,600		
	104,000 x 50%		52,000	
	104,000 x 10%			10,400
February invoices	140,000 x 40%		56,000	
	140,000 x 50%			70,000
March invoices	155,000 x 40%			62,000

2 Payments for food supplies

		Jan £	Feb £	Mar £
Food purchases	Jan 104,000 x 40%	41,600		
	Feb 140,000 x 40%		56,000	
	Mar 155,000 x 40%			62,000
Payments	December creditors	70,000		
	Jan purchases		41,600	
	Feb purchases			56,000

b)

MEMO

To: Gary Taylor
From: George Benson
Date: 4 January 2006
Subject: Proposed discount policy

The discount policy that is being proposed means that a significantly larger proportion of our sales will be received within the month of the invoice. For example if the discount policy had been issue from 1 January then £72,800 (£104,000 x 70%) would have been received that month rather than £41,600 as forecast. However it must be borne mind that this is partly cancelled by lower receipts in the following two months.

In terms of the cost of the discount the 2% deducted can be compared to the benefit received and we can use the January invoices as an example.

Cost of discount 2% x £104,000 x 70%   = £1,456

Against this there is an increase in cash flow in January:

Increase in cash flow (72,800 - 41,600)   = £31,200

This gives a *monthly* percentage cost of   = $\dfrac{£1,456}{£31,200}$ x 100

                                                 = 4.7%

As *annual* interest rates are only currently a little higher than this, 4.7% is a very high cost to pay for additional short term funds. If additional short term funds are required a better option would be to borrow short term from the bank.

Task 3

```
                                    MEMO

To:          Board of Directors
From:        George Benson
Date:        4 January 2006
Subject:     Financing method
```

It is anticipated that the company will require £300,000 in the near future for the purchase of substantial new premises. This could be financed either by a bank overdraft or a bank loan.

Bank overdraft

A bank overdraft is technically a short term method of financing which is repayable on demand, a disadvantage for a longer-term project such as the one we propose. The main benefit of an overdraft is that although an overdraft facility of a certain amount may be granted to the company, interest will only be charged on the actual amount of the overdraft used.

Bank loan

A bank loan can normally be negotiated between the company and the bank and these negotiations will determine the amount of the loan, the interest rate, interest method (variable or fixed) and the repayment method and amounts. The advantages of using a loan to fund the new premises are that it provides finance on a long-term basis (which is not repayable on demand) and the interest and repayments can be repaid from the funds generated by the assets purchased.

Preferred method

As the finance is to be used to purchase new premises which will be used for the medium to long-term in the business the preferred method of financing would be a bank loan which can be tailored to match with the cash flows from the new buildings.

Task 4

NOTE

When the company starts trading for cash from the factory outlet it is important that there is strict control over the cash taken for sales.

Physical safeguards

Any cash or cheques received must be kept safe at all times and must only be accessible to authorised individuals within the organisation. Therefore cash should be kept under lock and key either in a cash box, lockable till or safe. Only authorised individuals should have access to the keys.

Checking for valid payment

Payments received in cash will of course be valid provided that any notes are not forged. However if cheques are accepted as payment then they must be supported by a valid cheque guarantee card and be correctly drawn up, dated and signed. If credit cards and debit cards are accepted then basic checks should be made on the card and signature and authorisation must be sought for payments which exceed the floor limit. It would be best to use EFTPOS so that authorisation is automatic; the CHIP and PIN style cards provide better security than the old-style ones that require signatures.

Reconciliation of cash received

When payments are received in the form of cash, cheques or credit cards then a list of all cash, cheques and credit/ debit card receipts taken during the day must be kept. This list must then be reconciled at the end of each day to the amount of cash in the till, cash box or safe. The list may be manual as each sale is made or may be automatically recorded on the till roll as each sale is rung in.

This reconciliation should not be carried out by the person responsible for making the sales but by some other responsible official. Any discrepancies between the amount of cash recorded as taken during the day and the amount physically left at the end of the day after allowing for the cash float must be investigated.

Banking procedures

Any cash, cheques and credit/debit card vouchers not transacted using EFTPOS should be banked as soon as possible and intact each day. This not only ensures the physical safety of the cash but also that it cannot be used by employees for unauthorised purposes. It also means that once the money is in the bank it is earning the business the maximum amount of interest. All cash should be banked as soon as possible but if it is not possible for it to be banked until the following day then the cash must be left either in a locked safe overnight or in the bank's overnight safe.

(Note that only three procedures were required.)

Task 5

NOTE

Refusing credit to a potential customer:

- refusing credit must be communicated to the customer in a tactful and diplomatic manner

- the reasons for the refusal of credit must be politely explained

- any future actions required from the potential customer should also be made quite clear in order for credit to be potentially considered at a future date

- it should be made quite clear that the company is happy to trade on a cash basis even though credit terms cannot be currently granted

- the customer may be encouraged to apply for credit trading terms at some future date for example when financial statements are available for a new company.

Task 6

MEMO

To: Paula James
From: George Benson
Date: 4 January 2006
Subject: Debt factoring and invoice discounting

I understand that you are interested in the areas of debt factoring and invoice discounting. I set out below some of the major advantages and disadvantages of each.

Debt factoring – advantages

One of the main advantages of debt factoring if the provision of short-term finance in that the factor will normally advance up to 80% of the face value of the debts factored immediately. This is often a useful form of short-term finance.

Many debt factoring services will also take over the administration of the sales ledger both, improving efficiency, their expertise and freeing-up internal staff time for other activities.

Debt factoring – disadvantages

Factoring can be expensive as there is not only a commission for the service provided but also interest on any amounts advanced.

A further problem with debt factoring is that if it becomes known to customers that debts are being factored this may have a negative effect on the customers' view of the company. Although factoring is now a fairly common business activity it is still viewed disparagingly by some customers.

Invoice discounting – advantage

Invoice discounting is where the debts of a business are purchased by the provider of the service at a discount to their face value. The discounter simply provides cash up front to the business at the discounted amount rather than any involvement in the business's sales ledger. Therefore under a confidential invoice discounting agreement the business's customers will only be aware of the arrangement if they do not pay their debt thereby minimising the loss of goodwill.

Invoice discounting – disadvantage

Invoice discounting tends to be a high cost source of finance with a large discount payable on the face value of the debts.

Task 7

MEMO

To: Fiona Lim
From: George Benson
Date: 4 January 2006
Subject: Aged debt analysis

I have reviewed the extract from the aged debt analysis as at 31 December 2005 and have the following comments:

Havanna Ltd   This debt is now 11 days overdue and a telephone call should be made to the customer. It should be pointed out that the debt for £1,250 is now overdue and it should be established whether there is any query with regard to the debt. If there is no query then a date for payment should be established.

Jones Partners   This debt is now more than 30 days overdue and therefore the customer should be put on the stop list and no further credit sales made to this customer. A meeting with the customer should also be arranged in order to establish when the amount of £800 is to be paid.

Norman Bros   The debt of £700 is not yet overdue but the debt for £400 is 14 days overdue and there has been no response to the telephone call made on 28 December. Therefore a strongly but courteously worded reminder letter should be sent to the customer stating the amount that is overdue of £400 and that payment should be sent within 7 days or further action will be taken.

Task 8

NOTE

Trevor Lightman

The catering services were invoiced on 29 August 2005 and therefore the debt is now more than 90 days overdue.

Fundamental elements of a contract

There are three fundamental elements of a contract:

- agreement – this is made up of a valid offer and a valid acceptance
- consideration – something done in return for the bargain
- intention to create legal relations

If the services were carried in the course of business and there was a signed order for the services then it is likely that a legally binding contract has been created.

Action

The action Happy Chefs should take is an action for the price due to breach of contract by Trevor Lightman failing to pay the amount due.

Pursuit of the action

As the amount of the debt is £1,500 then this action should be pursued in the Small Claims Court.

AAT SAMPLE SIMULATION

UNIT 15
SUGGESTED ANSWERS

LUCENT LTD

ANSWERS

Lucent Ltd

Task 1

Cash budget for the three months ended 30 June 2006

	Workings	April £	May £	June £
Receipts				
Trade sales	1	200,000	239,400	200,475
Own retail sales		15,000	15,000	15,000
Total receipts		215,000	254,400	215,475
Payments				
Trade suppliers	2	120,000	78,000	81,000
Production wages	3	65,000	67,500	70,000
Production overheads		20,000	20,000	20,000
Sales department costs		11,500	11,500	11,500
Retail shop costs		6,200	6,200	6,200
Administration costs		25,000	25,000	25,000
Overdraft interest		2,200	2,549	2,112
Total payments		249,900	210,749	215,812
Movement for month		(34,900)	43,651	(337)
Bank balance b/f		(220,000)	(254,900)	(211,249)
Bank balance c/f		(254,900)	(211,249)	(211,586)

Workings

1   *Trade sales*

	April	May	June
Trade sales (units)	120,000	125,000	130,000
Trade sales (£) (× £1.65)	198,000	206,250	214,500

	£	£	£
Trade receipts			
Opening debtors	200,000	180,000	
Previous month		59,400	61,875
Two months previous			138,600
	200,000	239,400	200,475

2   Trade suppliers

	April Units	May Units	June Units
Sales			
Trade	120,000	125,000	130,000
Shop	5,000	5,000	5,000
	125,000	130,000	135,000
Finished goods			
Opening stock	(50,000)	(55,000)	(60,000)
Sales	125,000	130,000	135,000
Closing stock	55,000	60,000	65,000
Production	130,000	135,000	140,000
Opening stock	(100,000)	(100,000)	(100,000)
Production	130,000	135,000	140,000
Closing stock	100,000	100,000	100,000
Purchases			
(× 60p, paid for following month)	130,000	135,000	140,000

3   Production wages

January	130,000 ÷ 10 × 5 = £65,000
February	135,000 ÷ 10 × 5 = £67,500
March	140,000 ÷ 10 × 5 = £70,000

Impact of reduction in sales price

Cash

	£
Loss of sales receipts	
May receipts (59,400 × ((1.65 – 1.50)/1.65))	5,400
June receipts (200,475 × ((1.65 – 1.50/1.65))	18,225
Overdraft interest in June	
On 31 May balance (5,400 × 1%)	54
Increase in overdraft	23,679
Closing overdraft per original forecast	211,586
Closing overdraft per revised forecast	235,265

Closing debtors

	£
May debtors (125,000 × 70% × 1.65)	144,375
June debtors (130,000 × 1.65)	214,500
Closing debtors – Sales price £1.65	358,875
May debtors (125,000 × 70% × 1.50)	131,250
June debtors (130,000 × 1.50)	195,000
Closing debtors – Sales price £1.50	326,250
Decrease in debtors	32,625

Possible actions

a) Lucent could try to decrease the debtor payment period, so that all customers paid within their trade terms of 30 days.

b) Lucent could try to increase the credit it takes from suppliers, possibly paying within 60 days rather than within 30 days.

c) Lucent could try to decrease costs in certain areas, maybe there is some scope for reduction of overheads.

Task 2

MEMO

To :   Board
From: Pat Smith, Assistant Accountant
Re: Finance
Date: 10 April 2006

Amount required

The maximum amount of lending the company will require is £254,900, which is in excess of the current overdraft facility of £225,000. Lowering the sales price will not increase the maximum amount, on the evidence of the sensitivity analysis carried out above. However to be safe we should allow some slack and seek finance of £270,000 when the current facility runs out later this month. This will either be a loan or an increased overdraft facility.

Loan

Loans are normally taken out to provide long-term capital, for example to fund the acquisition of fixed assets. If Lucent takes out a loan, it will enter into a formal loan agreement, covering amount, repayment arrangements, interest and security. The bank will not call in the loan unless Lucent defaults. Interest will be charged on the whole amount outstanding. Loan repayments should match income from the asset acquired.

Overdraft finance

Overdraft finance is used by businesses which require short-term, flexible finance. Overdrafts are often used in the situation Lucent is in, when a facility is required to finance working capital. Overdrafts are repayable on demand. Interest is charged on the amount the company is overdrawn, and not the size of the facility.

Conclusion

I recommend that Lucent obtains overdraft finance, since the funds will be used to finance working capital.

Task 3

Briefing notes on gilt-edged securities and bank deposits

Gilt edged securities

- **Gilts** or marketable British Government securities are available at varying redemption dates. The gilt life that we chose would depend on our ultimate plans for the money.

- Gilts are low risk as it is unlikely that the government will default on them.

- They can be liquidated on the fixed interest market when we need the money, though transaction costs will be payable.

- The gross interest yield is normally higher than the interest rate available on a bank account.

Bank deposits

- **Bank deposits** are also available on differing terms from high street banks.

- As a general rule, the greater the interest, the longer the notice period we would have to give of withdrawal, and the greater the loss of interest if we withdrew funds before the notice period is complete.

- Interest levels are linked to the Bank of England base rate.

- Placing money on deposit does not involve any transaction costs.

- Bank deposits should be low risk providing the bank is reputable.

Security procedures

Gilt certificates should be kept in secure accommodation, and we should maintain a register of all gilts held. Only directors or senior management should be able to authorise dealing in gilts.

A list of all bank accounts held should also be maintained, and authorisation of transfers to and from the accounts should only be given by certain senior individuals.

Increase in base rate

If the gilt is fixed interest (most are) an increase in the interest rate will decrease the market price of the gilt, as the gilt will be less attractive compared with interest rates in the market as a whole.

An increase in the base rate should mean that the rate given on bank deposits also increases, and the company will benefit if the account is a variable rate account.

Task 4

LUCENT LTD
Tylers Trading Estate
Gloucester
GL15 3EW

10 April 2006

S Redmond
Director
Fancy Goods Ltd
20 High Street
Bristol
BS1 2FG

Dear Mr Redmond

Credit facilities

Thank you for your request for credit facilities. We are pleased that you are interested in purchasing from us.

We shall require certain information to be able to consider your request, which we would be grateful if you could supply. We shall need a reference from your bank, so please can you supply us with your bank's name and full branch address so we can contact it. We also shall require the names and addresses of two of your credit suppliers whom we need to contact to obtain trade references.

In addition we shall also require copies of your company's full accounts for the last three years.

Once we have received this information we shall be able to process your request speedily.

We look forward to hearing from you.

Yours sincerely

Pat Smith

Assistant Accountant

Task 5

MEMO

To: Trainee Credit Controller
From: Pat Smith, Assistant Accountant
Re: Refusal of credit facilities
Date: 10 April 2006

Reasons why credit facilities might be refused

■   The applicant for credit has only recently commenced trading, and cannot supply references or financial information.

■   The accounts of the applicant show a poor liquidity position or signs of imminent insolvency.

■   The bank has supplied a poor reference, along the lines of 'unable to speak for your figures'.

■   The applicant has been unable to supply two good trade references.

■   The applicant has suffered an adverse County Court judgement for failure to pay a debt.

■   There has been adverse press comment on the applicant's financial position.

Communication of refusal

Refusal should be communicated promptly and courteously, and we should state that we are prepared to trade with the applicant on cash terms. If credit would be granted when the applicant has fulfilled certain conditions (such as a new company supplying good figures for a year) the letter should state what these conditions are.

Task 6

To: Amy Williams, Financial Controller
From: Pat Smith, Assistant Accountant
Re: Review of aged debtor analysis
Date: 10 April 2006

Action to be taken with customer accounts

Candles Ltd

We need to consider if we should visit the company to see if we can obtain payment without legal action. If a visit does not prove satisfactory, I recommend legal proceedings be commenced on this overdue debt, subject to your agreement. We should provide for the whole balance of £12,500.65 due from Candles Ltd as it is more than 60 days overdue.

Lux Ltd

We should phone the company to remind them of the overdue balance of £1,000, and also to clarify the position regarding the £150 that is more than 60 days overdue. Non-payment may be due to a specific invoice that is in dispute, or which has been misposted. No provision is necessary at present.

Lights Ltd

All of the balance of £1,475 is overdue and £1,000 is more than 30 days overdue. We should consider placing this customer on stop and should arrange a meeting to discuss the operation of the account. No provision is necessary at present.

Flames Ltd

We should remind this customer by phone of the overdue balances of £7,540.25, out of a total balance of £16,815.75. We should consider placing the customer on stop because the balance of £1,420 has been outstanding for more than 30 days. However as the customer seems to be doing a lot of business with us, we need to consider the dangers of losing this trade, and only act if the balance more than 30 days overdue increases further. No provision is necessary at present.

INDEX